CRAFTING HISTORY

EXPERTISE

**CULTURES AND
TECHNOLOGIES
OF KNOWLEDGE**

EDITED BY DOMINIC BOYER

A list of titles in this series is available at cornellpress.cornell.edu.

CRAFTING HISTORY

Archiving and the Quest
for Architectural Legacy

Albena Yaneva

CORNELL UNIVERSITY PRESS   ITHACA AND LONDON

First published 2020 by Cornell University Press

Library of Congress Cataloging-in-Publication Data

Names: Yaneva, Albena, author.
Title: Crafting history : archiving and the quest for architectural legacy / Albena Yaneva.
Description: Ithaca [New York] : Cornell University Press, 2020. | Series: Expertise: cultures and technologies of knowledge | Includes bibliographical references and index.
Identifiers: LCCN 2020004383 (print) | LCCN 2020004384 (ebook) | ISBN 9781501751820 (hardcover) | ISBN 9781501752155 (paperback) | ISBN 9781501751837 (pdf) | ISBN 9781501751844 (epub)
Subjects: LCSH: Anthropology—Philosophy. | Architecture—Philosophy. | Architecture and anthropology. | Archives—Philosophy. | Material culture—Social aspects. | Design—Social aspects. | Knowledge, Sociology of. | Information organization—Social aspects.
Classification: LCC GN33 .Y29 2020 (print) | LCC GN33 (ebook) | DDC 301.01—dc23
LC record available at https://lccn.loc.gov/2020004383
LC ebook record available at https://lccn.loc.gov/2020004384

All photographs are by the author.

For Svet

Contents

CRAFTING HISTORY

INTRODUCTION

The Secret Life of Architectural Objects

Butterflies, Models, Changing Climates

Piano sounds gently crawl along the velvet green grass, savoring the sun in a lazy afternoon of 2014 in Montreal, outside a wide austere limestone building. A picnic in the garden. A young gentleman bends gracefully over the keys of the black piano, following a rhythm that only his ears can catch. Small bikes tour around the piano in amazement; children's hubbub; parents' picnicking; lethargic sunbeds enjoy the sunshine, and empty cups on the grass barely reach the reverberating piano sounds. Nothing suggests the nature of the building that affords the stage for that pleasant Sunday afternoon.

Designed and built by architect Peter Rose in 1989, this grey "temple of architecture,"[1] combining modern and postmodern elements, hosts the Canadian Centre for Architecture (CCA). It holds one of the world's foremost international collections of architectural drawings, plans, models, prints, and photographs of buildings, as well as the written archives and oral histories of individual architects. All of this material is accessible to researchers. The CCA also contains a large library and is host to various exhibits throughout the year. The study room is open to researchers; various programs and cultural activities are open to the general public. This explains the joyful scene in the garden.

A few days after that Sunday picnic, I find myself inside that building and within the world of a dynamic collecting institution. Founded in 1979 by the architect, student of Mies van der Rohe, philanthropist, and collector Phyllis Lambert, the CCA started gathering the archival materials of many significant architects after the building was opened in 1989.[2] The first Canadian archive acquired was Ernest Cormier's and the first international archive of a contemporary architect was Peter Eisenman's, followed by those of Aldo Rossi, James Stirling, Cedric Price, John Hejduk, and the artist Gordon Matta-Clark; more recently Álvaro Siza's fonds was acquired.[3] An archive typically consists of a multiplicity of working materials that document the thinking process of architects and firms, as well as the social and cultural issues that are entangled with architecture. The purpose of the CCA is to promote public awareness of the role architecture plays in society, as well as to encourage scholarly architectural research in the field and to foster innovative design practices.[4] Its ambition is to advance a novel intellectual agenda for architecture. As the CCA director, Mirko Zardini, states: "Architecture is part of the changing societal and cultural values. It is not driving, it is not driven, it is a part of this all."[5] In the galaxy of architectural institutions, the CCA collection forms one of those stars "shining brightly from afar off"[6]—so far off, in distant Montreal, that its brightness must be sustained by the skillful orchestration of institutional strategies and curatorial politics in devising mechanisms that can bring the collection closer to far-flung audiences. As Sébastien Larivière, technician in charge of exhibition display and gallery installation, puts it, the "CCA reaches out internationally to different architects, designers, graphic designers, and people who are really in different fields but are all very clever about how they work. We will not always use the same recipe. We will always think how we can do things in a different way, a bit more contemporary."[7] This ambition to be contemporary, relevant to distant audiences, ahead of the time, sets the tone of CCA's acquisitions and curatorial programs.

Once I am in the building, the piano sounds become barely audible from afar; the distant hubbub fades in sync with my steps. I follow the chief curator, Giovanna Borasi, for a tour of the vaults of the CCA. Silence. Sparkling floors—clinically clean. Dark, shiny corridors. We enter the lit vaults; silence supplants the piano sounds and outdoor chatter; order takes over from the disorder. I cross corridors full of drawers, boxes, and models; I stare at shelves full of treasures—small, big, strange, and amazing; I take a picture, walk again; the calm order is everywhere. The objects on the shelves remind me of pinned butterflies I have seen in different Museums of Natural Sciences.

Let us examine the shelves filled with scale models in the vaults and compare them with the collection of butterflies. What do we see? Just like the butterflies, the models used to "live" in their own "ecosystems" of architectural practices; gathered from distant places in the world, transported and staged again, they ended up in the museum. Every butterfly and every model had benefitted from the rich ecology of its biotope, but here, in the museum, they are on their own; we witness a reduction, a simplification. Compared with the unseen situation of every butterfly experiencing extreme temperatures or every scale model being part of an invisible frantic process of design trials, here, species and models become visible—what a spectacular amplification. A reduction yet a magnification; while something shrinks in one world, it grows in another. The entomologist could stay and compare all the butterflies in the museum; what was hitherto dispersed in distant sites and in specific biotopes, what was previously sitting on many different tables in architectural offices all over the world, now come together, unified and universalized. Inspect, now, for a little longer, the shelves with models. Imagine how these models (but also the drawings, renderings, and folders) travel to the CCA, detached from the natural environments of the practices, the office cultures, and the specific rituals of designing architects.[8] Once in the CCA, they find themselves on the same shelf, just like the butterflies that are pinned on a board, their power intensified as they share space together: Rossi, *next* to Stirling, *next* to Eisenman—each one amplified, empowered, by the other. Here, where the works are placed together, synoptically visible and synchronically assembled, a comparison is possible. Together, they can generate knowledge that cannot be extracted from one source only, from one practice only, or simply by visiting one architectural office and capturing its ingenious working ecology. When the objects are placed together under one roof, "pinned" to the same site, the architectural historian, curator, or theorist can zoom in, rearrange and unify these objects into some kind of provisional narrative of architecture. The reduction performed each time a model ends up on these shelves is compensated for by the intensification produced by having all these works together. Just as it would be difficult to understand the butterflies in relation to one another without the benefit of being collected in the Museum of Natural Science, so it would be difficult to gain the broader understanding of the models had the CCA not gathered them together on that shelf. An institution that hosts, classifies, and arranges these and other architectural materials in boxes, folders, and catalogues, the CCA preserves and frames them with labels and inscriptions to present them to scholars and exhibition visitors. Both the reduction and the amplification require specific expertise.[9]

Follow architects Siza or Eisenman, either of them in their practices, and watch them choose what will eventually become "archival"; each object will be subject to a very conscious act of selection of what could be of interest for architectural research. Then, although the structures of the archives remain the same, once they enter the CCA collection, it is the CCA that decides which materials to include in exhibits and publications according to its research agenda and knowledge production strategy. An amazing reversal of power relations has occurred. Just like the butterflies that become comparable and coherent in a museum collection, all the models of *that* architect, all the models from *that* period, and all similar architectural practices are rendered optically commensurate. They can be juxtaposed, mixed up, put in unusual relations in ways that make lateral comparisons with other models, other visuals, or sources of information possible. Here is an amazing intensification of knowledge: every new model, every new document benefits from the others, strengthening and magnifying the gathering. A surplus value is gained in their comparison. Moreover, the digitization of the sources makes it possible for every type of archival material to benefit even more from the presence of others. As such, they are not remote "symbols" of architectural processes, but compatible objects, optically coherent, standardized by codes, and all interrelated and connected to the world of architectural practice through a network. A collection. The objects' relations in the collection amplify their meaning and being. To combine both single objects and collated archives of firms and architects, to intermingle the scale models, the sketches, the clients' letters, the commercial catalogues, the quotes from contractors, all these materials, all traces of the complex social and cultural networks of production of architecture, all at once: there lies the power of an architectural collection.

First Encounter with the Collection

I continue following Giovanna and we stop in front of a table. The silence overtakes for a moment, brief and imposing; yet, the chatter of archivists gathered around overflows the vaults with life again. A humble theorist of architecture, I glance at some drawings. "Very familiar!" And before I finish whispering, I realize: "Is it the Chandigarh . . . [I say it aloud and I can barely finish my sentence] . . . drawings . . . [my voice trembles] . . . of Le Corbusier!" And before I even manage to end the sentence, my hands race, my fingers shiver in excitement, I imagine reaching the surface of the drawings and touching them—Yes! Yes, touching them! And, just as I imagine the touch, the silence is interrupted again by a violently spoken, vocal, energetic and collective: "NO!" My hands become paralyzed, I stop thinking, and I am lost.

I can still hear this choral "NO!" today: that moment at the vaults made visible for me the existence of a particular gathering of things and of archivists, curators, cataloguers, and visitors to the CCA—like myself—whom I had not noticed before. Reminiscent of a "society of friends" of architectural objects,[10] we form a special grouping around the precious Chandigarh drawings of Le Corbusier (see figure 1). We gather around objects of importance to the community of architects, believing that the objects can, in a way, respond to our admiration and answer our questions about architectural design and history. These drawings are not interpretable architectural objects per se. But because there is a group of people

FIGURE 1.   "Friends of architectural objects" in the vaults, CCA

for whom these objects *count* as interpretable, and who accordingly deal with them in a recognizable way, the objects matter, they talk back to us. The drawings are interpretable and describable only in the context of this particular "society of friends." When they are in danger, a "lawyer" comes to represent them and speak on their behalf. A "No!" resonates in the room. A "No!" spoken by friends. "Friend" has here a legal connotation: since friendship requires listening, under-standing, reciprocating, and answering, friends understand and are capable of rep-resenting and speaking on behalf of inanimate architectural objects. But are architectural objects inanimate, unresponsive? Can drawings talk back to us? Do they talk to cataloguers, curators, archivists, conservators, artists, and architects? If so, how? How is the society of friends of architectural objects being shaped by the practices of conversing with drawings, models, prints, and living files? The interdiction of my touch—the moment of "No!"—set an epistemological prob-lem for me as an anthropologist. What counts as legitimate "communication" with the object's desire to be known, or its maker's? The "No!" led me to reflect, and then later to begin this research project on the secret life of drawings and models found in architectural collections.

The "No!" I heard in the vaults followed me all the way through this study at the CCA and meant a lot to the entire society of friends of architectural objects. It denoted an acute awareness of the importance of archival objects of all sorts, and therefore the need to protect them. Within that "No!" one can detect several distinct voices: "Don't damage!"; "Don't destroy the drawing!"; "We care!"; "We are aware of its importance!" Two undertones slowly emerge: attention to preservation, on one hand, and worry about destruction, on the other. What stopped that innocent, iconoclastic gesture I was just about to perform was a statement of care and love for the architectural objects. This outlined even more the awareness of the archival value of the Chandigarh drawings. It is precisely that subtle balance between preservation and destruction that perseveres in archiving institutions; the way each of them regulates that balance defines their specificity. Preserving and caring for fragile objects of architectural creativity is at the core of the curatorial and archival practices at the CCA. The dialectic between idolatry and iconoclasm as forms of preservation makes us rethink the practices of architectural conservation in which, very often, "value," "usefulness," or "interest" explain the cause of preservation of entire collections.[11] Yet, the CCA is a special institution: it is not a museum, a place where exhibited objects are inseparable from the basic assumption that the objects signify something that the visitors see. While in some sets of practices the institution might appear to be a place where objects of design creativity are reduced to meaning—and subsequently defined as precious, valuable, of archival importance, and on which interpretation is performed—the CCA in reality has a hybrid nature as a collection and a center of research excellence, a unique combination of archive, library, gallery, publishing house, which together sets up an important intellectual discourse about architecture. Neither a museum nor a purely academic institution, the CCA engages that particular architectural "gaze on the world of today,"[12] developed through exhibitions, research programs, and publications, mobilized in an active semantic machine to identify issues rather than to solve problems, to be able to remain relevant in the future.

Phyllis Lambert started with a private collection.[13] Unlike most museums, whose appearances were historically accompanied by the presence of the state notion of culture, the CCA has no national mandate, no marriage with the state. The nature of its collection differs from those with national mandates that have a special focus on their own countries (such as the Netherlands Architecture Institute [NAI], the Cité de l'Architecture in Paris, the National Museum of Art, Architecture and Design in Oslo, the Deutsches Architekturmuseum in Frankfurt, the Royal Institute of British Architecture [RIBA] Collection in London, to name just a few), or form a part of university library systems that have a very precise collecting focus and tend to be geographically limited to their area (such as the Avery Collection at Columbia University, which focuses on the built environment in New York, or the Berkeley archive, which focuses on environmental design and landscape); the collection also differs from that of museums (such as the Museum of Modern Art [MoMA], the Pompidou Center, the Getty Research Institute) and individual collections (such as La Fondation Le Corbusier, the Frank Lloyd Foundation).[14] The CCA collects internationally; acquisitions follow specific curatorial interests or growing scholarly attention in a particular area, and thus shape agendas.

The specific CCA interest is in the intellectual production of architecture as a part of a broader social, economic, political, and technological context; it is concerned with the process of architectural thinking, not so much with the built environment per se. Phyllis Lambert was never interested in collecting or documenting the built environment, clarifies collection director Martien de Vletter.[15] This explains her interest in the Peter Eisenman archive, which contains very few buildings, but a great deal of thought. "It is about ideas, it is about thinking in architecture," reiterates de Vletter, and she sums up: "It is an archive of people that build less but think more."[16] At the CCA, more than anywhere else, the collected objects are marked by the essential ephemerality of architectural creativity. The process-oriented nature of the collection—products of design trials, working drawings, and models, still freshly keeping the traces of making—is reminiscent of the nature of the many objects I have witnessed as an ethnographer of architectural practices (such as those of the Office for Metropolitan Architecture [OMA], Moshe Safdie Architects, and Foreign Office Architects [FOA], among others). All these objects, as CCA director Mirko Zardini frames it, "offer enough material for the understanding of the evolution or the process of the architectural thinking in relation to the context."[17] They enter the CCA not just to be "contemplated" and "valued," but also as epistemological treasures that can ignite new ideas, nurturing further design creativity.

The Air of Archiving

Architects produce, assemble, and collect a massive amount of paper and visual objects over the course of their careers. In the process of creative making, designers generate correspondence, sketches and drawings, working models and simulations, reports and other written drafts intended for circulation among clients and larger audiences. As the documentation on a project accumulates, architects become "victims" rather that masters of their projects, argues Mark Wigley, while engaging in a "forensic" analysis of the documentation of the Casa da Música designed by OMA. What stays and outlives the architect as an author is *that* enormous "mountain" of documents accumulated through projects and the professional activities of an office; each project has its own internal life, surviving the office through successive mutations.[18] The last two or three decades have seen a very conscious effort by architectural practices to consider archives. As the computer entered the world of design practice in the 1980s, many architects developed an awareness and concern about their legacy. Offices and large firms began investing effort in organizing and cataloguing their archives systematically. Contrary to what some theorists say—namely, that "architecture as a practice is resistant to being archived" and that architects are "singularly adept in erasing their past"[19]—this book demonstrates a different process, showing how architects keep traces of the recent past, traces of practice, as they increasingly pay attention to the importance of archives. While the fate of established archives has been the subject of multiple studies, architectural scholars have rarely touched on the mechanisms of constructing these archives and the process of *archiving* as keys for understanding how historical sources in architecture are established.

While the everyday practice of archivists has been a subject of research and analysis since the 1970s, this body of knowledge is more an elaboration of a disciplinary discourse—that of archival science—than an accumulation of empirical detail. Analysis of what it means to be an archivist of architecture tends to come from the archivists themselves, rather than from professional architects or researchers interested in empirically examining the practices of archiving. As a result, the literature emerges from recollections and categorizations of archival practice, rather than a moment-to-moment observation of the moves of archiving.

Addressing this gap in architectural and anthropological scholarship, this study shifts the attention to the realities of archiving.[20] It aims at understanding the *becoming archival* of architectural objects by scrutinizing the specific mechanisms of production of archives in design practice (archive making). Tracing how architectural archives are assembled to reflect the nature of design as a collective, heterogeneous, social process, the study examines the situated and local practices of arranging (cataloguing, archiving, numbering) and taking care of archival objects (preserving, conserving, repairing, maintaining) and how they all happen to produce larger structuring effects in collections that resonate with greater epistemological anxieties, coming from the discipline or the profession.

Embarking in an anthropological study of knowledge production in architecture, I ask the questions: What constitutes an architectural collection? What are the tools, the documentary techniques, the experimental tactics, and the practices needed to produce an archive of an architect or firm? What are the different ways of knowing in archiving? And how do they happen to advance knowledge in architecture? How is the dialogue with current architectural practices nurturing archiving? To answer these questions, I follow archiving in its mundane, down-to-earth, and practical course, tracing how friends of architectural objects develop and practice the craft of archiving.[21] The book relies on ethnographic inquiry, which is attentive to the various sites of knowledge production and care, the attitudes, the forms of life, the conditions of enunciation, discursive and nondiscursive, all those little and insignificant things that little by little, step by step, allow us to understand what architectural archiving is. Tracing the everyday rhythm of archiving and its web of moves is a way to access the specificity of the current conditions of architecture making.

The book also contributes to the field of anthropology of knowledge and expertise. As it flourished following the boom in anthropological science and technology studies in the 1980s, "the anthropology of experts" advocated an approach to expertise that goes beyond the existing trends of "subjectivist anthropology" and "critical-historicist anthropology." Dominic Boyer offered an argument for a richer representational and analytical practice in the form of a five-point manifesto for ways for anthropology to overcome the understanding of experts as "intellectuals," knowledge specialists, or members of professional networks. Drawing on Boyer's dictum ("Pay attention to process! One is not born an expert") and the assumption that "the capacity to operate productively in a culture of expertise is acquired processually,"[22] this book explores the culture of archiving by following, meticulously and slowly, its specific moves, procedures, and instruments. Unpacking the process of archiving through the various moves of both professional archivists and a number of nonexperts involved in design, planning, construction, curatorial practices, and use, while following their wider networks that often cross confined institutional boundaries, the book traces how archiving expertise comes to be. Addressing the limitations of an analysis based on the logico-rational dimensions of archival expert practice (another challenge set in Boyer's manifesto), it advances the studies of "expertization,"[23] or the process through which knowledge becomes expertise and the process of becoming an expert, as an emerging prominent feature of the "anthropology of experts."[24] Furthermore, informed by the symmetrical anthropology of Bruno Latour, which does not prioritize any point of view (human or nonhuman), this study follows how architectural objects become archival as they get enmeshed in fine webs of relations.[25] Expertise emerges in concrete situations where the practitioners share doubts, anxieties, and fears, express desires, disagreement, and admiration, and talk back to objects, scripts, and instruments. These are situations where both the fragile bodies of archivists and the material granularity of archival objects are exposed, strained, and reconnected. Archiving appears as a way to emphasize the active and reciprocal nature of knowing, by appraising, preserving, and arranging architectural objects in relation to what is already known about them in architectural history, while also extracting new knowledge.

Building on recent discussions in "anthropology of knowledge,"[26] the book addresses specific ways of knowing that reveal architectural knowledge as inevitably situated in particular sites of design and archival practices. Such knowledge is activated by networked archival objects and knowers, and it is thus also emergent, evolving, correctable, "racing" simultaneously alongside the course of design. It argues for a difference in the dynamic between knowing "what" and knowing "how."[27] Archiving is considered here not as a way of establishing kinds of stable knowledge (knowledge as a certainty), but rather as an active ongoing process of exploring, testing, assessing, repairing, conserving, and reappraising the architectural connections of archival objects to the world, to other bodies of knowers and objects. It is mediated, collective, and distributed.[28] Knowledge is seen in a "continuous line of its reworking by human practice from one context to another,"[29] as well as by a variety of nonhumans that act on and react to it (there is a long list of nonhumans in archiving: instruments, chemicals, scripts, technologies, codes, and so on). Thus, following archiving, the study contributes to making visible the experiential tactics and spatial techniques of archival "expertization" by outlining how the dynamics of archival knowing connect to the dynamics of design knowing, and how these two ecologies evolve and redefine each other while simultaneously explicating what is meant by architecture.

Texts and Things: History

How is an architectural collection different from a pile of drawings and models, clients' letters and random documents lingering on tables in the offices of Price or Rossi, Eisenman or Siza? Is it simply an empire of signs, of texts only? A fortress of intertextuality? At first glance the collection leads us to texts. Here is a book on Cedric Price; a beautiful picture of the Fun Palace model from the CCA collection accompanies the writing. Reading the book, we learn about the creativity of the architect, about *l'air du temps* he shared with Rossi, Stirling, and Siza. But what would happen if the image of the Fun Palace disappeared, and so did the only model left from this project? Imagine that all texts, all documents, all books, all models, all archives on Price vanish in a fire: Would we be able to write about his architecture? Would we be able to think of Price and to think with Price in the same way? Would the disappearance of archival objects that constitute architectural history disrupt or deform knowledge? And after all, if architectural history bears such a remarkable material dependence on objects, why is it that we rarely examine closely how these objects come together in collections, get organized, classified, and preserved so as to form the epistemological basis of architectural history?

Collections, according to Michel Foucault, are places where we juxtapose, and all these juxtapositions, classifications and catalogues present a way of connecting things both to the eye and to the discourse—that is, a "new way of making history."[30] Juxtapositions and adjacency in a common space create epistemological anxieties, condition new knowledge. History "either picks out an entity and allows it to survive or ignores it and allows it to disappear."[31] In this book I suggest a way of approaching Architectural History and the production of architectural knowledge that is aloof from the big concepts of truth, uniqueness, durability, timelessness, and universality.[32] Rather, it follows mundane operations of knowledge extraction and care: the opening of crates, the writing of condition reports, the testing, the microscope inspection, the coding in The Museum System (TMS) databases, the cataloguing, the digitizing, all these documentary and experimental techniques necessary to make ephemeral objects archival. All these operations lead to specific ways of constituting and arranging archives relationally; and that is what determines at what point archives can withdraw in time or sparkle "like stars." Architectural scholarship depends on collections.[33] The architectural collection is embedded in a world of practice that without it would make the collection incomprehensible. It is a world of signs, texts, and materials, but also of practical operations of archiving. Instead of assuming that architectural knowledge and scholarship are simple works of intertextuality, I suggest taking a look backstage at the CCA to witness the practical networks of collecting and archiving objects. Opening its heavy doors, walking through its different sites of archiving (workshops, labs, and offices), we hardly get access to the big phantom figures of Zeitgeist or Creativity; we stroll, we pass by labs full of instruments, we watch the museum technicians opening a crate of objects that just arrived, we contemplate the conservators treating a model. A microscope sits in the silence, scalpels and spatulas all over the place; amongst solvents, crates and folders, digital and handwritten codes, we face diverse smells, we sense the fear of insects; we listen to an architectural talk in the exhibition rooms. An amazing work of transformation is performed here: not a storage space, but a mega laboratory opens up in front of us as we walk through the CCA building and we let the piano sounds in the garden fade away. The model of Price peacefully pictured in that book cannot be detached from the network of transformations, displacements, and translations that is needed for the model to be restored, maintained, and photographed for that book. The entire group of people working here—the curators, cataloguers, conservators, technicians, archivists—and their instruments and knowledge, the

network of institutions connected to the CCA, all this makes possible the double
game of reduction and amplification witnessed at the start of this chapter.

While archiving is not simply a process of interpreting signs, of intertextuality, it also actively produces its own textuality as objects in collections constantly
produce scripts.[34] When the objects arrive at the CCA, they are already accompanied by a dossier (paperwork from the loan, agreements with the CCA directors,
condition reports performed at other institutions). In sum, these dossiers testify
to a history that is to a great extent invisible to me as a researcher and to the other
friends at the CCA. Yet, the traces of that life are visible on the letter heads—the
names of institutions, architects, or firms—and through the very specific way that
the documents are written. Whatever the nature of the object and its importance
(a precious sixteenth-century century drawing or a contemporary scale model),
the accompanying dossier will be the same. Paper or cardboard will cover the object's dossier, and the dossier will be given a code, a combination of numbers and
letters, that will be inscribed on the folder and in the electronic system, and also
reproduced many times. Like every organization, the CCA creates records that
are part of its own institutional working archive—notes, minutes from meetings,
photographs, protocols, reports; the nature of these documents is different from
that of the archives that are trusted to the CCA.

Why shall we follow all these mundane details and the paper trail that travels
along with the objects instead of contemplating their aesthetic properties, unpacking their historical value, or revealing their unique architectural character? It is
because, by following the production of scripts, the experimental trials of an object and the caretaking and processing of it, we do not leave, even for a second,
the intellectual and cognitive foundations of architecture and Architectural History. It is by following specific dossiers that contain the instructions for opening
a crate and assembling a large model, the loan papers, condition reports, and
scripts from experiments and repair, and the manner in which they travel from
lab to lab, land in cupboards or move to shelves, rest *en attente*, migrate from written scribbles to digital data, and fly across workshops, offices, vaults, desks, and
carts that we witness the amazingly varied expertise that is needed in archiving.[35]
We thus grasp how people and skills, technologies and materials, scripts and procedures all get aligned, shaping a sound architectural collection of objects, a
foundation of history.

Friends, objects, and scripts all reside in specific sites of archiving. The work
of all the friends of architectural objects happens there, in a place that is either
lonely and secluded (when they need their special equipment, protocols, instruments, reports, and isolated environments) or highly collaborative and collegial
without any marks of hierarchy, age, or experience (when they need to talk to each
other and travel to other sites to discuss inscriptions). All these sites differ in

terms of access—restricted, semi-restricted, open, card-only—and doors and locks make the access slow or quick. The behavior of our friends is different there—dress code, attitude, tone, bodily position, voice, atmosphere, and noise level. There, the touch of objects is often mediated—gloves, scalpers, microscopes, carts, folders, zip files, and digital systems.

In this inquiry into archiving we will meet a very small selection of the objects residing in the CCA collection at the moment of study. Architects and firms such as Álvaro Siza Vieira, James Stirling and Michael Wilford, Vincenzo Scamozzi, Studio Mumbai/Bijoy Jain, Peter Eisenman, Victor Prus, FOA, Ernest Cormier, Ross and Macdonald, ANY, Alessandro Poli, OMA, Superstudio, and Morphosis perhaps never met in the CCA, yet they will be part of this account. Shows such as *The Other Architect, Out of Gas, Archaeology of the Digital, Rooms You May Have Missed*, and *Other Space Odysseys*, have very little in common. These random meetings of architects and shows are not unusual for the production of architectural history, and in bringing these contingent fragments, people and objects together, the book also tells a story about the mechanisms of history making, shedding light on its crafting. Tracing the moves of archiving also allows us to address questions such as: What counts as valid and licit knowledge in Architecture? How is a collection structured and preserved to operate as a precondition of architectural scholarship?

An Anthropologist at the CCA: Method

To address questions of archiving, I draw on ethnographic observation informed by actor-network theory (ANT) of the daily practices of conservation, cataloguing, and archiving, following curators, conservators, cataloguers, archivists, technicians, and others, accounting for the material and epistemic dimensions of their work, visiting their labs, offices, vaults, exhibitions, studios, and workshops, and shadowing them in their quotidian activities. As Michael Lynch argues in a pioneering study of archives in formation, "By pursuing detailed first-hand investigations of the proactive and retroactive work of consigning documents into archives of various kinds, it should be possible to supplement Derrida's etymology with a series of ethnographies."[36] By "ethnographies," he means descriptions of historical and contemporary cases that focus closely on "the work of assembling, disrupting and reconfiguring particular archival collections," thus reaching out to the archontic infrastructures of knowledge, to the power to control knowledge. Embarking in such an ethnography, I trace multiple daily choices of identifying, characterizing, valuing, measuring, documenting, coding, registering, and caretaking of archival materials; I also account for the techniques of handling and for the various trajectories of the CCA objects. I witness how objects get "entitled" to talk about/on behalf of a building, an architectural practice, or a style; how they circulate between the sites of acquisition, cataloguing, classification, preservation, maintenance, and exhibitions; how they are treated and selected for shows; and how they travel to other sites outside the CCA. Additional sources also help me to paint a full-blown picture of collecting practices: these include working materials (minutes of meetings, institutional papers) provided by the CCA directors, curators, archivists, and conservators; books and catalogues published by the CCA; and photo documentation of the process.

The role of specific events, such as exhibitions, that make curators go back to the archives and rethink their structure, logic, and raison d'être will be discussed as well. After all, exhibitions played an important role in the establishment of the CCA as a place of theoretical and historiographic knowledge production in the field of architecture. They rely on rare and precious documents contained in the CCA growing collection.[37] In the past fifteen years the dialogue between collection and exhibitions has intensified and developed in a cohesive and inventive way. Giovanna compares this relationship to "two people running"[38] so that sometimes it is the exhibition program that takes over, sets problems, and drives acquisitions of new objects for the collection; and in other cases, a new problem emerges in the architectural discourse for which the CCA collection has already some relevant objects, and so the collection in a way takes over and drives this new scholarly and curatorial agenda. Mirko reiterates that there is no linear causal link from acquisition/collection to exhibitions; in a traditional museum context we can expect that "exhibits follow acquisitions." Yet, what makes the CCA very different from a traditional museum is the way its curatorial strategy often drives policies of acquisition and informs research and publication projects. In this logic, "The exhibitions and the research publications are *tools* for developing a cultural discourse and setting the intellectual position of the institution. They are not objectives in themselves, used to measure the success of the institution; through them the collection is being built."[39] Thus, the lines of collecting, preserving, displaying, researching, and publishing are deeply interconnected and run in a versatile and nonlinear way under the drumbeats of the CCA institutional rhythm. The exhibits are not the end products, but rather active epistemic and cultural devices mobilized to explore individual archives, reshuffling their research value and extracting new meaning, thus enriching the collection.[40] Objects circulate in all these orbits without following established linear paths, without repeating conventional patterns. This makes the ethnographic study follow a roller-coaster pace at times, running through circuits that sometimes merge symphonically, sometime diverge unexpectedly, up and down, up and down, until a new kinetic energy is generated, boosting the machines of collecting and documenting, enhancing the power of archiving.

I did not spend a lot of time looking for the field. The field presented itself to me, by chance. In 2014, I was invited to participate in the CCA symposium en titled "Misleading Innocence: Tracing What a Bridge Can Do,"[41] and I contributed to the subsequent publication. During my visit, Giovanna offered a guided tour of the CCA. This very first guided tour captivated my attention; and in that very moment, I started constructing the field of a possible future ethnography of the practices of architectural archiving. If I had begun with the question "Where is the field?" or "Where is the best ethnographic site to capture archiving?" I would have been led to visit many different institutions, with different mandates and distinct archiving strategies. The answers to those questions would have led to a different format of inquiry—one that would survey various practices developed by different archival institutions. Similarly, the question of how specific forms of archiving can be ethnographically investigated could have led to a different construction of the ethnographic field, which would engage in a comparative analysis of various techniques of archiving. Thus, serendipity, exposure, the vocal "No" in the vaults, and the dazzling enchantment from a stream of practices that grabbed me from the start were the trigger for this project.

Unlike other ethnographic studies I have carried out before, I spent less time in this field. Conducted between 2015 and 2018, the work was organized as focused, one-week visits. However, a few specific techniques helped to intensify my presence and to maximize the time spent there. My project was greatly supported by key people at the CCA, such as the director, Mirko Zardini, and the chief curator, Giovanna Borasi. The assistant of Giovanna, Kimberly Davies, provided invaluable help with scheduling interviews for the duration of the study. At the start she produced a nine-page executive summary and distributed it to everyone prior to my first visit. This document provided a short outline of my project and my biography and an introduction to all participants in the study and departments at the CCA, as well as a detailed schedule of my visit. This saved a lot of time: I did not have to schedule the interviews, call and reschedule, remind and email; moreover, I did not have to introduce myself and my project at the start of each interview. All CCA participants knew why I was there and what the project was about, and some of them were even familiar with my previous work. The interview schedule, shared with all interviewees, ensured that everyone knew that other people were being interviewed as well: who, where, and at what time. A simple glance at that schedule was enough to inform them that at that moment of time I was sitting in the office of Martien or in the workshop of Sébastian or visiting the shipping area with Marie. This document helped me achieve greater presence in the CCA, while simultaneously multiplying the presence of others. It acted as a kind of mini-panopticon tool that rendered my attendance visible and traceable at all times—the kind of panopticon where the interviewees are placed in the governor's tower (while the researcher is strolling all around the "cells"). What a spectacular asymmetry! At the start, they knew more about me than I knew about them. While I could not oversee the activities of all the friends of architectural objects, they could track mine. While I could not check the many different timetables they had for the day, they could access mine. While I could not call anyone to warn her that she is overrunning a meeting, Kim would call to alert me that my next interview should begin shortly, and she would kindly help me get there. While my interviews made me move from one site of archiving to another, with my camera, notebook, and tape recorder, all participants in the ethnographic study continued to work in their dispersed sites, surrounded by objects, instruments, and tools at their disposal, knowing that another colleague was being interviewed at that moment and that a specific part of their practices was being revealed and ethnographically captured by me. Their movements in the CCA sometimes overlapped with mine: I occasionally bumped into people over the coffee break or in the corridor, and this resulted in spontaneous chats (outside the schedule). The interview timetable ensured synchronic visibility of all participants in the ethnographic study, a co-presence,[42] and maintained transparency of the multi-sited ethnographic inquiry.

It is this interview schedule, written by Kim in coordination with each participant, that positioned me as an ethnographer in the field and repositioned me every time I was at the CCA: it was not me trying to find a place to situate myself as a researcher; it was me-following-an-interview-schedule, running (literally running) after or behind it, recalibrating the positions of others, but also modifying it by negotiating new interviews, often exceeding the allocated time slots, rescheduling, losing myself in a detail and taking more time. If the executive summary and the interview schedules subsequently produced by Kim were a way to organize my presence at the CCA, I also found small techniques for recalibrating the ethnography further.

It is well known from science studies ethnographies that knowledge production is embedded in local environments, in bounded locales.[43] Whereas in previous ethnographies I had spent years living immersed in an office (OMA, Rotterdam) or frequently traveling to visit a practice (FOA, London), my study at the CCA included mainly ethnographic interviews during the short-term fieldwork visits.[44] Once I gained access to the "stream of practices" of archiving, all of the interviews took place in specific sites of archival practice.[45] They were either site-based or walking. All of them included elements of immersive observation. The site-based interviews involved going to participants' places in the CCA to gather qualitative data so as to be able to capture the natural setting of specific situated archival practices, witness how the participants work, and ask specific site-related, object-focused questions about what they were doing and why. Observing different friends of architectural objects perform various archiving operations and questioning them in their environments was paramount in bringing important details about their practice to light. Site-based interviews in labs, workshops, studios, vaults, and offices often happened to act as site-ing devices, recalibrating my presence and the presence of others. Very, very rarely would an interview have a script and a fixed scenario, a seating plan that would not change. Instead of engaging in a directed question and answer interviewing style, in a static situation where everyone and everything is seated, I spent time exploring the site, wandering, pointing to specific objects, opening folders, touching documents, and sneaking up on screens that were currently in use. Through this wandering around a site, I gathered specific impressions and arrived at questions that emerged from the contextual specificity of the practice that was unfolding and the socio-material circumstantiality of that site of archiving, streaming right from the world of objects, instruments, and solvents. Site-ing is thus a way of "establishing copresence." Site-ing is not a rhetorical device, trying to convince many others. Instead, it almost goes the opposite way, cracking "open" the black box of an archiving site and the practices typical for this site into many different associations; these specific practices that the archivist holds onto through the decisive and vocal "No!" Site-ing implies that nothing is still; it moves us all forward through new connections and additions. It entails work that gathers actors, both human and nonhuman. The interview becomes a way of producing words with things. Through my strolling in the site, the stream of new questions, the interviewees wandering around me, and the dance of the objects activated on the go, I experienced the folding contours of the site hosting the interview becoming reminiscent to a lively relational spatial "origami"—the traditional Japanese art of paper folding whose goal is to transform a flat surface through folding and sculpting techniques without any cuts. It is the "active" nature of the site that gathers talking objects, instruments, scripts, and friends together. That "site" is not a passive backdrop of an active ethnographer; rather, the site "activates" the interview. There, neither the friends of architectural objects nor the researcher is speaking; rather, the archiving processes are spoken through us. The site-ing interviews are thus reminiscent of the work of composing a musical piece, where the site is not a neutral locale of a relational composition, but rather partakes in the composing; it contributes to finding the right tones, the good arrangements, and it activates new connections, which, when aggregated together in the rhythmic flow of a stream of practice, will generate a full-fledged set of sounds that make sense: music. In these interviews the archiving site *sites* us all; it is active; the stream of the interview experience operates through me as a researcher, and the friends of architectural objects, as well as all devices and questions that amplify it further.

Still another type of ethnographic interview was needed: the walking interview. Prompted by the need to break the planned schedule, they were a good technique for situating the practitioners in the natural moving habitat of the daily trajectories that they follow in the CCA. In the walking interviews both researcher and participants are more exposed to the surrounding environment. Walking has long been considered an intimate way to engage with a place or a landscape, offering privileged insights into it; as such, it has been largely used as a method in urban geography and landscape anthropology.[46] Walking with interviewees, as anthropologists Tim Ingold and Jo Lee Vergunst suggest, encourages a sense of connection with the environment, which allows researchers to understand how places are created by the routes people take, by their intertwined trajectories.[47] Strolling produces richer data about place, and thus a denser nexus of connections between what people say and where (and in connection with what) they say it can be traced. Walking interviews in working environments are rarely conducted, but here, I was walking in an institution, not a beautiful landscape or an urban context. Walking in the structured and hierarchical space of the CCA, restaging the same kind of routine walks that practitioners take on a daily basis, provided an important source of information. For instance, visiting an exhibit with the conservator David takes him out of the usual site of conservation activities— the lab—and at the same time allows me to trace routine practices of the "follow up" and the maintenance of architectural objects that have been just treated in the lab. We stroll, we visit, we stop and discuss specific objects, the interview stages change as we move, and different objects appear and disappear from the misty scenes. Stopping by, site-ing around, and engaging in discussions that last longer than in a sharp question-and-answer rhythm, create specific settings where the archival objects can talk, and the interviewees talk *with* the objects, *through* the objects, *to* me but *via* the objects, and in many different sites. Walking interviews are ways of capturing events, or they are occasions themselves; as in the site-ing interviews, both interviewer and interviewees get situated, their boundaries become blurred, and the "being-in" a passive space turns into an active regime of "being-with" the site. If site-ing interviews involve strolling *within* a site and *with* it, walking interviews rely on many sites to be explored in an ethnographic journey of inquiry. Rather than isolating the ethnographer in an office, walking interviews situate her within the beating heart of archival and curatorial practices in the CCA, and within the vibrant worlds of many interconnected archival objects.[48] Thus, what looked at the start as a simple multi-sited ethnography took the shape of a dynamic multi-siting inquiry.

It is impossible to grasp all the sites all the time: so many fragments from practices, projects, time-spans are witnessed. Moreover, it is extremely difficult to continuously follow the course of a project from the beginning until the end—even impossible. Thus, transversal sections from the projects' flows reminiscent to crossing a river with fast running water were taken to seize the course of that river in different moments of time. The ethnographic sections provide a sense of what the river is—its speeds, its currents, its vegetation, and its living creatures, not in static freeze-framed pictures taken at specific moments of time, but in quasi-filmic sequences capturing a running stream of practice. While conducting a series of interviews in a period of time, I can crisscross events and sets of data produced by the different informants and compose an ethnographic mosaic that is far from recollecting the totality of activities. The ethnographic study also took place in specific windows of time between 2015–2018, thereby capturing a number of projects and activities of archiving being undertaken at those specific moments. Given the temporal limitations, some friends happened to be captured while performing operations that are not typically part of the daily business of archiving and preserving objects (such as dealing with a bug problem in the conservation lab); others were captured only in daily routines (such as conducting operations in the shipping area or cataloguing and processing an archive). In all ethnographic situations the individual ways of doing things mingled with institutional protocols, policies, and workflows, and there was no way to disentangle them fully. In the dynamic machine of archiving and curating that the CCA activates, change is constant; since 2015 some people have left, others have joined, institutional policies have been updated and refined, new collection objects have been added to the CCA holdings, and ways of working with and thinking of archiving have evolved as well. Following how specific people engage with specific archival objects in bounded locales and in a particular moment in time does not allow us to make any generalizations about the CCA as an institution. Nor is this the ambition: the CCA provides the perfect *locus* for an ethnography of archiving, but is far from being the ultimate object of this study. As an anthropologist I start neither from the observation of the individual specificity of the actual field explored (archiving at the CCA), nor from the general phenomena of archiving, but from many intermediate sets of knowledge revealed in specific situations of archiving. The goal is to grasp the process of the formation of architectural discourse not from the point of view of particular individuals who are speaking, nor from the point of view of the formal structures of what they are saying, but by tracing the unfolding aggregates of both humans and nonhumans that emerge within the practical application of archiving architecture.

Not being able to visit all sites of archiving in the CCA, to be present there at the same time and in the key moments of archiving, I abandoned the idea of

totality, an idea that made no more sense than attempting to study *all* architectural archiving institutions in the world. Although this project has taken me
to visit some of them, such as La Fondation Le Corbusier in Paris and the Bauhaus Building Research Archive in Dessau, among others, the purpose was not
to establish connections or comparisons with other archiving institutions or
collections. It was rather to bring fragments and experiences from different
sites together, assembling information from interviews, walks, and photo-
ethnographic sessions so as to produce a more vivid picture of archiving, with
bold contrasts and soft nuances at the same time. In addition, I visited some sites
of archive making such as the practice of Peter Eisenman in New York and of
Álvaro Siza in Porto, sites where designing and archiving tangle together in the
rhythmic dance of architecture making.[49] Many other "front" doors of architectural firms and archiving institutions could have been opened, and other sites
could have been revealed behind those doors. Yet, they remained locked. This
problem of closed doors, encountered many times in previous projects, was a
rather creative challenge in this particular study: some small internal doors
didn't open at the CCA because the ethnographic interviews, both site-ing and
walking, did not take me there. Nobody opened them for me; nothing suggested
there was a need to open more of them; thus, it was better to keep them closed.
Yet, as I engaged in site-ing and walking inquiries and discovered various sets of
archiving practices, these ethnographic techniques allowed the archiving world
to *open* itself up, with all its contrasting colors, boogying shades, pirouetting
moves, and lurking undertones. This presented a new challenge: how to capture
that world, and more importantly, how to relay it and make sense of it through
writing?

Writing Style

To capture the world of archiving in flesh, to bring together all these tones,
rhythms, and shades, I need a writing style reminiscent of a sketching technique
that provides the basis for painting specific scenes, profiles, and events. The art
of "ethnographic sketching" permits broader strokes to be made with fragments
of the distinctive archiving moves operating at various speeds, unfolding with different length and breadth of detail as they recreate the rhythm of the work of an
archivist, the intensity of the lab work in conservation, the anticipation of opening a crate in the shipping area, the silence and clinical elegance of the vaults, the
procedural precision of the cataloguers, and the laborious work of model repair.
Ethnographic sketching is more than "describing" in that it accounts for the layering of stories, brings together mixtures of colors and shapes, captures "dura-

tion." This writing technique increases the ability to augment bold, colorful, and vibrant fragments in the description and to create layered surfaces of stories clustered around types of moves or events. It introduces some aspects of archiving in an "impasto" style, with different contrasts, colors, and depth, each having its own narrative thickness and descriptive length, in order to contrast the different levels of visibility. It allows for the swift completion of a coherent and precipitously flowing ethnographic "canvas," a running river of practice, which gives more ontological volume to the narrative. All sketches, bold or shy, large or tiny, will enter the ethnographic log. Yet, just as in paintings, some ethnographic descriptions of characters and rhythms can appear unintelligible up close and can often be fully viewed only from farther away. Changing and recalibrating the ethnographic distance allow for a fresh look at archiving practices.

This writing technique gives the reader an opportunity to experience the strong and vibrant characters of architectural models, drawings, clients, solvents, smells, instruments, materials, temperatures, climates, archivists and architects, among others, being painted in an effective way when coated on the canvas of the whole narrative. Following this writing style, the book also makes an argument about the trans-particular knowledge transfer between cases and the mediated, multi-layered nature of anthropological writing.[50] To do so, the writing maintains a dialogue across cases, one that reflects on testing the boundaries between particular and trans-particular knowledge, as well as on making "trans-temporal" comparisons between "ethnographic moments" as they are also separated by time.[51] The profiles of all major protagonists in archiving are sketched on the basis of different appearances that they make in various sites of archiving; this sketch-based descriptive technique follows the daily rhythm of participant-observation and is presented as different logs in a diary, in a nonchronological fragmented way, yet, all painted. I, as an ethnographer, move across situations, and I capture their specificity; very often, my presence modifies the situations of observation.[52] Sliding across situations, the "brush" of ethnographic sketching produces a montage that ceases to be one construction from the point of view of a human eye, but is rather the vision of a nonhuman eye, "an eye that would be in the things."[53] The ethnographic montage inserts experience in matter, in a way that any spatial point of view can see all the others on which it acts and is able to act upon; it places archiving into the things, and situates us right in its heart.[54]

Structure of the Book

"Archive Fevers" (chapter 1) sets the scene for the book. I trace a number of recent developments in the social sciences and the arts that date back to the 1990s and motivated this study of archives as practice. First, the "archive fever" in the arts, with Jacques Derrida and Paul Ricoeur as key protagonists, led to rethinking the role of archiving as a tool of memory, yet, somehow arrived very late in the field of architectural scholarship. Second, the emergence of the trend of "archival ethnography" (which points to a technique of adapting ethnography to a set of related documents that account for the lived experience from the past) witnessed the advent of the "archival turn" in anthropology. Third, archival scholarship took an "empirical turn" in the mid-1990s, coinciding with the "archive fever" in the arts and the "archival turn" in anthropology, and this has opened up new, and previously unexplored, venues for investigating architectural archiving. All these shifts signal, for us, the direction for the development of an anthropology of archiving in architecture.

In the realm of architectural practice, the computer radically changed working dynamics and led to the practice's own "archival turn" in the mid-1990s. Responding to the archival impulse triggered by computerization, architectural practitioners gradually started to reflect on the formation of archives and the techniques of archivization, both traditional and novel. This development is discussed in "Architecture and the 'Fever' of Archiving" (chapter 2). Recent attempts within the field of architectural scholarship have shown more awareness—albeit implicit—of archive formation and the tactics of architectural knowledge making. From the incidental accounts of archives as sources, I suggest shifting the attention to archives as practices, as ways of scrambling epistemologies. This requires ethnographic attention to the daily work and care of professional archivists and conservators, as well as to archive making strategies employed by practicing architects to envisage an archive-based future. I advocate an anthropology of archiving that would scrutinize what constitutes an archive in architecture, what form it takes, and what systems of classification and epistemology it performs at specific times.

The following five chapters draw on ethnographic sketches of miniature moves of archiving and key characters, operations, and events depicted with different intensities in an ethnographic log. They all follow the natural rhythm of anthropological inquiry into the practices of record-keeping and collecting, as well as accounting for the multiple layers of the experience of the ethnographer and the many different mediations of knowledge. Boldly colored and richly textured human and nonhuman actors come together to recollect the moves of archiving: conserving, cataloguing, processing archives, archiving born-digital material, registering, and curating. All these characters when viewed from afar stand distinctively to tell specific stories, and when regrouped, they all configure larger figures and compositions.

The ethnographic log includes different moves of archiving, clustered as follows: visiting the vaults to open archival boxes (chapter 3), registering the objects in the shipping area (chapter 4), the conservation of objects (chapter 5), the long archiving and cataloguing journeys of paper archives (chapter 6), and the challenges of digitization and the archiving of born-digital materials (chapter 7). Every move is captured with a set of ethnographic sketches, which have their own rhythms, lengths, and narrative textures and reveal specific archival ways of knowing. They unpack the daily practice of friends shadowed in quotidian activities, the experimental trials objects are subjected to, the role of instruments and scripts, and the material and epistemic dimensions of archival work. All these mundane operations of archiving require description, careful identification, and scrutiny in terms of analyzable properties rather than in terms of aesthetic effects. Amazingly, in archival practice, all aesthetic judgment is suspended. Following different ethnographic sketches and pacing moves, we witness that all friends of architectural objects engage with the objecthood of the collection and its practical and epistemological application.

Drawing on the dispersions and clustering of moves witnessed ethnographically, the conclusion chapter brings together a number of moves under different collectors. This study makes us redefine an archive as a heterogeneous and relational aggregate that captures the distributed epistemic nature of an architectural oeuvre. Archiving points to the ontological complexity of architecture. Archival ways of knowing suggest that architecture can be grasped only as a versatile addition of built forms, *plus* the projections, expectations of the architects and other participants in architecture making, *plus* the materials and technologies, *plus* the site, the landscape, and the ecology, *plus* the anticipations of its future uses, *plus* all those humans and nonhumans who have something to say about these aspects of architecture, *plus*, *plus*, *plus*. Such a composite understanding of architecture makes us rethink what collections do to history, to architectural knowledge and its institutions. Archiving makes us discover a history of architectural forms that is far from being static, but rather unfolds as a diagram of active forces, challenging and reactualizing the distributed ontological boundaries of buildings, while also maintaining live connections to current design processes. That is, archiving is a semantic machine, continually evolving and developing possible futures for architecture.

Far from idealizing the archive as an ultimate source of architectural knowledge or a supreme technology of Architectural History, what I advocate here is the need to scrutinize the processes of archiving, to carefully explore the technologies of archive making integral to the practices of designing architects, and to unravel the underlying conditions of architectural knowledge production in all its forms.

ARCHIVE FEVERS

The archive often evokes a musty place full of drawers, dim lights, filing cabinets, and shelves overloaded with old documents. Either it is understood as a place enclosing records, a container of objects and other materials of historical interest, an institution; or it is just the collection of such materials from which History emerges, like that scent from old books, the "archive-as-source," the origins of History. In both these forms, is the archive an inert repository of artifacts of historical importance or sentimental value? Or is it possibly something more than just mute objects and documents—an active and regulatory discursive system, a semantic machine that produces historical meaning, the sure visions of our past? The dual nature of archives as storehouses of dusty objects and as active machines that transform structures and meaning has been the object of many studies by historians, anthropologists, and art and culture studies scholars during the past three decades.

As Michel Foucault provocatively observed in the middle of the twentieth century, the archive is neither the sum of all the texts that a culture preserves nor is it those institutions that allow for that record's preservation. The archive is rather the "system of statements" that shapes the specific regulations of what can and cannot be said.[1] Thus, it is also "the system that governs the appearance of statements as unique events, that is, as a discursive system."[2] More than a repository of documents, a series of images, a batch of correspondence, the archive, for Foucault, is what delimits normality, the average, and the field of the possible. While art critics, cultural historians, anthropologists, and historians have wrestled with this formulation to capture what renders archives as powerful documents of exclusion and as monuments to particular configurations of power, architectural scholars have rarely paid attention to the formation of archives, and even less, to the practices of archiving.

The study of archives as practice is motivated by a number of developments in the social sciences and the arts, dating back to the 1990s, a time when the "end of History" was officially announced.[3] First, "archive fever" (the drive to remember and store related to the fear of death, destruction, and forgetfulness) spread in the arts, with Jacques Derrida and Paul Ricoeur as key protagonists in rethinking the role of archiving as a tool of memory; yet, it somehow arrived late in the field of architectural scholarship.[4] Second, the emergence of the trend of "archival ethnography" (a technique of adapting ethnography to account for the lived experience from the past) witnessed the advent of the "archival turn" (the increasing use of archival sources and the need to conceptualize them) in anthropology and led to the rethinking of the role of archives, their formation, and their modes of existence. These two shifts signal, for us, the direction for the development of an anthropology of archiving in architecture. They provide hints for how to think about the nature of architectural archives, which contain both written accounts and textual products of architectural practices and visuals, models, videos, and films. Third, archival studies, performed mainly by archival scientists and rarely by architectural scholars, also took an "empirical turn" (the tendency to conduct empirical research to inform archival practice) in the mid-1990s coinciding with the "archive fever" in the arts and the "archival turn" in anthropology; this turn has opened up new, and previously unexplored, venues for understanding architectural archiving.

The Archive "Fever"

When philosophers and historians question themes of remembering, recollecting, and narrating the past, they look to the archive as a means of thinking through the problematic relationship between what has passed and what is to come. The archive is the site of epistemological questions that are tied to historical research, and how we write about our pasts; inevitably, archiving is caught within problems related to memory and testimony. While history and memory have been construed as two different ways of dealing with the past—history is written, documented, and "stands for" the past; memory is imbued with private and affective recollections—others have combined the two, treating history as a special case of social and cultural memory.[5] The fundamental objective of the good historian, according to Paul Ricoeur, is not just to consult archives, but to "enlarge the sphere of archives"; the conscientious historian should "open up the archive by retrieving the traces which the dominant ideological forces attempted to suppress."[6] Questioning the epistemological status of the documents that compose an archive, he distinguishes between monuments, documents, and traces. Insofar as the content of archives is thought to be more like documents than monuments, the critical approach advocated by Ricoeur aims at revealing "the monument hiding behind the document."[7] For Ricoeur, as well as Derrida and Benjamin, the archive is a way to resuscitate the "Angel of History." The archive holds not mere neutral traces of the past in the form of dead documents, witnessing for the mechanical reproduction of "progress," but possible monuments for enlarging "collective memory" and enlivening the past, of recollecting it differently; monument is what transforms the past and the possible future and thus is an "ethical" and "critical" device for the historian to act on what has passed and on what is to come. The archive is a tool for the critical historian to use to "narrate" the past differently in order to alter the future.

This awareness of the archive—its role, what constitutes it, and what it constitutes—is part of the increasing reflexivity of "history in practice"[8]; historical research often revolves around concepts and ideas, which were not known at the time of the construction of archives, whereby the archive becomes the catalysis for such concepts and ideas.[9] Ironically, the archive is thus also grasped and plagued with an anxiety related to uncertainty and the unknown. For Michel Foucault, the formation of archives and the practice of archiving prevent the amorphous amassing of things, thus controlling, even mastering, one might say, the fear of a frenzied accumulation, by establishing an "order of things."[10] Pointing to another fear, the fear of death, Jacques Derrida argues that facing destruction, and consequently forgetfulness, is what prompts, permits, and conditions archivization. The archive holds the possibility of memorization, repetition, and reproduction. The archive always works against itself, as the need to archive is connected to the fear of loss. Yet to archive something, it must be fixed in time (like a butterfly pinned in a glass case), and thus, paradoxically, to archive is also to kill what you fear to lose. Drawing on the analysis of Freud's own archive, Derrida coined the term "archive fever" or *mal d'archive* to outline that the archive is founded on an instant of death, a moment of passing into the past.[11] In other words, the death drive threatens every archival desire and leads to the destruction of traces and of the archives themselves. The archive, for Derrida, is aporetic: a desire to remember that is founded on the drive to destruction.

If Foucault sees the archive as unequivocally related to discourse production and allowing for a multiplicity of statements to emerge, Derrida in contrast, plays with the double meaning of "archive." The Greek origin of the term, *arkheion*, refers to a house, a domicile, an address, the residence of the superior magistrates, the archons, those who commanded, but it is also associated with *arkhe*, which is the commencement of history and the command of a people, an authority. Reflecting on the semantics of the term, Derrida regards the archive as having an important "archontic power," as it is what "gathers the functions of unification, of identification, of classification."[12] But Derrida emphasizes that this "archontic power" can be thought only in conjunction with another aspect of the archive, the "power of consignation." Consignation, as an act of entrusting, assigning residence, handing over for care, is also an act of con*signing*, consenting, and agreeing through the gathering together of all signs. For Derrida, "There is no archive without a place of consignation, without a technique of repetition, and without a certain exteriority."[13] Thus, consignation brings us back to the double meaning of the archive as what the dust settles on—storage, deposit, house, on the one hand—and, on the other hand, as that active circuit that scatters the dust—a mechanism of discursive formation or sign generation. The archive is, therefore, what gathers together things in a place, in a depository, in a building, and what simultaneously generates signs, discourse, and an authorized sequence of events.

The archive has been largely discussed and conceptualized through a semantic framework, that is, as language. Building on Foucault's theorization of the archive, Giorgio Agamben's work also locates the archive within language, in terms of the history of what is possible to say and as a collection of what has already been said, but also in terms of "testimony," or the *impotentiality* of speaking (the impossible passage of voice to speech and the difficulty in attaining the experience of language).[14] For him, the archive is "the mass of the non-semantic inscribed in every meaningful discourse as a function of its enunciation; it is the dark margin encircling and limiting every concrete act of speech."[15] The archive is also "the unsaid or sayable inscribed in everything said by virtue of being enunciated."[16] Maintaining a discursive understanding of archives as what "designates the system of relations between the unsaid and the said," the conditions of the possibility of speaking, that is, language as such, Agamben differentiates the archive from testimony; testimony is what points to "the system of relations between the inside and the outside of langue" and "between a possibility and an impossibility of speech."[17] In addition, the constitution of the archive presupposes the bracketing of the subject, who is reduced to a simple function or an empty position; thus, archive is founded on the disappearance of the subject into the anonymous murmur of statements, whereas testimony refers to the reemergence of the subject who is subjected to the impossibility of speech, and yet speaks. In other words, the archive, and here Agamben agrees with Foucault, constitutes the "historical *a priori*" (the fact that the conditions of possibility for thought are both necessary for us and also historically contingent) delimiting what is possible in speech; yet Agamben also departs from Foucault through the idea of testimony, which is what the speaking subject who witnesses that which is impossible in speech does.

By conceptualizing and problematizing the archive in different ways, the work of these philosophers has inspired art scholars, artists, and critics to rethink the role of archiving in the arts in the past three decades and precipitated the birth of what is known as the "archival arts." From the inception of digital photography as a medium that acts simultaneously as documentary evidence and archival record, the expansion of the use of archives in the arts has led to an "archive fever"; many art scholars have appropriated the term to describe the ways in which artists have seized, interpreted, reconfigured and interrogated archival structures and materials.[18] In fact, the abundance of literature addressing photography and film as the preeminent forms of archival material and the capacity of the camera to act as an archiving machine is an index for the extent of the spread of this "fever." The capacity for accurate description, the ability to establish distinct relations of time and event, image and statement, have come to define the terms of archival production in the arts as being proper to the language of those mechanical media.

In reflecting on what constitutes a photographic archive as a documentary source or as an artistic one, shortly before the art world caught "archive fever," Allan Sekula posited an understanding of archives as a territory of images shaped by different patterns of ownership, commercialization, and commodification (e.g., images for sale, copyrights, licenses);[19] the general condition of archives involves the subordination of "use" to the logic of "exchange."[20] Affirming that the semantic availability of pictures in archives exhibits the same abstract logic as that which characterizes goods in the marketplace, he advocates that an archive has to be read from below, "from a position of solidarity with those displaced, deformed, silenced or made invisible by the machineries of profit and progress."[21] Drawing on Walter Benjamin's philosophy of history,[22] Sekula argues that we can no longer consider the contents or the forms of archives, or the many receptions and interpretations of the archive of human achievements, to be innocent; for Sekula, archives are critical tools in an age of automation. Drawing on a detailed historical study of the first rigorous system of archival cataloguing and the retrieval of photographs invented by Alphonse Bertillon, with his nominalist system of identification, and Harold Colton's essentialist system of typology,[23] Sekula reminds us of the two poles of positivist attempts to regulate social deviance by means of photography. The photographic portrait, and the archives formed on the basis of photographs, are Janus-faced: they can act either as a socially repressive instrument or as a socially ameliorative one. What Sekula calls the "shadow archive," the inclusive archive encompasses social context and combines and contrasts seemingly disparate traditional archives into a social whole. This broader archive contains subordinate, territorialized archives—archives whose semantic interdependence is normally obscured by the "coherence" and "mutual exclusivity" of the social groups registered within them.[24] As a generalized, all-inclusive, open archive, it necessarily contains both the traces of the visible bodies of heroes, leaders, moral exemplars, and celebrities and those of the poor, the diseased, the insane, the criminal, the nonwhite, the female, and all other embodiments of the "unworthy." The "shadow archive," for Sekula, thus, highlights the potential of the archive to disrupt the hierarchical order of things, and thereby allows us to reflect on the social conditions that produce both the "good" and the "bad."

It is through the extensive use of photography that the "archival impulse" spread among artists in the 1990s and the beginning of the 2000s,[25] prompting them to produce "archival art" by employing more and more testimonials, images, films, footages, and documents accumulated through practice and research.[26] This impulse has led to the development of the genre of "archival arts," which "make[s] historical information, often lost or displaced, physically present. To this end [archival artists] elaborate on the found image, object, and favor the installation format."[27] However, according to Hal Foster, this international and general impulse is hardly new: it was present in the work of the early avant-garde in Russia and Germany between the World Wars—for instance, in the photofiles of Rodchenko and photomontages of Heartfield. The early modernist uses of the photographic index and archival attributes helped them establish a relationship between modernist dichotomies such as the public and the private, and between documentation and commentary, critique and analysis, power and subordination. Yet, archivization as a structural mode of organizing the proliferating images of photographic media was "even more variously active in the postwar period, especially as appropriated images and serial formats became common idioms."[28] What sustained the archival impulse for these generations of artists is the fact that the repertoire of sources was extended both politically and technologically. Politically, Foster argues, because "the paranoid dimension of archival art is the other side of its utopian ambition,"[29] this art developed possible scenarios of alternative kinds of social relations, which could possibly, he maintains, have transformative power. After all, the ideological struggle of the Cold War was as much a struggle over the past, the mythical origins of a society, as it was about possible futures. In addition, technological factors remain an important condition for the flourishing and acceleration of archives: for instance, the mega-archive of the Internet—its interactivity, its structures, and platforms—has been a crucial medium for "archival art." It would be a mistake, however, to claim that these art archives are mere databases because they are recalcitrantly material, fragmentary, heteroclite, and as such they call out for interpretation. The questions of who collects, curates, assembles, and makes sense of the archive remain, thus blending the figure of the artist-as-curator and the artist-as-archivist into one big profile.

Whether this happens in the form of projects dealing with real archival material or artworks in which artists use the archive as a theme (sometimes even inventing material), the idea of the archive continues to be an indisputable force and organizing structure in exhibitions today.[30]

As contemporary artists turn more and more to photographic archives in order to generate new ways of thinking through historical events, the "archival impulse" has become commonplace in the field. Interrogating the status of the photographic archive as a historical site that exists between evidence and document, public memory and private history, the artists generate a distinctive archive. Going beyond the traditional ideas of documentary evidence, Andy Warhol's work, for example, draws on the archive of mass media: by mobilizing images from media reports of misfortune and privation (suicides, car crashes, electric chairs, racist police officers, vicious dogs), and thus delineating a grid of social lives, he engendered some of the most sustained reflexive accounts on photographs as an "incunabulum of public memory." This is Sekula's "shadow archive" at work. Contemporary artists, more and more turn archival documents into monuments, to use Ricoeur's term. For instance, in Christian Boltanski's installations, the power of the archive is played as a fundamental site through which we remember; the images deployed and the narratives constructed are more allusive and evocative of an archive than representational of an actual existing archive. Exposing how photographic images and collections of objects trouble remembering, Boltanski poses philosophical questions by relying on the conceptual tools of archiving. Accumulating and reusing a variety of archival materials, the artist's works question the limits of the archive and its stability as a means by which we come to know and understand the past.[31]

Analyzing how contemporary artists retrieve, explore, and critique orders of archival knowledge, Anthony Downey turns from the content of archives toward its form, arguing that art practices create alternative, often speculative, archival forms, which have led to the production of "systems of archival knowledge that are often at odds with more formal, institutional archives."[32] As a dominant aesthetic strategy for contemporary artists, working with archives has especially helped artists in regions undergoing political upheavals, such as the Middle East, to express a political position or to articulate a civic concern.[33] Engaging with very specific regionally determined and historically localized forms of archived knowledge, these artists challenge the epistemological substance of artistic works and outline the crisis in institutional and state-ordained archiving in this region. Mariam Ghani, to use an example, retraces how the Afghan Left had imagined and reinvented the state by drawing on examples from the Afghan film archives.[34] By focusing on unfinished films produced in Afghanistan, she uses the archives as a means of thinking about and deciphering the sequential moments of revolution, reconciliation, and dissolution between 1978 and 1992. The gap between the complete and incomplete archives is a way for her to reflect on the relationship between the utopian imaginary of a political project, the completeness it projects, and its disrupted existence in reality.[35] Drawing on art practices in this part of the world, a growing number of authors discuss how contemporary art and criticism produce forms of archived knowledge that could potentially counter the instrumentalized, and often monetized, and politicized forms of knowledge.[36]

"Archive fever" has spread quickly in the art world, especially affecting visual and installation art for which collecting and archiving are inherent to their aesthetic media and representational techniques.[37] The "fever" grew so contagious that even those arts that are by definition anti-archival, such as performance art, thought and conceptualized archiving as an aesthetic form. In her seminal book, *The Archive and the Repertoire*, Diana Taylor explores how performed, embodied practices make the "past" available as a political resource in the present by simultaneously enabling several complicated, multilayered processes.[38] There is a need, she argues, to "reconsider how performance studies and historical studies construct and position themselves in relation to their objects of analysis."[39] That is, the activated *now* of performance and the performed *past* of History can be explored at once as entangled. Performance art is, for Taylor, a means of examining the continuity and discontinuity of tradition. The prevailing use of archives in the arts leads toward the interpretation of ephemeral and event-based forms of art as mechanisms of activating the past, and actualizing its again-ness, as quasi-archival aesthetic forms.

Daring to scrutinize their positioning in relation to their objects of study, artists and arts scholars, who caught "the fever" from the philosophers, have reflexively engaged with archives in the past three decades. In all these theorizations, the means of technical reproduction and how they affect the epistemic and the aesthetic values of art remain the foci. The archive appears, in its feverish plurality, as a powerful instrument of History, mobilized in remembrance and symbolic rituals, a critical device for activating the past, an apparatus for regulating social deviance, and a socially repressive instrument that could also be turned into a socially ameliorative, all-inclusive mechanism. It is, then, also a tool that could have a strong transformative power as it disrupts the hierarchical order of things, critically reflects on the existing social conditions, and enables the exploration of possible scenarios of alternative futures. While the archive often emerges in tandem with memory and history, through the lens of archives History itself, as an authorized sequence of events, multiplies from official to alternative versions.

The "Archival Turn" in Anthropology

At the moment when the art world, under the influence of the "archive fever," started hallucinating the ghosts and the angels of the archive and the archival impulse became a research focus and a reason for recalibrating the relationship of art scholars to their objects of analysis, the field of anthropology saw the beginning of an "archival turn." This "turn" registered a rethinking of the materiality and the imaginary of the collections used by anthropologists from a number of various vantage points and considered broadly what kinds of truth-claims lay in documentation. Such a "turn" converged with a profusion of new work in the history of science and specifically the history of probability theory, the social history of scientific truths, the historical production of "modern facts," and the history of statistics, among others.[40] The 1990s also saw the burgeoning of "archival ethnography," an archival mode of ethnography developing from within anthropology. The precise expression "archival ethnography" appeared in a book entitled *Historical Ethnography*, published in 1992 by anthropologist Marshall Sahlins, to denote the development of a historical research technique to trace the history of the island of Hawaii using written records, especially those of land tenure, but also accounts by traders, missionaries, and others.[41] Archival ethnography is a means of adapting ethnography to a set of related documents that bear witness to or contain explicit accounts of an everyday world of lived experience from the past; it is a way of proposing a mode of "being there." The document is a substitute for the anthropologist's actual personal presence and is a way to closely capture a past cultural world. Analyzing some of the oldest legal papyruses[42] and drawing on archival ethnography, Philip Esler argues that the distinctive nature of the execution of such a legal document allows him to imagine who was present and where and when the document was signed, just like a modern-day ethnographer who is able to observe what those present say and do.[43] Reflecting on archives as collections of documents, leading writers on ethnographic methods such as Harry Wolcott suggested that "for an ethnographer *any* document that proves valuable as a source of information can rightfully be considered an archive."[44] This concept traveled to the field of archival science, where leading authors proposed to further articulate and validate "a new tradition of inquiry for the field of archival research, that of 'archival ethnography.'"[45]

The publication of Elizabeth Edwards's *Anthropology and Photography* in 1992 (a seminal study on the use of photography in the recording of ethnographic data and a critical examination of the reflexive nature of the photographic "way of seeing" within anthropology) prompted a renewed interest in ethnographic photography archives, including discussion about their role "in the on-going construction of historical narratives."[46] A new interest in ethnographic photography archives converges within a special issue of *History and Anthropology*, published in 2010,[47] which focuses on the ways that archives come together, but opts for a historical, reconstructive approach rather than an ethnographic attention to the ways that collections are maintained. The anthropology of ethnographic photography collections stems from a humanistic interest in documents wherein photographs themselves serve as much of the empirical material. These anthropological writings demonstrate that anthropologists have become more interested in archives as research problems and this led to further developing the tactics of archival ethnography.

Demonstrating the potential uses of an archival ethnography informed by postcolonial theory, a growing body of scholarship emerged in management and organizational history in the 2010s.[48] It argued that archives were underused resources for organizational research and spoke of the need for developing different strategies by which historically informed research could contribute to the development of organization theory.[49] Advocating the use of archival ethnography, Stephanie Decker addresses practices of organizational remembering as a way to shape the meanings associated with architectural design; she demonstrates how archival sources can be used to untangle the ways in which companies seek to ascribe meaning to their architectural outputs.[50] The texts in an archive "are not used to report on the issues that they were ostensibly written about, but rather what they tell us about commonly held assumptions and intentions."[51] The archives offer important insights into the everyday practices of organizations for scholars who utilize archival ethnography in combination with other historical research techniques.

In fact, the most recent scholarship on archives has come from postcolonial studies, which have raised the question of the official status of archives. Whose history does the archive represent? How do archives intersect with questions of power and colonialism? Interrogating how archives are read and who writes History, Antoinette Burton draws on the writing of three twentieth-century Indian women and considers their memoirs, fictions, and histories as counternarratives of colonial modernity, which cross-examine and probe the status of traditional archive uses.[52] The memories that these women enshrined in a narrative act formed an archive, a historiographical opportunity in and for the present. A very influential thinker in postcolonial studies, anthropologist Ann Stoler shifted the attention of anthropologists and historians from archival ethnography to an ethnography *of* archives. Reflecting on the role of archives and archivization as practice, she notes that scholars working with reports and other archival sources rarely pay attention to their peculiar placement and *form*. Situating her findings within postcolonial studies and her specific work on document production in the Dutch East Indies, Stoler argues that archives should be viewed not as sites of knowledge retrieval, but as sites of knowledge production, as monuments of states as well as sites of state ethnography. Tracing the paper trails of the archives allows her to reflect on critical features of colonial politics and state power; the archive, she argues, is the supreme technology of the late nineteenth-century imperial state.[53] Shifting the focus of scholarship from "archives-as-things" to "archiving-as-process,"[54] Stoler looks at "archives as condensed sites of epistemological and political anxiety rather than skewed and biased sources."[55] This theoretical position requires a careful assessment of what kind of archive one is dealing with and how far the structure of the collection and the location of sources permits one to draw conclusions about the structure and intentions of the organizations that is studied.[56]

Historical geographers also engaged recently in reflection on their own engagement with different archives,[57] focusing mainly on the politics of the archive, debating about archives as part of their research practice,[58] and considering the different systems of censorship and resistance to research, as well as the ethical dilemmas they pose.[59] A clear shift from the "archive" per se towards an expanded notion of the archive and the multiple practices of "archiving" is also apparent in this body of work. For instance, through her research and website, artist and researcher Adeola Enigbokan brings together digital video, archival documents, cartography, walking-tours, and objects to explore urban experience and how the city is "built in layers of time."[60] Embracing a similar process-based approach, Paul Ashmore, Ruth Craggs, and Hannah Neate draw on domestic archives to explore how working with archives and collectors, instead of working in official institutional archives, actively reshapes and remakes archival materials and the stories that emerge from them.[61] At the same time, planning scholars have been reluctant to reflect directly on their use of archives in historical research. While they have rarely reflected on their own engagement with archival materials, the archive has been highlighted as a tool for unearthing the decision-making logics that underpin planning processes,[62] a way to develop a map for collective remembering of a community,[63] or as a means of facilitating policy analysis.[64] Here, as in the work of historical geographers, the "archive" as such is enlarged, and tends to be understood metaphorically to include "alternative archives," such as artefacts of the built environment,[65] and other urban spaces,[66] and thus to expand what the "archive" constitutes and to develop different histories of planning.

Thus, if in historical research archives are understood as sites of the (collective) imaginary and are institutions that have fashioned histories that conceal, reveal, and reproduce the power of the state and reinforce or weaken that authority of particular versions of History,[67] in architectural research the function of the archive remains to a great extent unquestioned. Is an architectural archive a simple depository of documents, or is it a set of discursive rules, a utopian project, a corpus of statements? How is it different from the visual arts or the literary archives?[68] For historians and anthropologists, the etymology of "archive" is a crucial indication for exploring the connection between the archive and the state; power and control, they point out, is inherent to the term's etymology;[69] the archive is both the house (as the Latin *archivum*, as "the residence of the magistrate" suggests) and the means (as the Greek *arkhe*, to command or govern, indicates) for ordering the past. However, how architectural archives are formed remains to be explored; they do not always follow the template for research of national or institutional archives as they seldom relate only to state power; alternative regimes of politics of creativity are at stake here, connected to the national mandates of archival institutions, private donors, the local markets of architectural drawings, the global industry of star architects, the Biennale events,[70] the gradual institutionalization of collections, and the birth of architectural museums,[71] as well as the current profusion of various institutions in charge of the architectural legacies of single authors or firms.[72]

Archival ethnography from the 1990s prepared the ground in history, anthropology, and colonial studies for an ethnography *of* archives that emerged in the early 2000s to scrutinize what constitutes an archive, what form it takes, and what systems of classification and epistemology it performs at specific times, depending on how it is put together and maintained and how can it produce epistemic effects, silence, or confusions. It is with these reflections on the archive from the early 2000s that the move from the "archive-as-source" to the "archive-as-subject" began. When the archive *as such* becomes a target of research, it implies the need to study archiving.

The "Empirical Turn" in Archival Science

In the mid-1990s archival studies, performed mainly by archival scientists and rarely by architectural scholars, also started taking an "empirical turn" at the same time as the "archive fever" in the arts and the "archival turn" in anthropology were unfolding. Yet, the everyday practice of the architectural archive has been the subject of research and analysis by archival scientists since the 1970s. While this body of knowledge is more an elaboration of a disciplinary discourse than an accumulation of empirical detail, the analysis of what it is to be an archivist of architecture tends to come from the archivists themselves. The literature is organized around the recollections and categorizations of practice, rather than a moment-to-moment observation of archival moves that might otherwise be missed. At the same time, this literature discusses the uniqueness of architectural materials and their implications for archival practice.

The architectural archive became a practical concern for archival scholars at least as early as the late 1970s. In 1976, for instance, James Knight noted that "literature on the subject of architectural archives is virtually non-existent" and summarized various issues the architectural archive might pose for an archivist: architectural records are valuable for a broad range of scholars; architecture might denote buildings as well as practices; and architects often do not maintain their own records.[73] In 1977, another archivist, Alan Lathrop, bemoaned the lack of architectural archives in the United States while observing that architecture as a practice is resistant to being archived, with architects being "singularly adept in erasing their past."[74] Further challenges include the sheer diversity of architectural documents and drawings. Despite the challenges, Lathrop called archivists to action. Delineating different materials and technologies through which architects produce records, he outlined ways of preserving these records in an archive.[75] In these earlier studies, archivists began to think about the specificity of architecture as a practice and how that specificity translates into a paper trail that archivists can engage with.

Another noteworthy moment in the architectural mode of archival scholarship is a 1996 special issue of *The American Archivist*. The introduction came from the then–chief curator of the Canadian Centre for Architecture (CCA), Nicholas Olsberg.[76] Here the architectural archive serves as a category for a problem of archival practice, a problem that a conference at the CCA sought to resolve as it "set out to establish criteria which institutions that collect and manage architectural records could use to develop common approaches to the documentation of architecture in the twentieth century."[77] A critical first step was an analysis that "looks at the whole process of architecture" and establishes "what gives evidence of its critical acts and movements."[78] It is important to note that architectural practice itself became subject to discussion among archivists, and at the conference, the archivist scholars listed principles, problems, and a research agenda for encountering architectural practices through the archive. As in the late-1970s and 1980s, archivists were interested in the figure of the architectural archive as something that poses unique challenges for archival work in the future.

As with the earlier wave of research, the critical concern at that moment was the implications of architectural documents for the practice of appraisal. Like Lathrop, other archivist scholars such as Nancy Carlson Schrock[79] and Richard Cox looked at different sorts of architectural documents and techniques for preserving them. Cox, for instance, outlined the concept of documentation strategy from archival theory and speculated on ways in which architectural archivists might make use of it.[80] Elaborating on the unique challenges of archiving architectural materials, Terry Cook echoed Lathrop's concerns.[81] It is not self-evident, for example, what an architectural archive even documents—whether it is "the building . . . ; the architect's firm; the broader institutional context in which many architects work."[82] Here we see archivists conducting an analytical procedure, dissecting architecture into several parts: kinds of materials, aspects of practice, firms, institutional contexts, and so on. The scholarly interest is one of delving further into architectural practice to assess its relation to something more familiar: archival practice as described in the professional discourse.

The self-reflexive theorizations of archivists in the course of their everyday work continue to dominate the theoretical arena; these archivists critically discuss the distinction between documents and the process of documenting/records-generating,[83] the value of analyzing records and reconstructing "the procedure followed to create them,"[84] the processes through which "records continuum" emerges and replaces the fatigued notion of "life cycle."[85] Drawing more attention to the processes of archiving, these accounts follow the style of professional self-critique; archivists conceptualize their practice in a self-reflexive mode, in the place of other scholars engaging in studies of archival practice.

When archival scholarship took an "empirical turn" in 1996 (the year of the publication of the special issue of *The American Archivist,* a year after the French publication of Derrida's *Archive Fever,* and shortly after Eric Prenowitz' translation of the book in English), scholars began developing case studies of specific archives. Basing his analysis on the study of the Northwest Architectural Archives with an eye for appraisal decisions made by staff, Lathrop concluded that "there are a few issues of general concern to archivists, but most can be resolved only on the local level because of the highly localized nature of research and user needs in every repository."[86] Both David De Long and Tawny Ryan Nelb agreed with Lathrop.[87] De Long's analysis was based on his experience in preparing archives from the offices of Bruce Goff and Louis Kahn, sorting paintings from photographs and cooking utensils, in the former, and interviewing colleagues about the authorship of drawings, in the latter. What he gathered was that "archives of individual architects should be organized in a manner reflecting, or at least, sympathetic to, the specific approach and method of the office in question."[88] Also referring to his experience as an archivist, Gilles Ragot analyzed the relationship between the materials within a collection and the time it takes to process them and argued that processing large amounts of architectural materials is necessary for resisting the canonizing tendency of architectural history and to "advocate the preservation of archival collections of ordinary architects."[89] What the archivists have found in these case studies are singular moments of archival practice. This encounter between architectural practice and archival practice produced reflections and conclusions that archivists could neither anticipate nor expect to repeat themselves. In other words, the specificity of architectural practice provided the means for them to think about archival practices differently.

Yet, one aspect of archival practice does seem to lend itself to more general theoretical focus: the shift toward digital technology and its effect on "appraisal" in archives. In a 1996 article, William Mitchell examined its implications. Given that architects may keep multiple versions of a single computer-aided-design (CAD) file, digital files accessible over a network may not have artefactual value,[90] and it is difficult to know how long the media and technology for storing digital files will last. Multiple authors have also pointed to one aspect of architectural practice, the existence of a building as different sorts of reality (projected, envisaged, anticipated, built) and in different kinds of documentation. Surveying architectural libraries since the eighteenth century, Alfred Willis argues that in representing buildings that both are and could have been, architectural documentation has an uncertain relation to history.[91] Alice Carey picks up on this tension between what is and what might have been and notes that the difference between early conceptual sketches and construction drawings persists, as architectural historians (such as Christopher Thomas[92]) are often more interested in documents from the early phases of projects, while architects looking to preserve historic buildings need to access more thorough construction drawings.[93] For lawyers, James Nowacki claims, the issues with appraisal become less relevant: it is most useful if the archive has everything, from meeting minutes to construction drawings, as possible evidence in case of a lawsuit.[94] Here archival practice can respond to a particular tendency of architectural production.

In the first decade of the 2000s, archival scholarship continued to look for the implications of architecture on the future practice of archivists. The rising awareness of the importance of architectural archives led archival scientists to rethink again their methods of study. Within the journal *Archival Science*, the empirical study of archival work was an emerging phenomenon, and the mood surrounding it was one of uncertainty and speculation. The journal has only existed since 2001, and the discussions on its pages reflect how archival science as an empirical investigation of archival practices was equally a fledgling pursuit. In a review of the discipline, Håkan Lövblad noted the reawakening of interest in approaches to archival science that look not only at records but also the processes through which records are created, emphasizing the objects' materiality, while leaving the hermeneutic vein aside.[95]

At the same time, scholarly interest converged on the question of architecture and digital documents. An explicit response to the 1996 discussion (documented in the special issue of *The American Archivist* referred to above) came in Laura Tatum's review of the contributors' analysis of digital files.[96] Commenting on a number of conferences on digital materials around the turn of the millennium, Tatum argued that the preservation of digital records was receiving less emphasis than it deserved. As she stated, "Architects, it seems, have given a great deal of thought to the issue of preserving digital records, while librarians and archivists remain primarily concerned with the electronic accessibility of current physical holdings."[97] One point of debate is the status of CAD files: the file itself might be more comprehensive than any printout, but at the same time the file itself elides the iterations that lead up to it. Elaborating on Tatum's argument four years later, Ann Armstrong noted that there was still no consensus among archivists as to how to handle digital-born documents from architectural firms, even though CAD drawings are central to architectural work.[98] In another response to Tatum, Kathryn Pierce surveyed a number of initiatives for preserving digital documents.[99] Basing her findings on interviews and observations conducted in one architectural firm, she concluded that to contribute to what was still a nascent body of knowledge, digital preservation was not a priority for architects. In Pierce's fieldwork, as in archival scholars' analysis at large, the interest seems to have been in grasping architectural practice, as it relates to its own preservation and documentation techniques, in order to mirror it within the practice of the archive.

Another crucial moment in the history of archivists of architecture came in 2010, in an issue of *Log*, which marked something of a departure from the issues previously debated. The question that emerged is less what architectural practice means for archival practice and more about archival practice itself as it relates to museum exhibitions. In particular, special attention was paid to the role of the archivist as it converges with the role of the curator. As Cynthia Davidson noted in her editorial, "Once focused on collecting objects and their documentation, and the relatively unquestioned mode of display, [the curator] is now confronted with the expanded idea of the object and the limited space of the exhibition."[100] While addressing these issues, scholars have focused more often on exhibitions than on archives. Mirko Zardini, the director of the Canadian Centre for Architecture, sheds light on this relationship between its archives and the exhibitions it produces:

> The character of CCA exhibitions is driven by the character of the CCA collection. While the collection may seem diverse and complex, it is coherent in its task of presenting architecture in a wider frame. The presence of very different media and heterogeneous materials is necessary to document and understand a project's various components and interrelationships. . . . In this sense, an architectural collection is more like an archive than a fine arts collection.[101]

Here we see themes that were foreshadowed in the earlier professional dialogue of archivists: the diversity of architecture and the heterogeneity of architectural materials. But the focus on the connection between exhibition and collection demonstrates a break from the concerns of the 1996. The upshot is that there is no self-evident technique for exhibiting architecture to the public. Historian Jean-Louis Cohen goes so far as to note that "the job of the curator can no longer be confused with the one of the archivist or the registrar."[102] If the debate in 1996 revolved around the archive's fidelity to architectural practice, now, with historians such as Cohen joining the debate, the discussion shifts towards the specific engagement of curators in the interpretation of architectural archives.[103]

The overview of the archival literature shows that since the late 1970s "archival scientists" have aspired toward a normative discourse regarding the production and maintenance of an archive; when they made an empirical turn in the 1990s, their studies mainly mirrored self-reflections on their own practices. Later on, in the first decade of the twenty-first century, the empirical turn materialized in historical investigations of a particular archival system.[104] As Randolph Head notes, this rise in historical analyses of archives accompanied "impulses from the history of science" as well as the "material turn" and "spatial turn" in the humanities.[105] Yet, what came out of this research was a problematization of the archive as a universal category, rather than examinations of particular archives as outgrowths of their own historical and situated trajectories. While archival science readily turned archival practice into a research problem, the "common sense" of disciplinary discourse appeared to stand in for the possible surprises of empirical fieldwork.

Rare are the studies that attempt to describe the cognitive processes involved in archival practice. In 2015, Victoria Lemieux noted how unprecedented her research was: "Surprisingly, a review of the archival literature on arrangement and description has revealed that explanations of the archival reasoning process, by and large, are absent."[106] Drawing on short moments of observation of how archivists conduct standard archival procedures on records—how they encounter these records, produce an overview of the fonds and refine their understanding of them, and then describe the final arrangement and document their description in an archival finding aid, Lemieux produces a unique account of archival practice. Her account is a way, to use the anthropological trope, of "making strange" the archival practice; it is an attempt to excavate processes that archivists cannot recollect on their own.

Even though some recent studies have begun to adopt ethnographic methods, archival science's interest in ethnography is still in its infancy and has yet to specifically encounter the architectural archive. A 2004 special issue of *Archival Science* on research methods brought to the fore one ethnographic study of film archives carried out by Karen Gracy,[107] which showed archive ethnography in its early days: the only precursors Gracy cited were recent PhD dissertations. Reconstructing various processes within the work of film preservation as "flow charts,"[108] Gracy's ethnographic observation resulted in one of the first monographs on film preservation.[109] Another study employing participant observation brought out the tensions and distrust between community-based archives and the heritage organizations that consult with them.[110] Again, the authors noted that ethnography "continues to be an unusual research method in the relatively new discipline of archival studies."[111] A decade after Gracy, Isto Huvila observed that "there are few comprehensive empirical studies of archival work itself."[112] Basing his work on interviews with archival professionals, Huvila argued that the "archival community is again in a period of competing paradigmatic views"[113] of the value and relevance of archival records and archival work. This brief overview of ethnographic accounts within archival science illustrates how it is too new to have produced any kind of comparative body of knowledge. Yet, it provides a starting point for an ethnography of archiving in architecture.

The archival literature on architecture reveals opportunities for ethnography to explore some unique challenges that architecture poses for archival practice. Far from self-reflexive theorizations and historical accounts, the "empirical turn" in archival science points today to a new avenue to explore architectural archiving—one that stays in the present and shifts the anthropological limelight to the archivists at work. Ethnography provides opportunities for reconnecting architectural documents and the decisions on what belongs to an archive with the ways in which architects act in and understand their own design worlds.

ARCHITECTURE AND THE "FEVER" OF ARCHIVING

The "archival turns" discussed in the previous chapter followed, in all their expressions, the newest technological developments and typically connected archives directly to history, to memory, and to state politics. In the realm of architecture, the computer radically changed the working dynamics and reconfigured the micropolitics of practice, thereby leading to its own "turn" in archiving. Although all these developments gesture in the direction of a study of archiving related to the current conditions of design practice, in architectural scholarship there is still a noticeable silence on the archival front; scholars rarely engage with the limits and the political relevance of knowledge production in architecture. Only recently did we start witnessing dialogues among architects, artists, theorists, and writers who began addressing the conditions for the production of good archives and questioned the need for their spatial permanence.[1] Some architectural historians have shown more—albeit implicit—awareness of archival constructions and the methods of historical knowledge generation; however, none of them explicitly addresses architectural archiving *as such*. Rarely do we find ourselves in the thick of the things and practices that constitute Architectural History. It seems that "archive fever" has not managed significantly to "infect" the field of architectural studies. While architectural scholars do critically address the limitations of different archives as sources of knowledge, they still remain silent about rethinking the conceptual and institutional machines of archiving as a vital precondition of Architectural History. These concerns outline even more the need of an anthropology of archiving that will pay close attention to the practices and tactics of archive formation in architecture—to their organization, classification, and epistemology.

Archiving in Design Practice

In the mid-1990s, at the time of the combined developments of "archive fever" in the arts and the "archival turn" in anthropology, as well as the "empirical turn" in archival science, architectural practice also started to reflect on the formation of archives and the techniques of archivization, both traditional (photography, film, printing) and novel (3D printing, digital-born archives), and gradually began responding to the archival impulse triggered by computerization. The new techniques of archivization instigated changes in the modes of archive production in design.

If artists interrogate the self-evident claims of the archive by reading it against the grain, bringing this interrogation to the structural and functional principles underlying the use of the archival documents to create new archival structures by establishing an archaeological relationship to history, evidence, memory, and symbols, the architectural archive is closely related to the inner logics and rhythms of design practice, to an active self-referential interrogation of *the now* in connection to the recent past. The "feverish pace" of pictorial generation and accumulation of images facilitated by computers in architectural practices has meant accelerating additions to the existing stocks of sketches, drawings, collages, and models. Pictures of models, of episodes from the life of a practice, of visits to the construction site, or of meetings with clients have supplemented the existing collection of documents and artifacts, prints and reprints. This amassing of archives happens as an underlying dimension of design practice, underpinning its existence. It is inherent to the creative process and not an ultimate purpose-built fabrication. The more architects create, the messier their offices get, and thus the greater the need for organizing and archiving the material becomes. Some practices keep "everything." I have followed boxes of models being packed now and again, traveling to storage, and coming back many times to the seventh floor of the Office for Metropolitan Architecture (OMA) during my ethnographic observation in the practice. A few years later I witnessed the same in Peter Eisenman's practice; he keeps everything, just like his friend Rem Koolhaas. Eisenman explains, "We do not do any selection. When it overwhelms us, we just put everything into the storage."[2] Practitioners mobilize the debris of production and reintegrate it into an ever-growing archive. We witness more often in architectural firms that the dividing line between the architect and the archivist is becoming increasingly blurred.[3] The active archive holds the possibility of repetition, of reproduction, or of reprints; repetition leads to creation, invention, new findings, and new forms. Copies have an important epistemological function insofar as they can be cropped, colored, and enlarged. Generating different prints, storing and amassing them are other ways of talking about design invention. The accumulation of series of copies and their variations drives design creativity.[4]

Architectural practice, thus, naturally results in an extraordinary accumulation of visuals and archival media that demand sorting, cataloguing, and organizing at a certain moment in time in order to avoid this amorphous accumulation from taking over the working order of a firm. Tagging, numbering, and classifying the accumulated traces of architectural creativity and data have become ways of organizing the log of creative options and scenarios developed in practice, creating a directory of successful examples and of failures, all arranged to be used as a self-referential working catalogue of options that may be mobilized at any moment in time: "We can do this bridge the way we did one in city A"; "The mesh developed for the façade of building C could be reused." Tracing how architectural practice functions today, ethnographers bear witness to an active mode of archiving working scenarios, which is gradually becoming a pervasive method of regulating the production of efficiency in practice.[5]

If the "impulse" of archiving that has animated modern art since the invention of photography and rendered contemporary art "feverish" was largely anticipated by the regulative order of the dispersion of photography and images through mass media, in architecture the technologies that facilitate the modes of image reproduction multiply. The emergence and proliferation of the digital, from digital photography to the development of new software, have radically altered architectural practice. We witness the first traces of this process unfolding in the 1990s. New versions of computer-aided design (CAD), form-generating software, parametric and post-parametric applications came to replace the tradition of sketching. A multiplicity of tools for video recording and data collection has added to the already diversified repertoire of archiving. The transformation and evolution of technology have hybridized the conceptual system of the architectural archive. Old floppy disks, physical models of different sorts, plans, sketches, and correspondence, which have filled the archival boxes of contemporary architectural practices, present us with curious and dazzling amalgamations.

The control over the flow of information in architectural practice is strengthened by networks of data generation and archival manipulation. Yet, these aspects of design practice are not empirically studied; instead, they tend to be considered insignificant or taken for granted.[6] Confronting these transformations of recent architectural practice, we must ask: What are the specific technologies of archivization in architecture? What are the technical mechanisms for reproduction that allow for archivization? How is archival techno-science changing the shape of architecture?

When archivization is at stake, one classic example is Sigmund Freud's letters: handwritten correspondence was an important material for psychoanalysis. An alyzing the landscape of psychoanalytic archiving, Derrida asks, "In what way has the whole of this field been determined by a state of the technology of communication and of archivization?"[7] Technology, in other words, conditions not only the form or the structure, but also the content. The medium is as important as the message, as per Marshall McLuhan's well-known argument. Following from this, if, instead of writing thousands of letters by hand, Freud, his contemporaries, collaborators, and immediate disciples had access to any number of new, different technologies, Derrida reminds us, the history of psychoanalysis would have been much different.[8] In a similar way, we might ask how the new technologies of archivization and the radical technological changes in the architectural profession (digital form finding, 3D printers, Building Information Modelling [BIM], parametrics) are affecting not only architectural practice but also the way architects think of the archive and their legacy?

A notable example of this transformation in architecture is provided by Beatriz Colomina, for whom new media and their related technologies transform architecture. The technology of offset lithography in the 1970s, for instance, made possible the printing of little magazines and brochures of Archigram (an avantgarde and neo-futuristic architectural group formed in the 1960s). Architectural names and concepts were first fashioned on the pages of these media outlets, such as Peter Cook's. The little magazines acted as "construction sites" for debate and innovations, generating new types of architecture and new conceptual frameworks, even new visions of architectural theory.[9] That is how the explosion of little architectural magazines in the 1960s and 1970s instigated a radical transformation in architectural culture. A more recent example, the fax machine, became an important "design tool," argues Mark Wigley, as it entered architectural practices in the 1980s and formed the heart of the recording/reporting/designing operations. Wigley tells a fascinating story about the OMA's domestication of the technology of the fax, a technology that relies on endless recording and communication "documenting the story of a project"[10] and greatly accelerates the production of documentation. Hundreds of faxes traveled to distant locations, connecting the OMA to other locales of practice and thus incubating projects such as the Casa da Música. Within the mountain of faxes and documents produced by a project, the working archive emerges as a repeated attempt "to diagram the evolution of the concept at each stage."[11] It suggests that there are many possible variations and offers a diagrammatic interpretation of design. And if the technology of offset lithography enabled the proliferation of little magazines in the

1960s and 1970s and fax technology accelerated architectural production, recording, and communication in the 1980s, the questions arise: To what extent do the new technologies influence (rather than determine) the archivable events now, thus gradually modifying the forms of the architectural archive and the practices of archiving? As archivization produces as much as it records events,[12] the new technologies accelerate this process, and the techniques of archiving have an impact on the structure of the archivable content.

The resulting reflexivity regarding archivization became very apparent among museum professionals and collectors of architecture in the 1980s and 1990s. As Phyllis Lambert recalls, "A particular challenge faced by museums of architecture everywhere is what attitude to adopt in relation to contemporary architectural practice, and in particular to the sheer escalation of the number of documents and representations (drawings, models, computer images, written documents) generated by the construction of buildings in the late twenty century."[13] That is precisely when the archive gained more importance for designing architects—and when architectural exhibitions "stormed" the field of culture, and more architectural museums were established.[14] This major cultural transformation began in the 1980s, as architectural historian Pierre Chabard recounts, and was related to the passion for the drawing in all its forms, and its growing aesthetization, or detachment from the cycles of design and the construction process. Architects started gradually realizing that their creative work had value. Peter Eisenman recalls, "People were telling me, 'Why aren't you signing your drawings?' Some collecting institutions would not take my drawings unless I signed them. So, I signed them after the fact, but I never signed drawings at the start. I was not conscious."[15] That consciousness Eisenman is talking about,[16] that awareness that the signed drawing can have an archival value, gained momentum in the 1990s.[17]

More firms began appointing archivists, PR officers, and record managers to help them organize their "mountains of paper."[18] This corresponded to the specific technological shift in design practice (from the mid-1990s on) when the computer became an essential tool for the exploration of new formal territories marked by continuity and smooth transitions.[19] Nineteen ninety-three was the "year of folding,"[20] a Deleuzian year of blobs, folds, bodies, and smooth transformations. In the 1990s, with the ubiquity of the Internet and the World Wide Web, digital materials moved into a dominant position. That technological moment and the digital design culture that emerged with it made architects become more aware of the importance of organizing both paper and digital archives and taking care of their legacy. These first symptoms of an "archive fever" in contemporary architectural practice were additionally catalyzed by the rapid commercialization of architectural outlets, the commodification of the archive, the proliferation of architectural museums and collecting institutions,[21] the Pritzker mania, and the unknown political and cultural orbits of star-architecture.

It is hard to imagine the act of design without thinking of the archiving gesture. Mark Wigley argues that "buildings themselves can be understood as archives, that is, mechanisms for storing, classifying, and making historical research available."[22] He goes so far as to claim that almost every design is in a certain way the design of an archiving machine. Architecture acts as a witness and storehouse of culture; every architect is making archives and in a way is an archival expert. I witnessed the entanglement of designing and archiving gestures during my visit to Peter Eisenman's office in New York. Known as a great collector,[23] surrounded by books and boxes of archival materials, pointing to them as we talked, he expounded: "As a collector I keep scraps of paper, letters, and other materials. I have for example, in a box here over forty letters from Colin Rowe. They are amazing letters. But I even did not know that I had them. I just kept the Rowe letters because they were important at the time from 1962–1963 till when I was doing my dissertation at Cambridge."[24] As we further discussed the role of archiving, he carefully traced the distinction between collection and conscious archive, claiming that all his collections (books, magazines, letters from Rowe, drawings by Palladio, and the like) are not "consciously archival." Collecting, amassing, and accumulating are inherent to architectural practice; archiving, however, requires an extra effort to organize, catalogue, take inventory, code, preserve, and maintain a collection.

While collections inspire design, the archive is a product of it, embedded in the design present. It is, as Wigley contends, "what is front of us, that towards which we move, rather than that we leave behind."[25] Taking his proposal to "unleash" the archive from the past, to place it between present and future, we can ask: How do contemporary architects employ an archival logic in their current work? How is the architectural archive produced in relation to design practice today? To what extent does experimental design work depend on intimacy with the archive? How is design practice changing now, in the heyday of the digital era—as archiving is becoming part of a broader culture of sampling, sharing, and recombining visual data in infinite calibrations of users and receivers?[26] What are the specific iconographic, taxonomic, indexical, typological, and archaeological means by which working architects derive and generate new archives in practice today? How are the analytical readings of the nebulous mass of materials from the daily work of a practice structured to become archival? How are the multiple times of designing and archiving producing different instances of the archive? The archival times of image generation, image reproduction, and image documentation are but some of these traces of the multiplication of temporalities. All these questions are important for understanding archiving in design as an active, actual mode of apprehending architectural practice.

This perspective differs from those brought to the artistic archive, seen as a way of questioning the logic of remembering a historic past, of bridling the past, a way of uncovering its hidden or unknown symbolic value, or as a semantic reading meant to create aesthetic ambivalence and project alternative futures. Far from an aesthetization of the archive, where video footage, diaries, documents become aesthetic objects to be exposed, the architectural archive is untidy and not very scenic. There, the materials linger waiting to swim again in the waters of making. Unlike artists, who transform the evidentiary and documentary modes of archival materials into profound reflections on the historical condition, architects are not mysterious agents of History. The taxonomies, typologies, and inventories generated by architects at work are practical shorthand for actively creating design memory and a sensible way of appropriating the recent past. The working archive acts as an active repository of materials that can be galvanized and reincorporated into projects at any time. The final archive, however, is a representative historical form, an enduring site of historical evidence, one whose methodological apparatus does not set "a condition of validity for judgments, but a condition of reality for statements."[27] As repositories and active systems, both the working and the final, the accidental and the purpose-built, architectural archives have an impact on the anticipation of design future.

The Restraint of Architectural Historians

We witnessed how "archive fever" glided simultaneously through adjacent disciplines. Spreading infectiously in philosophy and the arts, it caused the new technologies and the philosophy ways of grappling with them (Derrida's *Archive Fever*) to instigate waves of "turns": the "archival turn" in anthropology, the "empirical turn" in archival science, and the "archiving turn" in architectural practice. Yet, the architectural academic discourse remains barely affected,[28] as the shy reflexivity in architectural scholarship on the conditions of production of knowledge and the techniques of archivization indicates.[29] Historians "use" a large variety of archives on a daily basis—institutional, planning, construction, political, artistic, policy, among others.[30] Archives of architects and designers (whether self-curated and crafted by architects with greater awareness of their legacy or institutionally gathered) are just one part of the larger documentation that historians accumulate. While it is rare to find examples of historians' reflections on their journey to discovering an archive, there are a few that we can build from. In her seminal book, *Privacy and Publicity*, Beatriz Colomina begins her analysis with a reflection on the importance and limitation of the architectural archive in historical research.[31] She draws a powerful contrast: on the one hand, there is the slim archive of Adolf Loos,[32] whose destruction of materials left gaps and difficulties in recovering dispersed documents, which transformed the historian into a detective in her search for materials; and on the other hand, there is the abundant, even excessive, archive of Le Corbusier, who deliberately archived everything related to his private life and architectural work. Developing this juxtaposition, Colomina sheds light on how the historical accounts on the oeuvre of the two architects depended on the scope and accessibility of these two archives. Embarking on a reflection on the conditions of the production of archived architectural knowledge and the tools of the historian,[33] and scrutinizing the archive as an expression of the publicity of the private, she writes: "The archive has played an important role in the history of privacy, even in the history of history."[34] Take a walk, as she did, to visit the archive of Le Corbusier in Paris, and every aspect of the Laroche Jeanneret house (currently the site of the La Fondation Le Corbusier) appears before our eyes gradually fleshing out the distinction between archive as private and history as public. The experience of the archival place and the contrast between Loos's and Le Corbusier's archives instigates a reflection on the mechanisms of the production of architectural history: "'Out of the archive history is produced, but when writing history, the utmost care is traditionally placed on producing a seamless account of the archive, even though all archives are fractural and partial. The messy space of the archive is thus sealed off by a history. History then is a façade."[35] The architectural historian wanders in the archival material and between cities and countries to gather the fragments of archival sources, just as the *flâneur* ambles through an urban space.

Other architectural historians have reflected on the different techniques for constructing archives as sources, in both their limitations and epistemic possibilities.[36] It is here within these accounts that the problematics of the archive for architectural history come to the fore: the specific relationship between the document and the historian, the reflexivity on the role that archives play in the methodology of historical writing, the fragility and clumsiness of what is called Architectural History. The arguments that emerge from these accounts point to the emerging awareness of the archive's limitations or its proliferation in architectural studies, and a sensitivity toward the various historical techniques of approaching it and accounting also for some mechanisms of archival construction. These accounts also posit a special relationship that architectural historians have with time and History, one that needs further elaboration in architectural scholarship. Although these engagements are never explicit, and the archive appears only *en passant*, as a source rather than object of research, they nevertheless gesture in a direction that we can follow toward a careful study of the practices of archiving and the techniques of knowledge production in architecture.

The most recent reflections on the tactics of archiving have been made by biographers of architects who have either been omitted or deliberately excluded from or marginalized in official historiography. Drawing on Minnette De Silva's intellectual and architectural efforts of making an "archive" and her attempts to write her own version of history through text, and at times through architectural and material artefacts, carefully chosen photographs and materials, Anooradha Siddiqi examines "women's vexed relationship to the kind of history that archives typically house."[37] This problem, of how archives often write out voices from Architectural History, also lies at the crux of Antoinette Burton's *Dwelling in the Archive*. Burton challenges the conventional definition of "archive" and what constitutes typical archival "documents" by invoking a type of history written by women, whose diaries and personal archives produce counterhistories. Tracing De Silva's story, that of a woman architect shaping her own archive, while also addressing the archival deficit as a familiar problem among architects, Siddiqi asks, "how an architect's archive comes to mean, how its importance relates to its coherent form, and what aura or additional value a perceived archival integrity lends to an artist's or architect's archive in particular, beyond the confirmation of the details of the life and work intrinsic to the practice of connoisseurship."[38] Le Corbusier's *Oeuvre Complète* inspired the publication de Silva's autobiography, *The Life and Work of an Asian Woman Architect*.[39] Yet, de Silva's work extends beyond biography writing, through a material and visual practice through which she crafted an archive and began sketching a narrative for historians to continue. That is an epistemological intervention to a kind of historical writing. Engaging in a meta-project of history writing—through architecture, images, books, diaries—architects can construct, even craft their own legacy, emphasizing a localization, and a process of subjectification. This self-archivization, which mimics autobiography, is nevertheless unfinished—a work to be completed by historians and biographers.

Very often the act of unveiling a new archive uncovers a new dimension of the architect's profile hitherto unknown. Clément Orillard's work sheds light on the thinking of Gordon Cullen beyond his activities at the *Architectural Review* for which he was predominantly recognized and visible in historiography; through a careful reading of Cullen's notebooks, Orillard recollects his thinking on urban design and "psychological planning";[40] the personal archive sheds light on new facets of his architectural personality. If Orillard recollects a forgotten aspect of an architect, actualizing one possibility of the life of Cullen that his archive provided, the biographer Lilly Dubowitz rehabilitates an entirely forgotten figure in architectural history: Stefan Sebök. Sebök worked with Walter Gropius in Dessau and Berlin between 1927 and 1931, and his drawings for theaters and other buildings appear in many postwar books on the Bauhaus but are usually misattributed to Gropius. Attempting to learn more about her uncle, Dubowitz visited a number of archives including the Bauhaus archive in Berlin, the Busch-Reisinger Museum at Harvard, the Akademie der Kunste in Berlin, the Cologne University Theatre Museum, the archives of the Technische Universität Dresden, the Szolnok Museum, the Shchusev Museum of Architecture, and various archives in Moscow.[41] Recollecting the journey as another architectural detective assembling Sebök's archive, she brings us into the complex network of institutions and the multiple competencies of archivists, translators, researchers, librarians, and other facilitators who are needed for the construction of an archive that will resuscitate him and reinstate him in Architectural History. Similarly, Mark Wigley has recently followed the path of existing evidence on the Anarchitecture collective from the 1970s, assembling more materials while investigating "just like in detective story," to use his phrase, the foundational mythical exhibit of this group. For Wigley, "The forensic investigation of such an elusive exhibition would be less about trying to pin down work that by definition cannot be pinned down and more about understanding the formation of a mythology about a show, a mythology with much wider implications than the exhibition itself."[42] This formation can be traced, according to Wigley, by engaging in a meticulous study of the material traces left in the archive, scrutinizing details such as the number of prints mounted, series of images, handwritten captions, and other material traces from the selection of work for the exhibit. All these oblique archival traces and interviews with participants generate more archives.

Drawing on a case in Perrumbete in Australia, Karen Burns also outlines the importance of bringing repressed, illegible, and cryptic evidence into architectural theory and history writing and reflects on the archives commonly unused by architectural historians (such as juridical archives, oral testimonies, and large-scale mural paintings) and how they resurface, make a return and begin taking part in the rewriting of architectural history.[43] Architectural scholars also reflect critically on the role of photographic archives in the production of architectural history.[44] Most recently, Vandana Baweja investigates the circumstances that led to the creation of an eclectic photographic archive of Otto Koenigsberger in India and the role that this archive played as a historic artifact in Mysorean architectural histories.[45] This archive, she suggests, acted as a powerful tool for representing ideological tensions. Associating pictorial photography and documentary photography with the revivalist architecture in India at the time of Mirza Ismail, émigré Koenigsberger used avant-garde photography to archive his own ideas on modern architecture and mobilize them in the aesthetic battle between Revivalism and Modernism in India.

Besides dealing with an architect's oeuvre, archives have also been used to reflect on urban dwelling and urban culture. While designer-based archives are more often consciously and purposively built, urban living itself results in the accumulation of artifacts that can form "accidental archives" composed of handbills, newspaper pieces, train ticket stubs, fragments of letters and household lists, envelopes, postcards, theater programs, and receipts. According to Joseph Heathcott, the "accidental archive" should be read alongside the "purpose built" one in order to testify for urban culture and everyday life. Analyzing the archive of a *petit bourgeois* family at the beginning of twentieth century from a material culture perspective, he reveals tensions between their upward aspirations and limited means and illuminates how the artifacts expose a set of public enactments lived close to home, as well as the connections to the urban surroundings and to the lively civic and commercial world.[46] The "accidental archive" contains remnants of the banal, everyday life, which nevertheless hold important knowledge for understanding a particular urban culture in the past.

Archives can also contain traces of very specific architectural projects and play an important role in cases where authentic buildings are to be rebuilt and replicated.[47] The existence of physical documentation, in the form of both photographs and working drawings, is crucial when a temporary building is to be reconstructed (the example of rebuilding Le Corbusier's Philips Pavilion from the 1958 Brussels World's Fair is revealing in that regard). In other cases, archives that hold the original design, detailed plans, and drawings play a decisive role in the posthumous constructions of projects for the same site or the same client for which they were initially designed: for instance, Louis Kahn's Franklin Delano Roosevelt Memorial and other buildings were constructed by the Frank Lloyd Wright Foundation; the 1905 project of Yahara River Boathouse in Madison, Wisconsin, of Frank Lloyd Wright was completed in 2007; the Church of St Pierre at Firminy-Vert began construction six years after its architect, Le Corbusier, died and was completed in 2006; and the list can go on and on. In all these cases the construction process relied heavily on the existing archive and the interpretations of the architects who completed the job; while the choices were made based on the type and quantity of the remaining drawings in the archive, they also often undermined and betrayed the singular preservationist intention of the archival material. In his article on the role of the archive for posthumous architectural projects, Neil Levine argues that "in betraying the archive, the building of the unbuilt replaces its authentic record of the past with something that for many people will create not only a false impression of history but also ultimately debase the very legacy of the architect the building was meant to enhance."[48] Facilitating the construction of buildings from scratch and from designs originally intended for different clients, different sites, and even different programs, the archival record, so to say, enables the construction of buildings, not in terms of a perfect resemblance, but as one that rejects notions of authenticity. Without the archive, the building of the unbuilt is impossible.

Without the archive, maintenance and renovation of the built are also difficult. Kent Kleinman studies extensively the recent restoration of the modernist Villa Müller of Adolf Loos built in the 1930s; for him buildings and documents related to buildings have their own, very often divergent trajectories that at best cross only at the moment of construction or renovation and diverge relentlessly over time. In this way "the function of the archive is not to prevent this separation but to insist upon it; to quarantine certain records from the contamination of age, weather, and abuse."[49] Kleinman argues that the archive is more accurately described as a machine for forgetting that architectural projects are ontologically distinct from, and quite distant from, their representations. As buildings age and pass through political and social turmoil, they perform a "revenge" on their archive. He reminds us that historians always perform a fine archival detective work; yet, besides the detective metaphor mentioned in a number of studies above, in the prevailing historical accounts, the traces of deeper investigatory reflexivity regarding archiving remain scarce.

Archives, in architectural accounts, are often scrutinized in terms of their contents; yet, the practices of archiving remain to a great extent underexplored. David Friedman's study of one of the oldest kinds of architectural inventories with visual records constructed in the sixteenth century, the *libro delle case*, or house book, presents a rare story of archival construction, a unique account of the origin of the architectural archive.[50] The 1563 *libro* of Santissima Annunziata contained plans and inscriptions, with each page presenting a single building in a plan that was extensively annotated, with inscriptions that recorded dimensions, detailed the functions of rooms, and introduced data such as the name of renters drawn from the vast archive of textual documents on which the book was based.[51] This detailed information made the "house book" of the Annunziata an archive in miniature; this book and its many Roman successors set the archive in motion and acted as a model for the organization of future architectural archives. The appearance of the "house books" however did not emerge *ex nihilo*, but was tied to the dramatic transformation of the Roman real estate market, as well as economic instability and inflation. The emergence of this archival form was prompted by an urgency to find a new, more comprehensive method for inventorying property. The meaning of archive as inventory is born as a way of documenting what is built and constructed by others, thus allowing the study of architectural properties.

The architectural archive has traveled a long distance from being a descriptive inventory of Roman properties, for which architects played the humble role of measuring, estimating, and describing the physical features of existing buildings, to the purposively built archives, collections, and entire institutions hosting the monumental oeuvres of design creators, whether abundant (such as Le Corbusier's or Buckminster Fuller's) or deliberately destroyed and scarce (such as Loos's), to those assembled by the architects or by others, monographic or corporate, purposively built or accidental, national or private, easy to access or difficult to get to through complex geographies of travels and dispersion; they all marked the history of architecture, shedding light on dwelling and urban life. Archives are not just discovered, but also constructed by scholars according to different research questions, including the pivotal questions of "What counts as architecture, and how?," "Who is an architect?," "What sets urban life in motion, and how?," to mention just a few. In turn, a critical confrontation with archives results in different answers and, ultimately, in the rethinking of the discipline. Even though the attempts to grapple with archives and their logics of formation and legitimization are rare, in the existing accounts we can distinguish two modalities of being: the archive *of* and the archive *for*. The archive *of* an architect/practice—forgotten or present, star or mundane; the archive *of* specific buildings, projects, master plans, cities, movements—iconic or ordinary, groundbreaking or dull, destroyed or forgotten, never built, rebuilt, replicated, restored, never completed. Moreover, archives serve different purposes and ambitions, not just the scholarly ones: archives are used *for*—restoration, rebuilding, rehabilitation, renovation, posthumous construction, replication of the built, art and exhibitions. In all its variances, in all its semantic metamorphoses, and in all its epistemic anxieties, the archive remains a crucial source of architectural knowledge. Far from engaging in a feverish way with archiving—and there is certainly a contrast to be drawn with the impulsive way art, anthropology, and history scholars fell under the contagious influence of the "archive fever" during the past three decades—architectural scholars only notice the archive when it troubles them. The archive only becomes an object of study when an architect is effaced from official historiography, or when a facet of an architectural personality or practice is overlooked, or in situations of difficulty to find traces, of major lacunas, of accidental destruction or accumulation, of economic crisis and inflation, of striking contrast between abundant and poor sources, or the daunting threat that someone else will write that history. When it serves the historian, the archive is invisible, mute, unchallenged in a footnote or image caption, a source of materials "out there"; when it troubles, it resurfaces, it talks, and it interferes epistemologically.

Toward an Anthropology
of Architectural Archiving

All "turns" instigated by the "archive fever" in the 1990s gradually and slowly paved a new era for research on architectural archives. What do architectural historians, ethnographers of design, anthropologists, practicing architects, and archival scientists all have in common? All are concerned with the legitimating social coordinates of architectural epistemologies: how designers imagine they know what they know and how architectural institutions validate that knowledge. All of them are aware that the conventions and categories of analysis are neither neutral nor benign, and that these conventions necessitate addressing a particular set of questions about architectural knowledge. This raises a number of issues rarely addressed in the architectural scholarship. How are working archives and self-referential archives of practices kept and restructured according to different projects' dynamics, which activate them as epistemic forces and rearrange their relational regularities to avoid the "amorphous massing" of things in practice? How is architectural knowledge produced in relation to archiving? How are architectural archives assembled and arranged by collecting institutions? When do they appear and withdraw in time? Which archives remain?

The fear of endless accumulation, of amorphous massing, very prominent in arts and design, can become a driving force for archiving. And if the architectural archive is something more than what "collects the dust of statements that have become inert,"[52] but rather acts as a system of their functioning, how does it come into being? What sets it into motion, and how? How are statements and documents collected? According to what standards? How are they bundled together to make sense and according to which sets of relations? How does the process of archiving factor the nature of architectural archives as discursive and visual at the same time? The successfully composed archive (where a number of relations are established to make it work well) is an archive that "differentiates discourses in their multiple existences and specifies them in their own duration."[53] Archives also relate to a practice that "causes a multiplicity of statements to emerge." It is a practice that enables statements both to survive and to undergo regular modification: "It is the general system of the formation and transformation of statements."[54] This tension between the formation and the transformation of statements, the storing and the activating of the archive, is what I would like to explore here by focusing on archiving as a practice.

Archival institutions are not a popular object of study for anthropologists. They are perceived as dusty and mundane, as the containers for the interesting content we seek, quickly forgotten or reduced to a footnote. They hardly have the exotic appeal that attracts ethnographers to distant cultures; likewise, until recently, architectural practices were not in the limelight of ethnographic attention. Far from a critical appraisal of the archive and its relationships with memory, social identity, and time, and by extension, with History, the ensuing chapters take us into the pragmatics of archiving, shedding light on the ways in which archival documents get assembled in collections and the ways design strategies based on information gathering become a constitutive part of architectural practices. Diverting attention away from the ready-made archive and how it embodies ideologies, symbolizes power, acts as a repressive and/or liberating instrument, or operates as a historiographic source, the study illuminates specific moves of archiving: how ways of organizing documents and taking care of architectural objects constitute an archive and infuse the practices of contemporary architects. The moves are gathered in an ethnographic chronicle.

Architectural archives do not rest frozen in a historical past, to be thawed only for media appearances, for exhibitions in museums of art and architecture, in old libraries, in memorabilia concessions, as monuments and memorials, in private albums, or on computer hard drives. Instead, they are actively mobilized in contemporary thinking about design and in the production of architecture. The CCA provides the best site to witness this. Reflecting the taxonomy, classification, and annotation of the structured past of those architectural practices, movements, projects, and shifts that matter for architecture discourse now, the archives in its collection offer a way to observe, in real-time, the very making of Architectural History. The ethnography of archiving takes us into the world of an institution and into the world of a particular collection; both intersect and overlap as we witness the machine of archiving in action. Yet, as tempting as it might seem, the mere profiling of CCA-as-a-house, as an institution, or as a source is far beyond the scope of this study. Shifting our attention to specific practices witnessed at the CCA, we gain access to the mechanisms of production of architectural discourse and the technologies of architectural collections, and we engage in anthropology *of* archiving.

Although archives are full-fleshed actors in the making of Architectural History, little attention has been paid to the ontology of the archive,[55] as a collection of documents and artifacts that we, as architectural scholars, interact with. Architectural archives behave, look, smell, and sound different from art or literary archives; they have specific spatial arrangements and materialize in unusual embodiments. While anthropologists talk overtly about the difficulties of their fieldwork—the access, the obstacles, the limitations, the positioning of the researcher—for most historians this information is considered "noise." More detailed accounts of the construction of different archives and the specific ways that an archive is brought into the world of architectural scholars are needed. From the incidental accounts of archives as sources, I suggest shifting the attention to archives as practices, as ways of scrambling epistemologies, from archive *qua* noun to archiving *qua* verb, from collections as sites of enduring historical evidence to collections as sites of epistemological reshuffle. This move will require tracing archiving through the daily work and care of archivists and conservators in architecture, as well as the tactics of practicing architects to project an archive-based design future. This shift in attention to archiving gains its contemporary currency from a range of different analytic developments: first, the emergence of a reflexivity trend among architectural professionals and scholars as a key epistemological feature of architectural studies; second, the dependence of architectural history on organized institutional or firm archives (trends of interest in particular architects and periods very often depend on the availability of archives); third, the increasing realization of architecture as a social practice and the awareness of the highly political nature of all outcomes of architectural production.

Far from romanticizing or idealizing archives as sources, what I advocate here is the need to study *archiving* ethnographically—its moves, its mandates, its epistemologies—and the conditions of knowledge production that are facilitated by archiving and are integral to the practices of designing architects. For anthropologists of architecture, this kind of study can provide an opportunity for new fieldworks, inviting them to extend their methodological repertoire to the study of archiving as an underlying dimension of design (similar to some features of design practice that are studied ethnographically, such as modeling, simulating, and rendering). For architectural historians, it can bring a new awareness of how archives are made to serve as an epistemological basis of architectural scholarship; after all, research in archives is where historical science is marked with epistemological credentials. For cognitive anthropologists, it can point to new ways for exploring archival ways of knowing and trans-particular epistemological transfers. For practicing architects, it can signal a fresh way to grapple with the production of architecture: organizing a working archive in a firm is not an innocent matter, in that it reflects its creative culture, and its specific awareness of time and legacy. For those archivists who have already engaged in a reflection on archiving, this study can contribute to initiating new conversations with architectural scholars about documentary evidence, record keeping, archival strategies, conservation techniques, the politics of storage, and born-digital archives. The new reflections emanating from such conversations will have implications for the crafting of Architectural History in the future.

A MORNING IN THE VAULTS

Log: 10:00 a.m. I'm back in Manchester, UK, reviewing the transcription notes from the CCA visit. Paul, my research assistant, has written, "The acoustics changed, suggesting a shift of location: into the vaults." I'm immediately transported back to the vaults. To Montreal. To the CCA and its gloomy corridors. I walk there again, following Giovanna Borasi with my tape recorder; voices and noises tangle; the dancing resonance of Giovanna's and my steps down the corridors, the echoes of words spoken aloud, the effort of opening the heavy door; lastly, the pleasant sound of rustling paper and archivists chattering when we enter the vaults. This is somewhat of an unusual situation for Giovanna (see figure 2). She does not visit the vaults every day. As a curator she comes here occasionally when she wants to see some materials within the context of their archival arrangement. Yet, following Giovanna and sketching ethnographically this visit will provide opportunity for us to dive into the peculiar material world of an archive and grasp its ontic specificity.

We stop in front of the table in the vaults where I saw the Chandigarh drawings a year ago. Familiar! We pause. Giovanna opens a box from the Cedric Price fonds, a private archive acquired by the CCA. I look at the box and take out some of the documents to inspect them closely. YES! I hold them in hands. No vocal interdictions not to touch; no barriers between me and the 1970s-world-of-Cedric-Price. YES! It is a silent, timid but firm "YES!" I am *in*. In the archive. In the microcosm of Cedric Price's architecture.

Talking Boxes: A Note on Ethnography

Standing before the box, Giovanna explains that there are eighteen similar boxes like that one. I am surprised to hear that.[1] Somehow, involuntarily, I picture, just for a second, eighteen huge storage type boxes like the ones I have seen many times at the Office for Metropolitan Architecture (OMA) in Rotterdam.[2] Big bulky boxes stuffed with foam models, paper documents, tools, foam cuts, and other materials. Yet, the boxes we hold with Giovanna are slender, elegant cardboard boxes for files and documents more reminiscent of the smaller folders on the shelves of the bookcases in the OMA office, which designers at work refer to as the "working archives." I have inspected these folders many times while working on the NEWhitney project (a commissioned extension of the Whitney Museum of American Art), and I have seen many documents, press clippings, traces of research, coming out of them and "talking back" to the OMA designers. Yet, most of the OMA boxes are storage boxes for different sized objects; they travel back and forth between the seventh floor of the firm and the basement. At the time I had never thought about the distinction between these two types of archives (the working archives of designers and the archives that go into collecting institutions), nor did I write about archiving during my study there. The need to compare was prompted by an ethnographic similarity experienced and automatically enacted, resonating with the connection between designing and archiving, and my intention is to analyze and reflect on this similarity

At that moment at the CCA, a dialogue with the OMA case has begun; some patterns of knowledge, some analytics from that fieldwork interfered. I did not mean to transport anything from previous ethnographies to the vaults of the CCA that day. It just happened. Their effects appeared and were detected by all the friends in the vaults. And, it then happened again and again. At that moment, it was impossible to treat this fieldwork as separate from the other, to pretend that I lived on an isolated "island" that was never frequented by other professional "tribes" and that its exoticism was worth unpacking on its own without any connections with other distant "islands" that I have visited before and other cultures I have learned from. During my earlier ethnographic studies of architectural practices (OMA, the Foreign Office Architects [FOA], Mosche Safdie architects, among others), a number of key themes emerged: how humans share agency with various nonhumans such as models, software, and renderings; how publics are formed as a project unfolds; how content and context mutate as design develops; how architectural cognition happens on tables of models, not in the designer's mind; and how design messiness generates meaning. And now, while I am staying on the CCA "island," some of these themes have reemerged in an intra-objective

dialogue; the OMA fieldwork "talked back" without any intentional mobiliza-
tion of it. I am not surprised to see the OMA case interfere in my ethnographic
practice *now*, for it was the longest fieldwork I have conducted. It taught me
more about architecture than any school could do and left me with a big ethnographic archive. It was also formative, because it subsequently helped me to fine
tune my actor-network theory (ANT)-inspired ethnography tool kit and to adjust it to the rhythms of architectural "tribes." So, I let this intrusion thrive.

Recent studies in anthropology have suggested that anthropological theory
should not shut out these passages of knowledge from case to case, which allow
for trans-particular ethnographic insights.[3] To overcome the singularity of a case
study and encourage different cases to speak with one another can be revealing.
And here I am, witnessing past ethnographies interfere with a present one and
make analytics of significance transportable, while as an ethnographer-and-writer,
I am gradually absenting myself from the intense scenes of these intra-objective
exchanges. It is from the present study of architectural archiving that the appeal
of connecting to designing, to which the past responds, emerges. Previous cases
intervened in this fieldwork at the CCA without invitation and started operating
as a cryptological key to a larger information set that also began repatterning the
light and shadow around some broader problems of design making and architectural creativity. Not in an imaginary dialogue, but in a sensed reality. Not in a
prejudicial way, but rather played as an innocent recurrent pulsing timbre.

Following a number of friends of architectural objects at the CCA, drafting
their profiles via ethnographic sketches, as I do, I attempt to gain a better understanding of the changing nature of architectural archives and their vibrant connections to design practice. What follows will take us through some of these
sketches. Yet, the dialogue between cases will remain ever-present in the analysis
of archiving. It will also embrace reflections on different fragments from my fieldwork notes that retain the traces of my ontological disturbances experienced in
the world of architectural archiving, as well as the comparative dialoguing with
the OMA fieldwork. They all infused my ethnographic note-taking and my writing like unsolicited guests, and *all* piled up in the present narrative. Cautious of
the risk in making description "thicker" than it usually happens to be, to multiply the color shades before even reaching to the bigger tint clusters, the dense narrative could also paint an ethnographic picture that has more variable hues,
more flesh, with layers that transcend ontologically the two-dimensionality of a
painting, creating a 3D-image that has noises and fragrances, more coatings, not
a simple time-space, but a world.

Thick and intense as reality, this image can contribute to making a statement
against some commonly performed purifications of ethnographic writing, which

rarely involves comparisons between cases and ethnographic positions. Or, I will experiment here with a type of ethnographic narrative that will include the series of mediations that facilitated the writing: my fieldwork experience, queries, and struggles, interpellated by numerous objects of archiving, Paul's notes on the interview transcripts and their different mutations, all our inscriptions and recording and writing tools, the intra-objective dialogues between ethnographic moments of designing and archiving, between the OMA and the CCA, and the intuitive comparisons that emerge in situ. The ethnography follows the different rhythms of archiving work, integrating the techniques of capturing these rhythms that will follow the beat and amplify the breadth of the anthropological enquiry. The comparison "intensifies" the act of field observation, or what Marilyn Strathern calls the "ethnographic moment,"[4] the moment when the fieldwork is recreated in a reflective and analytical field (in the writing-up). This results in a narrative that has the ontological thickness of many reverberations of past fieldworks, foldable times of fieldwork, technical mediations of writing, of different noises, or better, echoes.

"Archiving" refers to the process of collecting observable traces, recordings, translations, transcriptions, and visuals—that is, a record-keeping process that is also central to ethnography and enables us to witness other worlds; these worlds are in themselves archival. Why should we remove the experiences of previous fieldwork, or appeal to a purity of isolated sites? Letting the different fieldwork cases speak to each other, in a lively intra-objective way, through the specific empirical givens of the local circumstances of fieldwork, will multiply the records, will grow the archives. As a result, the links between the particular and transparticular will become more distinct, more vibrant. However, additional methodological questions pile up: How is learning across case studies possible? Can ethnography analytics resist transportation? What is the nature of "transportable analytics" that migrate from one ethnographic "island" to another? How do they retain their invariance or internal structure as they move? How do they make sense in a new field? How do they exist as "trans-temporal"?[5] Attempting to answer these questions will bring both the "brutality" of the diary[6] and the direct spontaneous interference of other diaries and writings back from the past, into the tangible immediacy of writing *now*, embracing a foldable, reversible, and multi-layered course of ethnography.

It is an established anthropological wisdom that the particular, the specific, and the exotic can be better grasped in their immediacies, and by recurrently taking multiple distances from these immediacies. To the Geertzian multiple existence of the ethnographer-as-a-writer—that is, to convey in writing something that the anthropologist has experienced "elsewhere" in relation to what is said "now"—I add one more layer: another fieldwork "elsewhere" emerges in the ethnography "now" and interferes in the writing "here and now." What happens when we add the intensity of time to the varying spatiality of writing? It naturally adds to the narrative a degree of complexity, of laterality and multi-layerness, and makes it a richer canvas painted with palette knives. Not a problem of psychological nature, of exaggerated reflexivity, but rather a problem of literary nature[7]—multiplying even more the ethnographer's position, which, far from being relaxed, exists in different tensions and different distances, in a foldable Deleuzian time. This way of writing is a way to slow down[8] even more, and ask, when a trans-particular import from one case to another occurs, how do we take it into account into the immediacy of ethnography? What prompts past knowledge, gained in the complex specificity and intense circumstantiality of an ethnographic site, to become trans-particular now? How can patterns of knowledge and ways of knowing become trans-particular imports for our actors? All these conditions of knowing, and transport of analytics, all together, all at once, multiply the eclecticism of ethnographic data shaped by "our own constructions of other people's constructions of what they are up to"[9]—diverse, partial, circumstantial, and volatile, thus intensifying further the "ethnographic moment."

Another way to pose the question of archiving is: How can the past, which has presumably ceased to be, preserve itself? As the philosopher who accorded to the past its proper mode of existence, Henri Bergson stated, "Practically, we perceive only the past, the pure present being the invisible progress of the past gnawing into the future."[10] The OMA's talking back and intervening in the CCA means that immediate parts of the past push into the future and seek to realize and associate with it. The integral survival of the ethnographer's past experiences is not to be excluded from the process of tracing archiving, sketching an unfolding of the different states of archiving and its multiple dynamics. Tracing moves of archiving now, by sliding into past ethnographies of architectural practice, constitutes an ever-renewed present: this is the direction of travel of this ethnographic study. And present is the only tense an ethnographer can master for "only the ethnographic present preserves the reality of anthropological knowledge."[11] As the awareness of some current processes of archiving reveals itself as recollection of past experiences witnessed in design, the ethnography becomes a place of passage of the movements received from past and thrown back, a hyphen, a connecting link between the things, between designing and archiving. Tracing the everyday rhythm of archiving and its web of moves in the present is a way to re-activate the design past and access the *current* conditions of architecture making in order to be able to reach out to its future.

Wonders in a Box

At first glance, the archival boxes of Cedric Price's fonds appear in a rather cluttered state. The messy archives keep the traces of design process as they were left by the practice, while the well-organized archives, or the "sanitized archives," as Mirko Zardini calls them, keep the fingerprints of an archivist who has translated the design process into an archival order, a true mediator between designing and archiving. The recently donated archive of Álvaro Siza is an example of such a well-structured archive (as discussed in chapter 6). The order in the archive reveals the degree of archival awareness of each architectural practice. As Espeth Cowell, who is in charge of collection and program services at the CCA, elaborates, "Whoever gives you the archives has a specific awareness or lack of awareness of what an archive is. In some cases, they give you too much. In other cases, they don't give you enough."[12] The quantity and the arrangement of the archival objects received reflect a specific concern about architectural legacy, as well as all mediations, human and technical, that have facilitated the production of the archives.

Giovanna and I start opening more boxes of Cedric Price's fonds together. "An archive is like a box of surprises,"[13] observed the CCA head archivist Robert Desaulniers many times. Look at Giovanna. Look at the box. Can we for a moment forget the existence of Giovanna without what she holds in her hands? And does the box make any sense if Giovanna is not holding it, pointing to specific materials in it, flipping through pages, expecting to be surprised?

She takes a red folder out of the box, the McAppy report—a proposal by the British architect Cedric Price in the 1970s on how to improve labor conditions on the building site by increasing the mental and physical conform of the employees. Then, she shows the different documents in the box (see figure 3). The numbers correspond to different subjects/themes covered by the report. Number fifteen is "lighting," sixteen is "safety and security"; she goes through all the folders until twenty-three. The structure of the report reflects all the research areas Cedric Price had to cover in his work. As we flip through the sections of the McAppy report, we learn about the architect's research of lighting; we see a paper cut from a "Health and safety at work" seminar, then images of safety equipment and fire protection clothes, among other things. What an amazing range of things come out of the box! What a dazzling entangled world of Cedric-Price-and-1970s-British-society is stored in that box! This brings us again to the OMA and the amazement of all the architects observed, startled as they were to see an ethnographer following architecture in the making. Back to Giovanna, and her own amazement at being part of an ethnography of archiving. She adds: "Archives are brilliant because there are so many funny things, you know? So especially with

FIGURE 2.   Giovanna in the vaults, CCA

Cedric Price it's really a delight to go through the boxes. You always find strange surprising things." Blending social, design, and technical features, these objects are reminiscent of wonders; the archival space appears as a site where the hybridization of particular features of British culture, societal concerns, and architecture design have been intensified further before cementing marvelous tangles of design content and context in a box.

Let us contemplate the effect that opening the Cedric Price box has on Giovanna. She is silent for a moment; then, forgetting my presence, she spends more than a few minutes staring at a document, turning it around, getting lost in some details. Is she talking to it, questioning its nature in a mute way, dialoguing soundlessly with its hidden history? Is the document taking her back to a moment in her curatorial practice when she happened to interrogate it in a vocal way or when she made it speak openly? Or is the document talking to her the way that architects, models, and sketches talk to one another in design? I interrupt the silence. Afterward, we spend some time looking at military images (radar reflective survival jackets; see figure 3). Contemplating all these materials, we also find letters with quotes and prices, written as a result of an enquiry from Price on specific costs. There are also catalogues. We flip through the letters written to Cedric Price (see figure 4), and we can find out what exactly he was searching for and

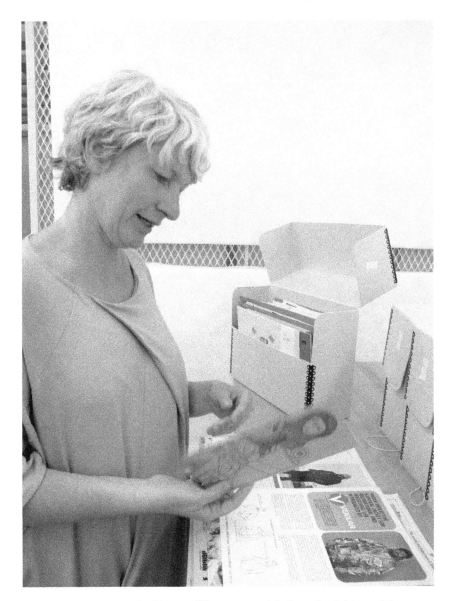

FIGURE 3. Giovanna looking at different materials from the folders of the Cedric Price fonds, CCA

why he was asking for specifications for different kinds of things. In another box we find a folder with Price's Aviary project in London, 1963; we look at the plan for the park and the structures for animals. We inspect all the books he collected for the project, trade catalogues about animals, some letters, and so on. The archive contains heterogenous materials that Giovanna tries to decipher as signs,

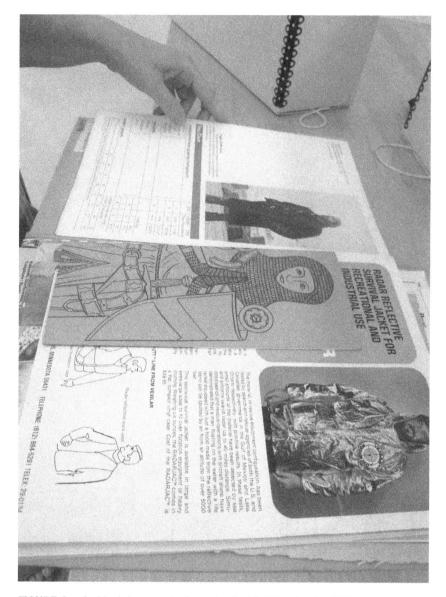

FIGURE 4.   Archival documents from the Cedric Price fonds, CCA

as "hieroglyphs," and in opening the box, she begins thinking through them, interpreting and translating them.

Giovanna's profile is sketched here with a big brush: she becomes the spokesperson of Cedric Price's archive; the archive shrinks into a number of boxes, and the boxes shrink to folders and disparate documents. Yet, as we go from Giovanna to red folders, to scruffy letters written on tracing paper and colorful leaflets, we do not descend from the Master of Archives to the small archival items, from the genus of archiving to the specifics. Instead, what we witness is Giovanna emerging through the successive minute operations of archive reading. Sketches of her will appear at other sites; for instance, we will see her making decisions on objects in the shipping area or discussing the curatorial program in her office. Here, though, what we see is a particular Giovanna who is attached to the archival boxes; in other sketches, she might hold different objects—exhibition drawings, budget letters, scale models, conservation lab reports—and appear attached to them differently. In these situations, her engagement varies, the modalities of action of the objects in her hands multiply, and so does her expertise—distributed, aerial, positioned, and compound. Tracing her attachments, we also trace her way of becoming part of the institutional expertise.[14] In fact, she is one of CCA's key assets. Her expertise is also multi-sited, yet, situated and traveling simultaneously, multi-siting and so are the composite entities that we discover: Giovanna-and-the-archival-boxes, Giovanna-picking-objects-for-an-exhibition-project-on-the-table-in-the-shipping-area, Giovanna-in-her-office-with-her-curatorial-team. All these sketches, all together, paint the portrait of Giovanna; tinted and bundled; brushed and retouched, outlined and reshaped by swarms of all these situated actions, dispositional—involving both a manner of arrangement and the potentialities of the things so arranged—and so is the expertise that will be activated as she moves from one situation to another.

During the box "inspection" we witness a strange magic trick, where amazing things come out of a simple enigmatic treasure box full of wonders. Yet, the nature of the materials coming out of the boxes in the CCA differs from those in the OMA. What "portable analytics" have been brought *here* to the CCA? How do they help the immediate ethnographic experience *now*? How do they add to the immediacy of writing? While in the thin CCA boxes we see files and paper documents only, there is a greater multiplicity of foam cuts, paper drawings, and tools hidden in the square storage type of archival boxes at the OMA. They differ in quantity, in weight, and in the degrees of heterogeneity of the materials contained; hence, they testify to a distinct ontological thickness of the assorted nature of the design processes reflected there. When compared to those in the CCA, the boxes in dialogue talk about specific analytics: the course of a design process, its rhythms and various streams, generates a collection of objects with variable ontology; when gathered and enclosed, they become an assortment that is meant to preserve the momentum of architecture making, to contain and prolong the duration of making, yet detaching it from the excitement and spurs of many spontaneous moments of creativity. The heterogeneity of archives is related also to the fact that, as Mirko elaborates, "architects are not the best people to deal with the archives, and the archive is what is left of a lot of actions, and a lot of material is lost, or destroyed, and not considered valuable."[15] What appears initially like a strange magical box, we hear from Mirko, is rather a selection that bears traces of destruction and hazards. In addition, the boxes we open (and intuitively compare with the boxes from the OMA) testify to the original ambition of the CCA to collect material that will be able to reveal the process more than the products of architecture making. This dialogue with the OMA comes to question the process that makes a random collection of heteroclite materials, still distilling the smell of freshly cut foam and holding imprints from the warm hands of many designers, shrink, lose weight and thickness, and fit into a box.[16] Archival objects have a different mode of existence when contracted to the size of their boxes. The archive hosts an assortment of architectural materials that once had a life in an office, objects that witnessed excitement and suffering, objects that had "experienced" the whirlwind of architecture making.

Original Order, Apparent Disorder

Back to the red folder, we read "McAppy, Angel Court Story, June 1975," and with a felt-tip orange pen someone has added a note on that same label: "office copy." And then, as the folder comes out and rests for a few minutes in Giovanna's hands, we are suddenly transported to the past in a flashback, as Giovanna recounts a story:

> In 1973, following the strikes that beset the British construction industry during the early 1970s, Alistair McAlpine commissioned a design program for his construction company, Sir Robert McAlpine & Sons, that aimed to increase production efficiency and improve labor relations. He asked Cedric to look at the years when in England there were all these strikes on construction sites, safety issues, and so on, so as to rethink the construction site, and to actually look at how they can facilitate the work but also make it more efficient. Cedric took this much more seriously, and he really wanted to look not only into how the organization of the site as a kind of production is run, but also what happens with the health of the workers; he looked at the safety issues, what workers will eat, etc. He started to kind of design everything. And he ended up having something that is called a "maquette report," a kind of full report.[17]

As soon as the story stops, we return to the present, to the archive room, to the here-and-now, and yet, the story still resonates in the background. Now, Giovanna and I can look soberly at the archival nature of that folder: we look at the acquisition numbers, letters, and codes on the box and carefully try to decipher them. The letters "DR" stand for "drawings." In the beginning, as the CCA collection was partitioned into photography, prints and drawings, books, and various kinds of ephemera, they were all numbered with a different code. Now it is one collection. But even as it is one collection, the numbering or identification continues to reflect the different parts of the collection. One collection means that it can be searched and used as one, but the different objects are still defined in media terms: photos, drawings, archives, books. The code reflects the different internal organization of the materials. Yet, when this particular box was acquired, it was part of "prints and drawings," which is why we read "DR" on the box, the photographs have "PH," the books have "BIBL," and so on. Then, we read "1995": the year when the archive was acquired. This is exactly twenty years after the McAppy report was written. What an interesting gap to explore! Another number follows: "0263." This is the project number and also, explains Giovanna, a series number. All these codes and numbers suggest order. But what kind of order is this? If the different codes situate archival material within the spatial flatness of the CCA collection, the years indicate time that is far from being chronological, synchronic, and linear; it rather "gallops" in a disorderly way. Polyphonic, multilayered, and foldable, it emerges in terms of meaningful events: the year of acquisition or donation, the year of the project, the year a letter was written. These are hints as to the nature of the archive as a specific spatiotemporal organization of a quasi-autonomous body of work.

While inspecting carefully the content of the folder, we find many similar documents. Mirko's words resonate: "When you go into an archive, in reality, everything looks like a mistake."[18] It is a messy place, a place of total disorder on which a first layer of order has been imposed. I am trying to grasp this ordering. Giovanna points to the maquette and the copy, then numerous photocopies, and many numbers added to the project. It was initially organized in this way, she explains, meaning that all copies and repetitions were part of the workflows and ended up in the archive. All repetitions were part of the original order, and this order has to be preserved, we are reminded. The idea of an original order along with the idea of provenance (the ability to trace the creator(s) of an archive, a fonds) are key principles in archival practice, and that is why it is important "to reflect as much as possible on the original order in which the documents were created, gathered, or used."[19] The archivist, as Robert puts it, is "the professional who is preoccupied by maintaining the archival qualities of a group of documents received."[20] The main task of the archivist is to try to understand how the documents were produced and how exactly they were used in the context of a design practice, and their original arrangement; the archivist is very cautious not to disturb that particular order in which the records were made, and tries to maintain it as such.

There is a significant epistemic dimension that matters for both the archivist and the researcher: "The original order is important as there is a lot to be learned from why you [the architect] kept certain things."[21] In some cases, it is difficult to interpret the original order, and the archivist is required to arrange the material in a "way that will make sense."[22]

Knowing what original order implies, we now flip through the materials in the box, and we notice several more different copies and originals all together and that they are kept and bound in a specific way. Clarifying the repetition, Giovanna explains: "Often what we have in all these folders is actually the preparatory work to arrive at the report. You might see the same thing many times. Here you have this original. But you might see the same thing photocopied, re-photocopied, different versions."[23] Giovanna finds some logic and order in that deceptive untidiness and apparent disorder. It points to a relational arrangement in which the materials were generated through design in the culture of the practice of Cedric Price. Reading the internal irregularities and repetitions enables archivists and curators to recollect the process and track back design research. As Robert puts it, "The archive is a group of objects in which all the documents have an organic link."[24] The multiplicity of things accommodated by an archive reflects the irregular course of design process; both quantity and interrelations are important to be able to fully recollect that process. Redundancy is common for an archive, and in particular for the Cedric Price fonds. In that aspect, too, the archive mimics the turbulent course of design, full of precipitations that create duplications and result in significant variations.

Flipping through the repetitive versions, the curator and the archivist perform a reading of the surface that confirms the power of all variations and heterogeneous series; for the variety of versions "in rising to the surface, causes the Same and the Like, the model and the copy, to fall under the power of the false."[25] They create a nonhierarchical assembly where through the series of repetitive documents with variations, a kind of internal reverberation is produced that can overflow the series themselves. Opening the box, Giovanna performs a reading of all signs on the surface, thus enacting the power of all heterogeneous series as what stays on the surface and dilutes the binary of original and duplicate, of appearance and essence.

However, as soon as we question why one type of document is so present in the archive, we are inevitably led to another set of questions: "What challenges were at stake?," "Why did they have to make so many copies?," "What did they struggle with?" None of the repetitions we witness in the box is random; the extra copies point to a moment of difficulty, a significant battle in the practice that led to many attempts, many trials. The discernible material accumulations of things allow archivists to speculate on why so many versions of the same were produced at a particular moment of the development of a project, to interpret how these repetitions were significant for the design practice. I begin to grasp this implicit sense of order behind the apparent disorder, the timid, slow and creeping change that many versions not of the original, but *in addition to it,* are able to produce. Giovanna warns, "We should be very careful when we go through the material in the box as we should not disrupt the order."[26] Looking at the "maquette report," we find all the preparatory material, all the sketches that helped Cedric Price's practice to organize it, and the materials they took from the general report. The text documents referenced by the report are in separate sections, numbered differently. Thus, in the box, all the bits and pieces that helped produce the McAppy report—drawings, copies, images, working drafts, letters, calculations, quotes, magazines, press clippings, trade catalogues—are kept in the exact disorder in which they were found in Price's practice. What might appear as a joyful messiness is rather a meaningful ordering, and as such it is jealously preserved. Here, the archive presents itself as a particular space that accommodates traces from various flows, intensities, and irregularities of time; the foldable, fast-running, disjointed time of design creativity has left its scars on it. What also makes it special is the fact that it is "qualifying a set of relationships between the objects that is very different from taking ten drawings from a project."[27] It embraces varied working materials maintaining their togetherness according to their very specific inherent collaborative dynamics. This is what makes an archive very different from a collection of drawings. It is neither a random assortment of things, nor a linear sanitized collection of objects, but a body of work defined by design-driven connectivity, forces and tensions, interventions and inventions. Here lies another feature of the archive: a relational entity, assembled to host, juxtapose, and preserve the traces of making *in addition* to the objects and the intrinsic creative dynamics of a practice; it is a way of connecting things both to the eye and to the discourse.

Examining further the question of redundancy in the box arrangement, Giovanna explains: "This is the way it has been put together. It is exactly how it came from the office of Cedric Price. We are trying to respect how the box was in the office. The sequence stays exactly the same."[28] This is precisely because the archive strives to maintain the connection to design practice and the particular order of things generated there, keeping the imprints from Price's and his collaborators' hands, the echoes of design hubbub, the hidden patterns of the office routines, that it is never catalogued at the object level. The McAppy report and the drawings are not classified as individual objects; it is the box that remains the discernable unit and that is numbered, and through this number gains an existence. Giovanna warns me: if I select a document out of the box, I can pull it out, and I will give that document a specific number that will carry also the same number as the box; singling out that document, I will give it an object number while the other materials in the box will remain unnumbered. A marker indicating where the object was taken from should be placed in the box. When an object is taken out of the dormant and well-ordered spatial arrangement of the archive, it gains visibility; it becomes distinct, numbered, it counts, it exists. That number also indicates traceability—that is, the reassurance that the document will return to the right place in the folder, in the box, without the risk of any disruptions in the initial organization. No matter how messy the ordering appears to be at a first glance, there is a logic behind it that is precious, and that is why it is cautiously preserved. Watch Giovanna taking the yellow document, putting a paper saying "GB Lisbon" and a number next to it to indicate the place where it was found and where it should return. Both the object and its specific location (page, placement in the box) get demarcated by numbers, allowing the initial archival ordering to be reestablished. What may look as a random set of gestures of flipping through, pointing out specific documents, selecting, pulling out, numbering, tracing paths, making their coming back possible, all these series of moves and the traces they leave also enter the box. Making the objects' "journeys" traceable, these molecular operations *add* more records to the box (through paper cuts, numbers, post-its), more paper, more traceability; they make history themselves, and they become archival.

Misleading Similarity

To find out what similarity means in this context, I question Giovanna to better understand the status of copies in an archive. She explains that what appear to be photocopies of the same are "not just [the original] photocopied ten times." The careful eye is able to discern tiny variations: "You see that the dates may be changing but the text is always the same. There is this idea that among other materials, that particular one was quite important, because throughout the process it was always there, that thing."[29] One document, many dates, many changing dates. Why this repetition? What varies and what remains invariable? And what does this mean? Inspecting the box, I see that it is important not just to have the document and understand its positioning in the relational set of the archive, but to comprehend why it repeats itself in so many variations, and how it builds a meaningful accumulation of things.

The question of archival repetitions reveals the dynamic intensity of the design process. Intensity brings me back to the OMA, where architects frantically produced many alternative scenarios for developing a building, many options, many variations of foam models and drawings following an invariable pattern of constraints, regulations and client's demands.[30] The same models made and re-peated many times, in different scale, with small variations. All of them placed on the table of models, storage boxes, or in presentational books. The obsession with many-ness hints at a moment of intense experimentation resulting in reit-erations that are kept; they uphold both the options and the process that gener-ates them. They also refer to a flash of forceful brainstorming, a detour from a so-called linear course of design; there, the intensity of time drives toward sig-nificant accumulations of trials, foam pieces, diagrams, cuts, letters, stuff. Amaz-ingly at the OMA, architects do not produce "one huge realistic model of the whole," one successful prototype that will endure throughout the design process and be gradually transformed into a building or end product. Rather, they pro-duce options, variations; the building exists as a collection of these, as a concen-tration of things, as added intensities of detail. It is designed and perceived as multiple, not one.

Back to the CCA boxes. Giovanna now explains that in the archive of Abalos & Herreros, the curators found many collage pieces—similar cut-outs found hun-dred times. This excessive repetition eventually indicates an office struggle to find the right colors, the best shades of blue, the ones that match the clouds. While the collage is kept in the archive, the hundred repetitions give an idea of the pro-cess of its making; the innumerable cut-outs render the process traceable, recol-lectable. That is another way to tackle many-ness, and the multiverse that a building is.[31] It takes us back to that practice, even though we have not been there ethnographically; yet, its specificity is brought by Giovanna through the "cone of time"[32] bringing thousands previous experiences right into the plane of action of our current conversation in the vaults. What we witness, surprisingly, is that in that particular moment, Giovanna also transports analytics from her curatorial work. Those same analytics—design is the product of many repetitions with vari-ations; a design object exists as many, not one—travel in an involuntary way in her response; all these unsolicited "guests" brought by the act of questioning ar-chiving end up amplifying the narrative. Giovanna pictures what "option mak-ing" means in an OMA context; similarly, I imagine Abalos & Herreros architects designing a fictional landscape, and the frantic process of testing colors, print-ing, and trying to figure out "if the building should have the same color as the sky as it could run the risk to melt into the landscape."[33] Dark blue follows light blue hues, tested, printed, reprinted, cut out, juxtaposed, growing into new shades. Hundreds of cut-outs pile up in the office; kept, superimposed, amassed, rear-ranged relationally, they form an archive. Repetitions can help us make assump-tions about the nature of a design process. They tell the story of how, eventually, a hundred shades of blue came together to shape an imaginary landscape in the practice of Abalos & Herreros.

There is indeed a resemblance between the way the OMA is interpellated in the act of ethnographic questioning of archiving here, and the way Abalos & Herreros's practice comes to Giovanna's way of responding to it. In this dialogue we discover the similarity, and we witness that "portable analytics" retain some invariance or internal structure as they move into a new site (design is an option-making process, and options co-exist with, produce, and extend the original, whether an initial sketch or a building). However, they could also gain a new form as they are transported from one set of particulars to another. When we are ethnographically tracing the phases of design at the OMA, they manifest themselves as a process of option making. Option making appears at the CCA in the form of readable traces of an ordering of things that contains "copies, not *of* the original, but *in addition* to it." So, when a "portable analytic" is used, it does not aim to return to an initial, genuine design experience to clarify some meaning of it, but rather to elicit differences in the here-and-now. In addition, the archive made out of disparate parts of the architectural past, heteroclite and uneven, bears a striking similarity to the practice of the ethnographer, tracing, keeping record of this process, memorizing, recollecting, going back, repeating, and thus integrating past ethnographies into the present "now." That is how "portable analytics" start operating as a "cryptological key" that works in a dynamic way, recognizing the similarities and repatterning light around the issues of design creativity.

Flipping through these repetitive documents, we understand that when the CCA collects archives, it collects design processes, not individual artworks. As Giovanna sums up, "The challenge with architecture, as you know, is that you cannot have the final work. You just collect surrogates or traces of that in the preparation for the process of thinking."[34] If the drawing is taken out of the archive, isolated, separated from the relational ordering of the box, its mode of existence will be similar to that of an artwork; artistic outputs of architects would commonly constitute fine art collections. Yet, as architectural archives are collections of documents and artefacts created jointly by big practices, not just one author, they are more complex than art collections; the architectural collection does not contain the work (building) but the ideas of the work, and many versions of it, the process. That is why the archive that we witness here is not a final resting place for a number of outlandish objects; it is rather an active tool for recollecting the practice of creative making that led to them. From the inspection of the box we learn: when you as an architect archive, you collect materials that capture the repetitive, eclectic, contingent, and relational nature of design; when you as an archivist, curator, or theorist of architecture interpret an archive, you make sense of traces and rhythms of design process, as well as worlds interpellated involuntary. At the CCA we find the realm of design practice deployed in its extremity: working models, traces of experimentation, surrogates, lines of investigation undertaken by designers, in *addition to* the drawings and sketches. And, that is why, quite understandably, the OMA comes to speak to the CCA, why designing and archiving reconnect.

Surprisingly for some, no sketches of single masters are seen in this box. Surprising, because architectural process is easily mythologized before being subjected to empirical analysis; a sketch is often canonized as "first" or as "final" in design theory in order to enhance the mythology of the architect's genius. Yet, this is a predictable finding for an ethnographer of architecture—she expects to see working copies not mythical originals. It is by tracing the networks of design making that we can demonstrate the fallacy of some beloved and well-established myths of creativity in architecture: the belief in the original sketch or initial idea, the magic of the creative moment, the idealization of the final product—that is, a logic that places the design process in a linear progression of achievements. We can see all these myths collapsing spectacularly here, again. Flipping through the pages of an archive, we see a myriad of working sketches and documents; while the early conceptual or presentational drawings "can be very boring to a certain extent,"[35] they are of greater interest than the final ones as they bear witness to the development of design ideas and speculations; their flow demonstrates the epistemic complexity of architecture making. Examining the archive, where so many reiterations coexist in a condensed way, design can be defined only as what emerges in the relational world of a practice, through many variations, collective experiments, and in a frantic dialogue with materials and shapes, bodies and technologies, not in the solitary mind of one creator. The multiplicity is valued here; that is what connects designing with archiving. Far from reflecting one iconic work or the oeuvre of a single author, an architectural archive subsists as a dynamic relational aggregate, celebrating repetitions, tolerating irregularities, reproducing many-ness, generating wonders. Bathing in silence, where only the "sounds" of juxtapositions and reverberations of proximity can be "heard," the archive does not rest in the shiny vaults, but is rather constantly alert and alerted by the renewed epistemological anxieties of all those who open these living folders.

How Repetitions Make Differences

In the boxes of Cedric Price's fonds, I inspect the documents that came out of the box and its folders. In addition to the traces of design thinking and research; these folders also keep traces of the social and cultural networks that Cedric Price considered in his architectural work. The technologies at the time, the developments in Britain in the 1970s in the field of mobile electricity or lighting, the economic rationale behind costing specific technological equipment, the relevant lighting, health, and safety regulations—all these developments are also stored in the box. And when Giovanna and I start taking the documents out—the strange costumes, the technical objects, the price lists, the letters, the accounts of conditions at the construction sites, the paper clippings—all these beings, objects, their times and spaces, all at once come out of the files. A world in a box!

Reflecting on the multitude of things we flip through and discuss, Giovanna states that "it's not that this object per se is so important, but actually the entire bundle of things Cedric Price was looking at sheds light also on the practice of the industry, technological developments, and other spheres."[36] That is, context is not artificially isolated there; it is rather part of the whole process of thinking, visualizing, and assembling the ingredients needed to imagine an architectural intervention. And it is by flipping through the traces left from Price's practice that we get to grasp "drops"[37] of contextual mutations that happened simultaneously as the architectural thinking on a project unfolded. And thus, we find ourselves here in a regime of experimentation and technological innovation that is not necessarily related to an end product. In an archival box we uncover a body of work consisting of heterogeneous pieces and presented relationally—drawings, but *also* the correspondences, the budget, the refusals, the nasty letters, the quotes, the paper clippings collected by the architects that all hint to the context. The heterogeneity of that "bundle of things" reflects not simply the composite collective nature of a design process, but also the entangled relationship of design with social and technical factors. The architectural works of Cedric Price emerge from the society's anticipation of architectural design, rather than flowing from the architect's fantasia. Giovanna adds, "You can actually look at this [the box and what multiple materials come out of it] and you can forget it's about Cedric Price."[38] It is a world on its own; it is a microcosm.

Thus, the archive does not simply reflect "the leavings of an architect showing his thought."[39] Defying all laws of gravity, it rather holds a carefully coated aggregate of those "drops" of social, technological, and cultural worlds that make architecture possible and are so dense and colorful that we "can forget it's about Cedric Price" or, indeed, any other particular architect. The first Canadian archive acquired by the CCA, the Ernest Cormier fonds, for instance, contains his paintings, correspondence, collections of photographs, tools for making books and book covers, sculptures, paint boxes and paintbrushes. It also includes photographs he made, which reflect the social and political influences upon his work, and his library, which is an index of the cultural influences. And we can continue the list. All these materials matter for understanding the creative world of Cormier.[40] They also tell us a story about the air of time and the cultural and societal energies setting Cormier's creative machine in motion. And indeed, since its beginning, the CCA (and first Phyllis Lambert) collected primarily a multiplicity of working drawings and materials that document the thinking process of architects and the social and cultural issues that are entangled with architecture—never just single drawings (first or final). The archive emerges as a broader entity: "It's drawings, plus, plus, plus, and drawings in a different way too. And it [the archive] gives you a chance to think differently, think out of the box, think about how architects relate to society."[41] It also outlines the contextual entanglements that makes architecture possible. Here the archive echoes the fallacy of another myth, the myth that architecture is just architecture, for its autonomy tale often exists as the twin brother of the genius myth.[42]

Is this relevant to the archives of contemporary architects and practices? The relationship between the folders of Cedric Price's fonds and the folders at the OMA labeled as "research" resurfaces again. When archivists explain that the CCA is more interested "in offices which have a strong research component," the box comparison that brings together Carol Patterson, the project manager of the NE-Whitney at the OMA, and the project files from 2001 in dialogue with the files of Cedric Price's projects from the 1970s appears more boldly and materializes ethnographically as a comparative appraisal. Yet, Giovanna explains, the McAppy report was a "very special project of Cedric Price where he was working on something like designing a system more than an object, a flow of things inside a construction site."[43] Therefore, the research conducted is very specific as it is related to the flows of things, rather than buildings, moving systems rather than fixed design products, which summons another similarity with the OMA. To develop this contrast further: in the Universal Studios project, for instance, the OMA is concerned with a number of research questions that have a wider cultural and social resonance: "What is entertainment now?" "What is a movie?" "What is a theme park?" While designing the Seattle Public Library, the OMA architects tackled questions such as "What would it mean to read in the twenty-first century?" "What is the future of the book at the time of digitalization?" "What kind of cultural practice is reading?" "What should the library of the future look like?" Therefore, designing a building is not just about form and function, or program and aesthetics. It involves a wider reflexive questioning of the technologies of the time and a critical engagement with the cultural and social consequences of design. This is what defines research in firms such as the OMA, and the specific answers to these questions "land" in the folders of many archival boxes, as witnessed here at the CCA. Designing and archiving reconnect again. Full of various, sometimes surprising, "strange things" as Giovanna calls them, the archival folders have a life of their own; they "talk" and tell stories about the perplexing nature of what designers call "research"[44] and the pitfalls of architecture making.

What we learn, as we conclude the visit of the vaults with Giovanna and from the slow ethnography of that particular scene of archiving, is that an architectural archive reflects to a great extent a specific understanding of architecture. Architecture, considered as a building, will require its archive to be a composition of representations of it, such as elevations, drawings, and other visuals. Yet, a different understanding of architecture not just as a building, but also as the social conditions, cultural context, the information and technologies available for the architect at that moment inevitably emerges from an archive that echoes that wider idea of architecture; far from including documents *of* buildings, *of* final works, it captures buildings-in-connection-to-societies-and-cultures, through materials that will account for the process of design, *plus* the conditions of production and consumption of architecture, *plus* the contributions of other participants in architecture, *plus* the technologies that make architecture possible. An archive is, thus, a much bigger and complex, relational, *additive* entity, rather than a simple projection of the mind of one architect, of "a heroic genius, acting as the lightning rod for the storm of forces that goes into the making of building."[45] It emerges as the product of the work of many; what transpires along with the wonders coming out of the folders of Price's fonds, is a colorful crowd of contractors, clients, industry people, manufacturers, planners, engineers, military people, inventors, commercial agents, all speaking *on behalf of* and *in relation to* architectural works; they resurface from letters, legal documents, quotes, contracts, and newspapers, all contained in the box. They are all witnesses to the growing realization of architecture as a collective social practice.

Conclusions: Closer, but Not Too Close!

What is the nature of the objects in Giovanna's hands? Can we define them as "design," or as purely "social" or "cultural" objects? None of these definitions will give justice to their peculiar nature. Blending social, design, cultural, and technological features, these objects merge aspects of all these realms. Neither purely design nor social materials, they are rather "hybrids" in which either society has begun the work of architecture or architecture has extended the work of society; it is that process of mutual imitation that is wondrous.[46] Inspecting these objects, we see that context is part of the archival boxes of Price's fonds, not outside of them defining his architecture. Here, architecture does not usurp or reflect society, but rather completes and assists it. This points to the fallacy of yet another mythical position in architectural theory: namely, that there is an opposition between design and society, which thus reduces architecture to a reflective surface of active societal forces. Exploring the ontology of the archive challenges the reflectionist paradigm in critical theory once more, enticing us to further rethink the conceptual apparatus of design theory and architectural history.

Tracing the moves of archiving reveals the nature of these wonders as well as a number of wondrous characters: Giovanna, the archival box, Cedric Price's archive, and Cedric Price and his practice (as seen through this very quick "stroll" through the archival boxes). How often do we learn about Price's work without looking at some of these materials? How often do we see a curator flipping through boxes with disparate materials? How often do we call boxes "archival," if they do not contain and reveal the context for others? When I explore a situation of archiving, I am neither facing Giovanna and her pure subjective expertise as a chief curator of CCA, nor am I facing the boxes in their pure material cold objectivity; in a situation of archiving, we are rather seized by the correlation of boxes and curators (humans and nonhumans), a correlation that shifts when witnessing the moves of archiving in their fullness. This situation talks about one phase, one site of archiving—that is, a space-time, a number of sociotemporal coordinates, the humans and nonhumans involved and all the real connections among these entities. On this site of archiving we witness Giovanna engage with the objecthood of architectural drawings or documents from Cedric Price's box, and their practical and epistemological applications. Rather than embarking on a regime of valuing them for their exemplary character as an attempt to make contact with their intrinsic properties, aesthetic, functional or other, Giovanna is involved in a practical, elaborate exercise of making the objects speak and responding to their speech; she is concerned with the ephemeral nature of these material and epistemic entities as archival. In other situations, she opens the boxes in the vaults to select material for an exhibition, and she can be led occasionally to engage in valuing the objects for their aesthetic appeal and selecting those that are more eloquent in conveying a particular curatorial concept. Her actions are in no way determined by the situation, or by the CCA as an institution; it is instead what comes from these moves that reveals both the nature of the archives and the expertise of Giovanna. In other words, Giovanna is defined by what she does through these moves of archiving during that particular morning in the vaults, as well as in many other situations depicted in this book. These actions, like many others, including the curatorial events, the molecular interactions, and the archiving moves, are what make the CCA specific.

Reflecting further on the peculiar objecthood of the CCA wonders witnessed in the vaults, I ask: How can I make sense of the trans-particular dialogue between the OMA and the CCA, between other design practices where many archives are being generated now and the CCA that collects them and preserves them for the future? How does this connection inform a better understanding of the ethnographic data collected at the CCA? How do "portable analytics" prioritize more flexible, multidirectional, and plural connectivities that accelerate epistemic exchange? None of the cases voiced directly its originality; instead knowledge emerged *in between* the cases. This allusive and indirect dialogue between people and architectural things, which somehow started simultaneously with-me-and-without-me as an ethnographer, suggests that meaning lies *in the movement* between objects in similar modes of existence, between articulations, gestures, voices, or silence,[47] and the embodied responses generated by the situated ethnography of the case-of-the-present.

Watch Giovanna opening a box, just as we can watch Matisse painting à la Merleau-Ponty, and we see that there are two sides of the act of archiving: the documents, the codes, the folders, the numbers, the lines of order, all in a box, and their effects on the whole arrangement. If you, as an anthropologist of creative practices, decide to put your focus on Giovanna's hands as a phenomenologist would do, you would see only the wrong side of her work. Slow ethnography, yes! But not too close into Giovanna's emotional and bodily reactions! Changing and recalibrating the ethnographic distance would bring us a fresh look at these practices. The distance regulator here emerged through the OMA case and varied many times. Thus, if in addition to the hands of Giovanna and the slight movement of pen, we also catch a glimpse of the noises, the neon lights breaking through, which that movement releases; and the OMA stories and the related analytics that reemerged, we will get a fuller, more colorful picture of the process of archiving as it connects to designing.

When followed ethnographically, Giovanna moves without hesitation; yet, when slowing down even more and trying to capture her moves, we see her hands appear to pause and wave over the surface of the folder, creating the impression that she is considering and weighing different possibilities before laying her hand on a folder. Thus, we could ask: "Did Giovanna consider all possible ways of showing the materials in the files of this project, all documents of the epoch possible?" "Did Cedric Price choose between all possible lines of investigation when preparing the McAppy report ?" No. Both Cedric Price's practice and Giovanna Borasi's curatorial team, and the multiplicity of their moves, the folders, the documents, the codes, and the series of copies, all contributed to assembling and making sense of a special assortment of things. A mixture of design contingency and context. A relational entity. An archive.

OPENING THE CRATES

Log: 8:30 a.m. I enter the shipping area, where the material is received, and as such it is often the first place that the architectural objects "visit" upon their arrival at the CCA. In the well-lit, nondescript space, I began to wonder about the nature of the operations performed there: How are the objects themselves welcomed into the CCA? What does it really mean to register an object? What happens on this site of archiving? To begin, as I did, let us examine this small room (see figure 5), which is a hybrid of office, storage, and workshop facilities, full of shelves and crates, computers and boxes, gloves and folders, and let us inquire more about the particular nature of activities that take place here. How different is this shipping space from the vaults, the library, or the conservation lab? What kinds of objects reside in here? How do the friends of architectural objects engage with them? What do they hold in their hands? What are the conditions for speech enunciation? How do friends interact with and talk about the objects? In order to engage with these questions, meet Marie Gouret and Alexandre Phaneuf,[1] two technicians with different backgrounds and expertise who work together in the shipping area; following them, we can attend to the specificity of archival objects at the start of their archival trajectory at the CCA.

On the Move

Marie and Alexandre each start the working day in the registrar team's office. Depending on the current curatorial or research projects, each of them goes her or

FIGURE 5.   The shipping space at the CCA; Marie and Alexandre opening a crate

his way, finding or following objects. If there are any incoming materials (on loan or by donation), they open the boxes to make the first inspection of the objects, finding out what is inside in order to record their condition. These are the objects, registered and accounted for, that Marie and Alexandre spend their days with. It is by paying close attention to their relationships with the objects that we can come to grasp the specificity of their practices. Although they have different roles, they often do things together with the objects. Alexandre is in charge of the reception of objects that arrive in cases, crates, boxes, and all the other matters related to the exhibitions. His time is devoted to their preparation for shows or for archival accessioning, following them to other places in the CCA, gathering other friends of architectural objects together around them to share expertise about them, and helping their installation. Marie deals with all the requests for the transfer of objects, and her role is to prepare the documents requested for consultation. Together, they are the very first friends of the objects here, receiving them and following them through the CCA.

Yet, Alexandre and Marie rarely remain in this locale for the whole day; they are constantly on the move at the behest of the objects. Holding them or pushing loaded carts, they visit the reserve, the conservation lab, the galleries, and the study room. When needed, they go off-site to the Centre des Collections (CDC). Alexandre often accompanies objects in the exhibition, taking them upstairs into the gallery, occasionally helping Sébastien to do the installing, taking the objects to the conservation lab or to the staging. A recent addition to the fonds of Victor Prus, required him to travel to the house and the offices of the donors, who are still alive, to collect documents. While he was there, he spent time observing the objects with the donor to find the ones that they wanted to donate; then he took plastic and cardboard materials to the house and helped pack the objects before moving them with the transport company to the CCA and to the CDC, where the most voluminous objects are stored.

Responding to different requests, Marie is often on the move, too. She prepares documents and objects requested for loans by friends at the CCA, by scholars in residence, or by external institutions. She also travels with the objects from one CCA site of archiving to another, transporting them to different places so that these objects can be consulted or treated. When the request is internal—for instance, a request for a reproduction—she takes the item to the curator or to the cataloguer's consultation room. When there is an external request for a reference, she takes the object to the study room. As Marie travels back and forth between the vaults, the study room, the shipping area and other sites to respond to requests, and Alexandre travels in and out of the CCA to accompany the objects, to pack and transport them, we witness another group of internal and external actors forming around the many displacements of architectural objects and the trails left by their trajectories. Strolling across sites with a cart full of precious objects, pushing it cautiously through dark and lit corridors, opening the heavy doors of the study room and the vaults, back and forth, or visiting the galleries, the conservation lab, the houses of other collectors, Marie and Alexandre are like their objects: migrants, travelers. Yet, just like the folders on Marie's cart and the model in Alexandre's hands, both technicians come back here again and again, to this hybrid of office, storage and workshop, shipping and reception; that is what makes the shipping area their main working place and constitutes it as a site of archiving.

While they often work in isolation from other friends, collaborations nevertheless happen on a daily basis. People from other institutions visit, sometimes traveling with cases and accompanying objects, and stay for a while at the CCA to supervise the receipt and registration of the objects; likewise, CCA technicians travel with the objects on specific occasions. The objects are often surrounded and comforted by those who look after them and follow them. Varied also are the trajectories of travel: between institutions and sites, but also within sites. Just like Alexandre, who often helps Sébastien in the galleries, Marie helps other operations in places far from the boundaries of the registrar's office and the shipping space. In fact, we can often spot two Marys in the vaults: Mary Louise Gordon, who is a library cataloguer and also processes archives and describes objects, and Marie Gouret from the registrar's team. Mary-the-cataloguer is doing a consultation in the vaults; Marie-from-registry helps her take out the folders and place the objects on the counter, take some of them to the conservation lab, or prepare them for special presentations. What do we see? There are two Marys, four hands, hundreds of different moves, flying folders, and the few objects on the stand, standing guard, all *en attente,* waiting impatiently to continue their journey.

Cycles: Marie's Mornings, Alexandre's Days

8.30 a.m. Marie starts her day by opening her special email address for "displacement of objects." She stays for a while at her desk to check if there were any requests that were received in the evening. At 9 a.m., she rises to go down into the vaults, taking the cart with her; she fills it with documents, books, and materials that are to be consulted by the researchers at the CCA and then brings the cart to the study room. The consultations are supposed to start at 10 a.m., and they run until 4.30 p.m. Marie's cart must appear in the library by 9.30 a.m., before the three large tables there are filled with archival materials for the researchers who will arrive shortly. Perhaps tentatively, she leaves the objects to bathe in the silence before the empty room becomes bustling with scholarly life and then continues on her way down into the vaults. As one type of silence replaces another, she begins to arrange, with enjoyment, all of the objects that were requested the day before into their respective places on shelves, then begins to prepare the requests for the following day. Depending on the number of requests and researchers, her mornings differ. Since I am following Marie in June, in the middle of the busy research season, her mornings are long—so much so that she has someone to help her during the summer to prepare the requests. Two carts tour the building with documents and books, back and forth between the vaults and the study room, the photography lab and the registrar's office, a continuous machine of circulation in the archives. All of the objects, books, and documents moving from site to site, on a conveyor belt of architectural history, must be put back into their place so that the rhythm of the requests can be refreshed. As a result, this mechanical dance of objects that follow Marie, and that Marie follows, caught in its rhythm, repeats.

That particular morning in June is very busy for Marie. She is working simultaneously on two separate requests for the reproduction of particular images. One of the requests is internal, for the catalogue that will accompany the exhibit *The Other Architect,* and the second request is from someone outside of the CCA, who had come to consult objects, and had made a selection and requested permission to reprint a certain number of objects for a publication. Practicing architects also come to the CCA for requests, to consult documents. A practice in charge of a renovation project, for instance, may request copies of building plans that will help them work on the restoration. The CCA sometimes works with Montreal Printing, a reproduction company. Marie accompanies the objects, handles them with the technician, and remains there with them for the scan and the printing, if needed. Thus, no matter how good the partner is, and how established the collaboration is, as a true friend, Marie "cannot leave the objects with them"[2]—although she cannot constantly stay with the objects either. Another job, for instance, is to deal with a reproduction request. Caroline Dagbert, the coordinator for reproduction requests (as part of her administrative coordination work for collection), shares the request with the registrar's office. Marie works with her to number the objects and the folders to create a database. Caroline generates a work order (*bon de travail* [BT]), a script that facilitates the next object's move, and makes a request so she can transfer the object, updating also its location in the database. In all these cases, the travel of an architectural object cannot be reduced to a simple movement from point A to point B. As the aggregate Marie-and-the-object circulate, a number of other actors are enrolled: Caroline, the work order, photographers, codes, databases. As simple as it might seem, Marie's trajectory oscillates between the silent vaults and the busy database digits, passing continuously through different sites of archiving, back and forth, producing new scripts.

While Marie is touring the premises of the CCA with the cart loaded with archival objects, Alexandre's day continues to unfold somewhere else. Unlike Marie's mornings, Alexandre's days might be more unpredictable; they depend on whether he knows what is in a given case. Normally he knows what to expect. Once the case is opened, Alexandre takes pictures. The first picture captures the box when it is full of objects; then pictures of the lending numbers follow, as well as individual pictures of all the objects inside the case. Taking pictures is his way of getting to better understand what kinds of objects have just arrived at the CCA; it is his way of getting to know the objects, of becoming acquainted, and also of knowing what to do next. These pictures suspend aesthetic judgment: they are not used for exhibits or publications, but rather serve the purposes of identification and internal documentary tracing. They help Alexandre remember the state in which the objects arrived at the CCA, what they were packed in, and how they were arranged. This all matters because he eventually has to prepare the objects for their next trip and pack them again as they had arrived; Alexandre should know exactly what to do. The pictures instruct his actions and facilitate his work; they are shared with other friends of architectural objects and travel along with other objects across the CCA. The pictures also constitute a part of his own working archive, stored on his computer and shared with others. The act of photographing is a way of taking account of these architectural objects in a way that has an epistemic dimension: it helps Alexandre to gain knowledge of the objects; that technical, peripheral and surface knowledge of their state, condition and packaging will help him to prepare the objects for another journey into another set of relations. Here, we witness again how the architectural object multiplies and "recruits" a fresh crowd of new allies just as it did, moments ago, in the request for a reprint. Archival objects, observed here, are not coherent and composed, certain and solid; they are tentative, fragile, decomposed, and mutable; they produce traces and proliferate feverishly. Here, too, is a situation that generates scripts in addition to the initial scripts that accompanied the objects when they arrived (such as contracts, agreements, documents on the provenance and history of objects, or instructions of how to open a crate), and these newly generated scripts (work orders, requests, pictures, reports, minutes) constitute an evolving working archive as the process of archiving unfolds.

Alexandre's use of photographs is reminiscent of my own ethnographic use of photographs: hastily taken shots that aim to help me recollect ethnographic situations and retain details, atmospheres, and flavors of actions, speeds and rhythms; far from any aesthetic engagement, these shots gradually constitute a working ethnographic archive.[3] For instance, as I write these lines, I read carefully the many transcriptions of interviews, while at the same time matching my ethnographic notes and flipping through these images; in these multifold moves, I retrace the connections between the words of Alexandre and his gestures captured on the pictures, and I can distinguish between the wooden cases, crates, and cardboard boxes. Far from the search for any aesthetic value, the images assist the recapture of ethnographic situations of archiving in their specificity and minuteness. Ethnographic photographs are usually "raw," just like the research data collected in situations of observation and ethnographic site-ing interviews; they too can overflow with meaning. Yet, they possess the potential to open up new knowledge perspectives, sometimes due precisely to this raw quality; they can "spring leaks" to show alternative viewpoints, unnoticed details, or alternative interpretative strategies. In both sets of pictures, Alexandre's and mine, the aesthetic judgment is suspended; objects multiply, visual and written traces frantically dance around them, and the scripts proliferate; grasping and coming to terms with architectural archives indeed produces more working archives. Each of these moves, together, this toing and froing from object and text to image, give a working pace to Alexandre's days and provide a rhythm for my writing nights.

Numbering

Earlier this morning, I saw a mysterious red truck containing crates arriving at the CCA. Now I expect to see these objects in the shipping space, but they are not in there yet. Instead there is another case: it arrived from Boston on Monday and

FIGURE 6.   Alexandre describing and numbering objects in the shipping area, CCA

contains objects from Nicholas Negroponte for the exhibition *The Other Archi-tect*. These are the objects that we have the opportunity to observe as they are being received and registered at the CCA.

The objects are neatly arranged in their cases on the table in front of Alexan-dre. First, he takes pictures to better "identify" the objects, then removes the ob-jects from their cases and begins to number them (see figure 6). All the pictures then migrate to his computer, and the files are renamed in a database called "The Museum System" (TMS).[4] Every object that had traveled from Boston—or from distant monsoon India and Studio Mumbai/Bijoy Jain—to the quiet and warm microclimate of the shipping area in Montreal, "landing" on the wooden rectan-gular table, is now about to perform another migration: from the 3D object to 2D files, from case to pixels. These pictures are also shared with the conservators who use them to prepare their condition reports so that the curatorial team can gain a better idea about the state of the architectural objects. Alexandre arranges the files that refer to each object into folders; on the folder we find the number that corresponds to the object. Here again, a new script that documents the pro-cess of archiving on Alexandre's computer is produced. A dossier is also prepared to provide an overview of the contents of the box. The numbers are placed: loan number 2015.4.2, loan dossier numbers, exhibition dossier numbers. The num-bering points to the importance of keeping a good ordering of things because of the huge amounts of objects arriving at the registry, begging for attention and care.

The careful documentation allows for better traceability.[5] If, years later, there is some uncertainty about an object—for instance, it could have been damaged when it arrived[6]—the friends would be able to find the pictures taken upon the arrival of the object at the registrar and would be able to trace its transformations. The picture documents the initial condition of the object; as such, it has the potential to gain a quasi-legal status and could be used to solve legal issues, in the case of conflict between institutions, or in the event of damage. That is how more friends are recruited through the script-generating activities.

Numbering constitutes a major part of record keeping. It is done at the level of the box; it keeps a recollection about the number of boxes and cases available, and it is also a way to trace the objects—both those that stay in the CCA and those that go to the CDC. The Foreign Office Architects (FOA) material, for instance, contains primarily models in boxes with textual materials; in this case, only the number of containers (cases and boxes) are counted, and this number is entered into the database ("50 boxes with models, 150 cases with documents, thus 200 containers"). While this process of inputting the objects into the database shows that the boxes are numbered, it registers only that the boxes have been received. Opening a box requires another process. As soon as a box is opened during processing, a detailed description of the objects from this box has to be made. Processing means arrangement. Processing requires moving from the level of the box to the level of the objects, and it connects to their provenance, sorting out similar documents, finding out repetitions, while striving to preserve the original order in which the documents arrived at the CCA. When the objects are described at the level of groups, they are connected to the box and numbered accordingly. It is important, for them, to retain this division between the box (where a multiplicity of objects is kept) and the object. However, the box is the currency of the registrar's office; it is the scale at which organization and recollection occurs.

Let's return to Alexandre opening the box that had arrived from Boston (see figure 7). He is still taking pictures. Following this box of documents for *The Other Architect* will provide an opportunity for us to witness the beginning of the processing. Alexandre inspects all objects arriving at the shipping area; then he looks at the objects and documents that have been "flagged" by the curators for inclusion in the exhibit. The numbers on the objects are crucial and come originally from the lending institution, which has already given them numbers. The CCA has to give them a new, temporary, OL (*objet loué*) number, which corresponds to the logic of the exhibition list. The OL number, which is typically a code of four letters and a numeral, simplifies the process of identification. Alexandre carefully removes each "flagged" object, places it in a transparent folder, and gives it a number. Afterward, he takes these objects to the conservation lab, where the conservators Karen Potje and David Stevenson can examine their condition. The

FIGURE 7.   Archival objects from a box displayed on a table in the shipping area, CCA

number accompanies the object all along its travels. It designates its belonging to a certain order of programming—curatorial projects, specific exhibits; it point to its status—loaned or borrowed; it shows the material arrangement—a box or folder. The codes vary according to the specific ontological category—"DR" for drawing, "AP" for archives (*archive privée*), "PH" for photos[7]—while the numbers show quantity in sequential series. If an object is acquired by the CCA, after a loan, its number changes again.

However, the registration work does not follow a strict and predictable linear path. Objects overlap, shows intersect, and they all follow the overlap of different programs. "If an object needs to be reproduced before it goes to conservation," explains Alexandre, "we need to engage in the work in the quickest possible way so that the other departments can start their 'coming and going' in the quickest possible way too."[8] This is the start of other engagements for objects. Those from *Archaeology of the Digital* are still waiting for archival processing. They remain *en attente*, in transit. Meanwhile, Alexandre is labeling the box for *The Other Architect* and carefully gives temporary codes to all objects. Numbering the objects is a way of demarcating their belonging to a certain documentary order or a specific material arrangement that has its own epistemic value. The code allows objects to be traced and becomes a *tracer* of different objects' lives and states of transit. Marking their beginning as archival objects, delineating their paths, tracking fading traces, the code makes objects traceable and traced both materially and digitally. The different codes provide instructions for the objects' movements: the "flagged" objects travel to the exhibition galleries to enjoy a life in the limelight of public attention and cameras; the rest stay in the shipping space, waiting for Alexandre to place them in boxes on the shelves ready for their next journey.

The Dance with Catalogue Codes

To understand the process of coding, we meet Mary Louise Gordon. We have already crossed paths with her in the vaults, where she was working alongside Marie from the registrar's team. Mary's work with both published material and archival materials can be understood as she travels between desks, counters, large computer screens, between vaults and office spaces, CCA spaces and offsite locations. When Mary works in the vaults, where we have seen her moments ago, she looks at objects to make sure that those in the folders correspond to the description in the catalogue, she checks the medium, the size, the type of drawings, the information written on them. She also often finds herself in the vaults when there are fairly large drawings that she cannot bring to her office to describe. For instance, the drawings we have seen in the vaults are 78×110 cm, and she requires more space to move them and to be able to see them better. The vaults provide that space.

Now, we surprise Mary in her office (see figure 8), which she shares with other cataloguers. At her workstation, we spot an inviting computer screen, with two open windows: one to the system called "Horizon," used to catalogue mainly published material; the other to TMS, the system used to catalogue the archival objects. A tape measure is also placed on her desk, among other common office objects, and I wonder what its purpose might be. Let us zoom into Mary's large screen to understand what cataloguing implies. Various codes appear: DR, AP, and others, followed by sequences of numbers supplied by the registrar's office.

A few clicks on the computer, and we access, following Mary, the James Stirling and Michael Wilford fonds, through "collection online."[9] We see the classification scheme of this archive—that is, the overall conceptual framework of the archive that can vary according to the different framings of the objects. It is organized in series that typically reflect groupings of material according to different types of activities of an architectural practice. The Stirling and Wilford fonds is organized into four series: one for James Stirling's own papers, one for professional papers, one for Michael Wilford and his papers, and one on Stirling's obituaries, memorial, and foundation. When we open "Professional Papers" (Series

FIGURE 8.   Mary cataloging objects, CCA

Two [S2]), for instance, we read a content note that says: "This series documents the professional activities of James Stirling, James Gowan, Michael Wilford, and the successive firms of Stirling and Gowan; James Stirling; James Stirling and Partner; James Stirling, Michael Wilford, and Associates; Michael Wilford and Partners; as well as the firm of Michael Wilford GmbH." The entire collaborative universe of Stirling and partners is here. Ten architects and firms are listed as "creators" of this series and thirteen as "creators" of the fonds. The content note describes the kind of material contained in that series, including, for example, conceptual and design development drawings, publication and presentation drawings and panels, working drawings and models, photographic materials, textual records, film reels and other audiovisual materials, and artefacts. The "date of creation" points to "ca. 1948–2004?," the language of the material is mentioned: "English," "extent and medium" are described (35,919 drawings, 173 film reels, 49 models, and so on), and the subseries are listed. This hierarchy is what cataloguers and archivists refer to as a "classification scheme." This series is divided into ten subseries: "Projects," "Dead Projects," "Exhibitions," "Publications, Lectures and Writings," "Awards and Honors," "Professional Activities and Associations," "Photographic Materials," "Audiovisual Materials," "Administrative Records," and "Office Records." The Stirling and Wilford fonds is coded as AP 140, which indicates that this is the 140th archive in the CCA's possession. And since we are looking at S2, we are in the coded space of AP140.S2. The subsequent numbers for the ten subseries go farther down in the hierarchy:[10] AP140. S2.SS1, AP140.S2.SS2, and so forth. If we open subseries 1 "Projects," we find 180 projects coded as D (dossiers) and in each of them numerous files coded P (*partie*); one *partie* can correspond to one design object, say, a coffee table or a house, and can contain, for instance, twenty-four photographs, six drawings, and five negatives. Similarly, Series 1 (S1), "James Stirling Papers 1947?–1990," contains three subseries (AP140.S1.SS1 to SS3), each of which contains dossiers. In the first of these, "Student Work" (AP140.S1.SS1), we find eleven dossiers, numbered AP140.S1.SS1.D1 . . . D11, and when we open the first dossier, AP140.S1.SS1.D1, titled "Community Centre for a Small Town in the Middle West," we find three files—elevations, views of presentation drawings, and plans—numbered AP140. S1.SS1.D1.P1 to P3 and dated 1948.[11] When we open P3, "Plans," the object proliferates again—this time to eight design development drawings.

Now we understand why Mary talks about a hierarchy that goes from the AP to the series, then to the subseries, dossiers, and down to the level of the files; rarely does it go down to just one single object. The architectural object remains multiple and the archive cautiously maintains this inherent multiplicity. Here again, just as in Cedric Price's fonds, no glorious first sketches, no memorable final drawings, no heroic originals are singled out of the aggregate of materials. The archive is the "cross over between a person and a professional practice,"[12] the outcome of a group activity that spans multiple professional practices and countries. Architectural projects are described at the file level. As Mary elaborates, "Inside the file, at the lowest level of the hierarchy, you'll start to see the list of objects, if individual objects have been identified. If not, the lowest level is a group of materials."[13] In the files we open with Mary we find an inventory of photographic materials and publication drawings: twenty-four photographs, six drawings, five negatives, which constitute a group record or set. Information on objects such as dimensions, technique and media, stage and purpose, is added here; some of this information is obtained in the registrar's office in the process of identification. The archival object, we witness, is always part of a larger grouping, a larger series, a larger formation. It is never on its own, singular, at odds.

The content of the archive starts shaping the classification scheme. Yet the scheme is never fixed: as the cataloguers work through the material, they discover things that might shift the content in an unexpected direction and cause the cataloguers to modify the classification scheme. We find notes in the finding aid that tell something about the process of archiving: when and how the material was processed; what the initial arrangement was, what was changed, who edited the finding aid. When processing the Pasanella & Klein archive, Mary finds out that Joseph Merz was the consulting engineer who worked with the firm. It is by carefully inspecting the drawing that she discovers this information; it is written on the drawing itself, on the title block. Then, she updates the system, and this information is *added* at the level of the file in the inventory. Working through the Stirling and Wilford fonds, Mary opens "Professional Papers" and in the subseries "Projects" finds 180 projects listed in chronological order. As she goes through the long list, she discovers a project that she does not know, and she has to adjust the classification scheme. "I do like very much working with the archival material, because it is unique. And you do feel like you're discovering a little universe,"[14] she expounds. There is always an element of surprise when finding out something that others have not seen before. Cataloguing, we witness as we follow Mary, is not just about identifying physical objects (their media, dimensions, material features) for the sake of an accurate description and truthful record keeping. It is also about "discovering that little universe" that the object holds. The cataloguer dives into the world that the object has opened up, extracts knowledge, and adds it to the system, thus perfecting the objects' descriptions, refining the classification scheme. If you watch Mary and her screen, you can see the inventory as a record for a group of objects; "They are true objects, actual, physical objects," Mary emphasizes. There is little content description. The reference number comes from TMS; that is also the box number needed to request a document. At that level it is the cataloguer who has to "meet" the objects "in person" and measure them. We understand now why that tape was on Mary's desk. Taking it occasionally to measure dimensions and surfaces when inspecting the archival objects, Mary writes the information down in her notebook, and then travels to the screen to insert this data into the cataloguing system; that is how through the many moves of Mary's measurements and data inputting on the computer, in addition to Alexandre's photos in the registry, new knowledge is gained. Material objects gradually become signs.

Let's follow her working with some models of the Japanese architect Shoei Yoh, which were received for the *Archaeology of the Digital* exhibit. Mary goes to the CDC, where the technicians help her to take the bulky models from the shelves and unwrap them; she looks at the models, measures and describes them, identifies the materials ("plastic and paint," she writes down in her notebook), takes some photos similar to Alexandre's, which will be entered into the system as identification photographs. That is how a record for the models is being produced, then incorporated into the rest of the classification scheme of the archive. As Mary elaborates, "We refer to all these objects as virtual objects, because they are records describing things in a collective way."[15] Cataloguing, as we witness here, is an object-based activity (it could include objects within an archive) and differs from the activity of processing an archive, which is the act of describing and conceptually ordering the material (as we will see in chapter 6). As objects are catalogued, many signs pile up in a hierarchy developed by the cataloguers; TMS gets updated; that hierarchy gives shape to the classification scheme; the scheme will suggest an epistemological framework that will serve as a precondition of Architectural History.

Paths

Turning back to Alexandre in the shipping area and watching him prepare some packaging for materials and arrange cases for loans, both outgoing and incoming, we can see him open the crates and inspect the objects, then go back to his computer, back and forth, just as Mary did moments ago. Once on the computer, he goes in the databases to input the new data and register the objects. Every object, whether it is part of a new acquisition for the CCA collection or it is on loan for a specific exhibit, has to find a place on the large wooden table in the middle of the shipping space and on the shelves around it. They also find a place in the computer database. Receiving and registering the objects, we witness, is about finding more than one base for them: one physical, one digital; and, it is also about this passage from the physical to the digital, and back. This is not a lonely journey either: Alexandre is there to guide them. Displayed on the table, they are constantly on view; it is important to "take over control, as we [at the CCA] do not wish everything to be dispersed in four or five different offices"; the registrar technicians try to ensure that "the objects follow the same path; they pass through here."[16] Yet, from here, the objects could follow different routes: after the cataloguers have made descriptions, they can be sent to storage.[17] Placed on the cart, they can also travel back to the registrar's office, where Alexandre can prepare them for the next trip; he can pack them and send them to the CDC building.[18] These are just a few possible trajectories.

Another important reason why objects pass through the shipping space is that in the case of contamination, the source has to be identified quickly and measures have to be taken accordingly so that the affected objects do not infect others.[19] All archival lives, whether healthy or sick, start in a shipping area. Yet, this is also the place where the fear of the objects' death—or the concern with not destroying other objects' lives—begins. Contaminated objects are first identified visually: "There are things that look a bit suspicious sometimes." But the provenance of the objects can also help: "This sometimes gives us [the technicians] hints."[20] For instance, when objects arrive from tropical countries, the technicians are even more on alert, and, resorting to other senses, they conduct an olfactory inspection when the package is opened to look for "the signs by detecting a smell."[21] Smell is a very useful indicator. Alexandre opens a huge wooden box and says:

"Here is the box, do you smell that?"[22] I am hesitant. I have been warned about that smell. Shocking as it was at the start, I have grown used to the idea that architectural objects smell; still I have never actually sniffed an object. Alexandre takes my faint, yet noticeable grimace, as an answer that I have recognized the odor. "It is this smell that will be present in the galleries and that is why we need to send these boxes to companies specializing in the deodorization of objects."[23] The treatment is done either outside the CCA or in the conservation lab (see chapter 5). Smell is something we commonly associate with other types of objects (food, flowers, bodies), but rarely with architectural objects. Here, though, smell is an important *tracer* that allows us to follow objects from site to site, and through various journeys. The mention of smell brings me back to the OMA again where I have witnessed architects discussing, at length, the smell of foam cutting and its possible hazardous effects; smell connects them to volume, and volume links to design rhythm. If smell in practice means a certain intensity of making,[24] smell in archiving points to hectic archival lives: long trajectories, troubled journeys, different climates; "smelly" objects "talk" about explorations.

Smell, dirt, rubbish: all these conditions tell us stories about the trajectories of archiving, which are reminiscent of the trajectorial nature of design, and provide a perspective onto the ways in which these activities are organized.[25] In one of the boxes are some objects from an exhibit that just ended, *Rooms You May Have Missed*, featuring the work of architects Umberto Riva and Bijoy Jain. The donation of Studio Mumbai/Bijoy Jain for this exhibit arrived from Mumbai, India. The objects reached the registrar's office and began "telling" a particular story about that trip: packed up in India during the monsoon season, they traveled a long way by sea and by air to arrive in Montreal, where they emit a pungent odor. Marie explains that these objects have a type of dyeing that smells very strong. "The smell makes a difference," both Marie and Alexandre expand, and it is disturbing for them as they find it unfamiliar; it seems out of place. They are worried that it "could pose a problem for the exhibitions because . . . if a gallery is entirely infused with that smell," it could create an unpleasant experience for the visitors.[26] As a result, they have to clean the objects before the exhibit, to "deodorize some models" and even use pesticides to eradicate termites and pests that could present danger to the collection of objects. A company from outside is hired to conduct the deodorization before the objects enter the galleries. Thus, getting rid of the traces of travel, of long journeys and patchy trajectories, requires a lot of additional work. This happens rarely. Yet, when it does, a number of other friends of architectural objects are mobilized in the fight against the environment that appears here as a set of conditions and of entities (monsoons, humidity, dirt, insects, pests) that can interrupt the routes of objects from design to archives, shipping space to exhibits.

This struggle is very apparent. Both the codes and the smell within the shipping space make it more present than in other sites of archiving. At the OMA, for instance, such a struggle is missing. Monsoons and stars, winds and insects are not part of the cosmologies of designing architects witnessed there.

En Attente

When the truck arrives at the loading dock, the cases are transported to the shipping area, where they have to remain for at least twenty-four hours before being opened; they "wait." A point of "landing" and a point of departure for all objects, this space marks the trajectory for all CCA objects as archival. Here is also where objects pause for a while, before they depart again; they remain *en attente*, to use a term often used by Alexandre and Marie (see figure 9). In many other CCA sites of archiving, you can see the label: *En Attente!* Objects are waiting to be opened, to be identified, to be prepared, to be transported, to be included in an exhibition; expecting a decision on their destiny to be taken, waiting for the show to start, anticipating new lives. Let us continue to follow the work of the technicians in the shipping area for a little longer to understand what the regime of *en attente* implies.

Wait, just like the archives *en attente*, and contemplate some objects from Studio Mumbai/Bijoy Jain on the shelves farther down. Some of them were acquired at the end of the exhibit and are currently lying on the shelves *en attente*, awaiting special attention at this site of archiving. Objects that dwell longer in the shipping might shortly be acquired by the CCA and be "waiting" for negotiations with the lenders to unfold and a decision to be made. They might also be waiting for a treatment. These objects often compel friends to gather in the shipping space to discuss their status, their pertinence, or their next journey; waiting on the shelves as they are, the objects wordlessly assist these meetings. Quietly anticipating a verdict: Will they be part of the CCA collection, or returned to their owners? All of the objects on the shelves await the chatter of that meeting, a decision, a clear destination.

This is a transit space that bridges different sites of archiving, distinct institutions, or different material orderings of objects, as well as between the ontology of designing and the ontology of archiving. While in transit, architectural objects exist in between countries, owners, and audiences, in between the nature of monsoons and the culture of exhibitions. During this time, they take multiple short journeys between sites, between the registrar's and the cataloguing offices, the shipping area and the conservation lab, the vaults and galleries, returning to the shipping space after one or another of these destinations for a short rest before

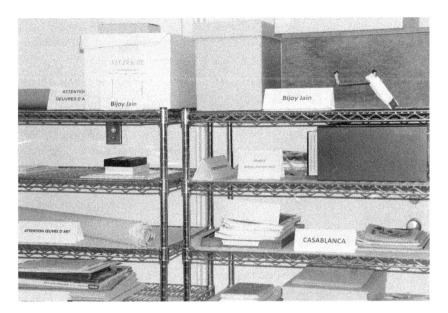

FIGURE 9.   Objects *en attente*: a display in the shipping area, CCA

they depart again. It is important to note that there are no common, or typical archival trajectories. They are all just different.

The Studio Mumbai/Bijoy Jain objects illustrate the possible diversity of these trajectories. Once they arrived in Montreal, the contaminated objects were sent immediately to the CDC, where they resided in a special quarantine room; the cases were opened there (instead of being opened at the CCA shipping space). Traces of mold and insects were found on the objects, and the conservators treated them in the premises of the CDC. Eventually, a truck returned the objects to the CCA building; the cases, now clean, were opened in the shipping area and the objects were sent to the conservation lab for inspection. Condition reports were made, minor treatments done, and preparations completed. Then, the objects went up in the galleries and back to the registrar, to the shipping area, to these shelves, here, where they remain *en attente*.

The huge wooden table of Marie and Alexandre is often full of objects from donations, too. "Sometimes we receive drawings, models, photos from people who wish to donate."[27] Instead of receiving a label, the objects that are accepted and remain *en attente* hide behind another paper note that says: "*Attention, œuvre d'art!*" If a decision is still to be made, they wait in shipping, on consignment. The head archivist Robert Desaulniers receives them and signs their donation papers (*offre de don*). This new script will now accompany the archival object and will become a new "tracer" in conjunction with the code, the smell, and sometimes also with specific written instructions for opening the crate (for instance, "Do not incline the case on one side as the objects should come out in flat"). Equipped with scripts, the objects are brought into the shipping space where we have just seen Alexandre receiving and registering them: taking a picture, numbering the folders, updating the database. A closer look at these shelves and we see all sorts of other objects: drawings, models, books, documents, photos; they have different types of lives, some less glorious than others. My eyes stop on a pile of books. I wonder how they landed on these shelves. These five books were part of the exhibit *Archaeology of the Digital*, explains Alexandre. They were bought on eBay and Amazon after the curatorial programs decided to include them in the show; the books took part in the exhibition and now they are back in the shipping space, overhearing our conversations with Marie and Alexandre. They too, are *en attente*, waiting to enter the institutional archive of the CCA.[28] Where are they going? In the collection, or in the library? It is not clear yet. Alexandre explains that this decision is also *en attente*. It is most likely that they will go to the library or the curators' offices (or the institutional archive of the CCA). The fact that they can go in any of these places illustrates the stasis state of objects, of being *en attente*, holding possibilities, while expecting to be realized in another set of relations.

The swift shelf inspection brings us back to the OMA again, to the offices of practicing architects, and reminds us of the many shelves with heterogeneous materials lingering there *en attente*. Some of them have been waiting for years before going into the boxes with foam models, then into the cellar, waiting even longer to come back onto the shelves and the tables in the office and to become part of design making once more. These trajectories are there, a visible, constitutive part of design creativity. *En attente* is an ontological status inherent to the design processes witnessed at the OMA, whose traces are kept in material form, *there*. Cutting foam, experimenting with materials and shapes, retouching an image with Photoshop or sketching things on tracing paper give rise to something admirable, something that sparks the architects, inspires them, and talks back to them, something that troubles architects and consumes their energy through the course of design; it is that unknown "angel of the work," as Etienne Souriau calls it,[29] that compels and surpasses its makers. All traces of everyday making, experimentation, and enjoyment of design remain and account for that specific state of latent creative potential, waiting to be activated and enticing activation; models resting on the adjacent tables, tools and visuals, more foam pieces scattered around the studio and stored on the ground floor in bigger boxes, ingenuity in recess, the arrested development of many potential projects, amassed and dormant, all there, all at once, *en attente*. Designing connects to archiving again.

Blue Gloves, White Gloves

A swarm of supporting objects crowd around the architectural objects in the registrar's office at the CCA just as they do at the OMA. packaging and isolation materials, gloves and folders, cases and crates, cardboard boxes and transparent sheets, all mediating the contact between the friends of architectural objects and the archival objects. The existence of these supporting materials reminds us that the contact to architectural history is always highly mediated; objects are precious and require protection. For protection and safety, archival objects travel securely packed. Whether the receptacles are big or small, crates or boxes, wood or cardboard, packaging designates precaution and good care. It multiplies the object, adding new layers on it. Objects on loan require even more care and precaution. Every detail matters: "I cannot return the objects in a bad state," explains Alexandre, or "in this kind of package." With a frown on his face, he shows the poor quality of a package; he explains that he cannot keep this box: "I will change it and I will pack it also in plastic as we need to take responsibility when we return the objects."[30] In case anything happens and the object reaches the lender in a bad state, the liability rests with the CCA. The package has to be done in a professional way so that the objects can travel safely. Packing well is Alexandre's way of caretaking; his way of saying "STOP!," "Be careful not to damage!" It is his way of showing respect to the architectural objects and maintaining the delicate balance between idolatry and iconoclasm in archiving operations. That is also a way of juridically reinforcing his friendship with them.

Usually, the objects are packed in wooden boxes. Although these wooden boxes tend to have a similar shape, they serve very different purposes. Let's open a few of them in the shipping area. In the first one we see objects that have traveled to the United States and back and are now waiting for the conservators to check that they have been returned in a good state or require treatment. In another one, we find objects that have traveled to Paris as a part of a traveling exhibit and have come back to the CCA. In a third wooden box, we observe objects that are not part of the final selection for an exhibit that will be staged shortly, so they stay in the shipping area as it offers a highly controlled and secure space. As simple as they might appear, these boxes are not mere containers for transporting archival architectural objects—while they serve as "suitcases" for travel or controlled safe spaces for storage, they are also important "tracers," numbered, labeled, and present during the objects' journeys of becoming archival.

For shorter trips, when objects tour the CCA, they are accompanied by carts. Along their journeys with the objects, Alexandre and Marie weave in and out of the crowd of people coming and going, visitors, researchers, numerous doors to open and close, heavy gates, controlled entries. As a result, there is the ever-present risk of people bumping into Alexandre or Marie, and worse, of damaging the objects. To avoid this, the objects are secured on the carts. In addition to the wooden cases and the carts, CCA objects are accompanied by numerous Solander boxes. Named after the renowned Swedish botanist, Daniel Solander,[31] these boxes are black and very solid; handmade, expensive, they create an acid-free environment that protects the contents and are considered the most suitable cases for storing and viewing prints, drawings, and photographs. While these were largely used at the CCA in the past, now there is a cheaper version: cardboard boxes, which allow for storage at the level of the folders and are variously sized to accommodate the varying parameters of archival objects (for instance the dimensions and the size of the drawings, as well as their folding vary according to national contexts).

Cases, boxes, folders, paper dividers, wood, cardboard, plastic—the layers that cover an archival object multiply. Neither friends nor visitors (nor potential enemies) are allowed to have direct contact with the objects. Every touch is mediated by layers; every manipulation, every encounter, requires additional layers to be added, layers imbued with caution. Since the more an object is touched, the greater the risk for damage becomes, the number of people who have access is restricted. Yet a simple vocal "No!" is never enough, and a written interdiction never suffices to protect the collection from damage. An entire material support system is put in place to ensure that the objects reside on the sites of archiving safely and that their circulation from one site of archiving to another is secure.

Similarly, the friends require a support system to survive the sometimes harmful conditions of archiving. Often you see these friends wearing different types of gloves, depending on the type of object. Just as the cases and the boxes that protect archival objects vary in size, materiality, and shape and are endowed with different properties, gloves can vary as well. The blue rubber gloves, preferred by Alexandre, help him handle the objects; there are skills *in* these thin gloves, their materiality and color; these special gloves allow him to do specific things. With the gloves on, he "manipulates the paper without touching the object" and arranges photos without touching their surfaces; the soft and thin blue gloves afford a gentle handling of fragile surfaces, a delicate flipping through photographs, and the fine and precise execution of numerous dexterous operations. However, the blue gloves are not convenient for the manipulation of hard wooden surfaces; there is another type of glove for that, a thick, white, cotton gloves, which allow both Alexandre and the objects to remain safe, to endure longer. To the multiplicity of archival objects, we add the variety of support objects and instruments crucial for caretaking. The multiplication of the archival object is in full swing; it is never one, single and isolated. Both in the cataloguing and in the shipping sites of archiving the archival object exists as multiple, as many—never one, but in sets (in the classification system), never single and easily accessible, but always enveloped by an entire support system of materials and technologies mediating the complex relations with humans, both creators and archivists (in the shipping space). Just as the online catalogue access to a particular archival object make us flip through the hierarchical levels of series-subseries-dossiers-folders-sets, the physical access to the object is also layered as gloves-folders-boxes-crates.

Conclusions: Chatter around the Shelves

Like architectural objects, people, too, constantly move around the CCA and often pass through the shipping space; like the archival materials, they come, they pause, they wonder, they are *en attente*, they stay for a little while, and they go. I have seen many friends of architectural objects coming here, into the registrar's office, the "empire" of Marie and Alexandre, of conservators, directors, and curatorial teams (see figure 10). Often, other friends crowd the registry to see the new arrivals. "They have waited for the objects to arrive for months and that is why they will come straight here, impatient, and eager to be present for the opening of the cases."[32] Not everyone is allowed here, passing by spontaneously, and knocking on the door is not an option; it is a "restricted" space. Only a limited number of friends can witness the opening of the crate (the directors or friends in charge of the program or exhibitions). The rest of them can come only by appointment. No matter what their attachments to the objects are, all friends suspend their aesthetic judgment; they are not there to judge whether this object is good or bad aesthetically. Instead, they mobilize their effort to control the environment, to secure the space and to provide a series of mediations through support structures; all of these are part of the process of registering.

Record keeping permeates the activities of registrar technicians and cataloguers. The working archive proliferates throughout the everyday moves of cataloguing and registering the objects. There is a record of all the travels and trajectories of the objects kept, of all the instructions, interventions, and the additional scripts produced in situ—hence, more written instructions, the donation papers, the work orders, pictures, codes, TMS databases. The generating of new traces that are assembled as scripts is a generic feature of archiving, witnessed here through the specific scripts of registering and cataloguing archival objects. Every move of archiving generates traces: Alexandre's camera, Marie's cart, the curators' post-its, the "flags" on objects, Mary's measurements and notes, the discussion minutes. Then, too, smells, codes, digital photos, documents, boxes help the archival objects travel, producing even more traces as they do so and as they are

FIGURE 10.   Curatorial meeting in the shipping area, CCA

being traced. It is with these additional traces, the traces forming records, composing scripts, that pile up in addition to what is already officially "archive-able," that we are able to have more hints as to the varied lives of these objects. Record keeping adds mediations, and necessary precautions produce additional mediations, new scripts, to enable handling the objects with care.

In the registrar's site of archiving, friends, objects, and scripts all reside in silence, interrupted only by the chatter of a selected group of friends who enter the shipping room. Registering the object happens at this site, but also simultaneously at many other sites, and through the synchronized site-ing of the movements of archival objects, friends, and support objects across all those sites simultaneously. Marie's and Alexandre's work can seem lonely and secluded, especially when the objects that come out of the crates happen to shout out at them about their needs for treatment or the danger of contamination. Isolated as they are in the dark misty space of the shipping office, they need to follow special protocols, respect package instructions, use specific equipment, honor agreements of donors and lenders, produce reports and images, add new codes. Despite the silence of the room, they are surrounded by things that "talk" and that they must respond to and follow. Their work remains highly collaborative without marks of hierarchy, age, or experience; roving along with their objects and scripts, they travel, discuss, transport, take care, intervene, adjust, install, help. This site of archiving differs from the others as the access is highly restricted, and while a very few people come in, a large crowd of objects leave. There is also a contrast of rhythm: while crates and people come quickly and do not remain long, the objects going out of this space move slowly, gracefully, equipped with boxes and carts that slow them down, they march with purpose through doors and other sites of archiving, like soldiers. While the touch of objects is mediated by gloves, carts, folders, instruments, tape measures, and cameras, just as it is at many other sites, the behavior of our friends Marie and Alexandre is different here: dressed casually, enjoying the silence of the office, they move cautiously in and out and according to the spatial arrangements prescribed by the objects just registered as archival.

There is an important quasi-corporal work of materiality (taking care of packaging, the smell, and the different climates) and intertextuality (instructions, reports, and scripts that pile up and fill new dossiers) in the work of the registry friends, and in the cataloguing work of Mary, which is indispensable for creating a collection. An archival object is one that constantly multiplies; far from being independent, autonomous, composed, and emancipated, standing on its own, the archival object is highly dependent, since the moment it gets registered, it relies on the support systems of scripts and devices that gather its traces and that enable it to be traced. Its multiplicity is enhanced by the classification hierarchy, in the catalogue space, as well as by the material support network that keeps it safe, in the storage space. An archival object is also one that travels constantly and, if not on the move, rests *en attente*, waiting for another journey; from immediate it becomes mediated, from material it becomes a sign. Registering implies a way of knowing archival objects that entails obtaining knowledge "by the smell," "by the case," piece by piece, just as cataloguing implies extracting knowledge of dimensions, media, materiality, and size—that is, temporary, fragile, and tentative knowledge gained *in* the process of opening a crate, of sniffing a package, of placing heavy objects on carts, or of taking pictures or measurements. Each time one of these operations is performed, new knowledge is added, knowledge that, little by little, furthers our understanding of *that* type of architecture, *that* epoch, *that* architectural practice, technology, or zeitgeist. Knowledge about the object—its specific trajectory marked by journeys, institutions, countries and continents, cultural events and archiving mandates—and knowledge about the contexts are gained simultaneously. This epistemic multiplicity highlights the ontology of the archive and the discrete processes that make it architectural.

POLITICS OF CARE

Log: 2.45 p.m. Continuing to trace the life of architectural objects at the CCA, we move to the conservation lab. The conservation lab creates the impression of being the most isolated place at the CCA; it is hidden behind heavy doors on the ground floor; in order to find it, you must pass through large and unremarkable corridors, and down a flight of slippery stairs. After carefully descending the steps, there is yet another corridor. Suddenly, in front of a giant metal door I have for a moment a feeling of *déjà vu*. We knock. The door is heavy, extremely. Even though Kim Davies, Giovanna Borasi's assistant, helps as I try to press the horizontal handle that will release this burdensome pressure of opening the door, we have difficulty. The heaviness of the door makes me wonder about what we will encounter on the other side. Once we finally pry it open, on the other side, there is another corridor. This time it is different. It is bright and narrow, a stark contrast to the heavy door. There are office spaces on the one side; behind open doors active computer screens shine brightly (these are the offices of the conservators). Again, we come across another door at the end of the corridor, this time, much lighter and much easier to open. At last, I am in the lab. What a journey! As soon as we enter the conservation lab, the sense of *déjà vu* flashes again and I remember being here with Giovanna and talking about the possibility to study archiving at the CCA. But there is also a recollection of the many scientific labs I have seen before and the many labs I have read about. As soon as I find myself in this one at the CCA, I am immediately taken by its scientific mystery: objects on trial, experiments in progress, protocols, tests results, a giant microscope, and the lingering smell of unknown chemicals (see figure 11).

FIGURE 11.   A table in the conservation lab, CCA

The heavy doors and long corridors indicate how difficult it is to access the lab; access is in fact highly restricted. The doors constitute barriers and aim to prevent random visitors from entering the lab. Access is extremely mediated and slow. The lab itself contains a few large tables, which are surrounded by cupboards and shelves and form a scenic center for the space. There is a very charming working "disorder"; paper is sprawled over the table next to objects undergoing conservation care; next to them a huge silent microscope resting like a statue, which is beside a number of carefully dispersed instruments, some of them in use, like the spatula, and small containers with different solvents. The table is overstuffed and busy. Scientific principles seem to guide the flow of actions here: the ideal of disinterest, the absence of prejudice, the distance from the objects, the precision of the activities, and the esoteric languages spoken. I can sense that everything here is done with caution. Despite the busyness, nothing happens lightly. The apparent disorder knows its order.

The objects on the table focus everyone's attention. They are carefully examined, diagnosed, and treated. Here we move from the laboratory to the hospital. The use of quasi-medical terminology is striking: conservators "examine" objects, "predict risks" (of falling apart, of mold, of infestation), do "treatments" and "tests," use "instruments," plan "interventions," take "care," write "protocols" and "reports," sign "decisions for treatment." Objects in the conservation lab are treated like patients in need of special care. Karen Potje, the head of conservation, tells me without irony: "We get a full health and security check of the objects." On clean, white lab tables, under bright fluorescent lights, drawings, sketches, models, and photographs are spread out, cautiously "inspected," "examined," and "diagnosed." Reports of each object's experiences and reactions are carefully made and travel with the objects, like a medical report. This record is necessary as it allows the objects to be inspected at the beginning, in the middle, and at the end of an exhibition to ensure that they have not changed. The conservation lab provides an environment where objects undergo a series of operations to improve their "health," so that these "patients" can return to the boxes or folders in the vaults in perfect condition. Nevertheless, the primary concern for conservators is the impact of the environment and time on these objects. Instead of treating the object itself as a separate and static entity, they are concerned with its relations, to itself in time and to other objects. In what follows, we will first discuss the fear of time and hazards of climates and environments, and then, we will follow how the affected objects are treated by tracing the work of conservators Karen Potje and David Stevenson, along with that of the museum technician, Anne Gauthier. Wandering around together in the lab, multi-siting the inquiry, we will discuss the specific challenges of architectural conservation and the politics of care—not politics as power, but politics in a Latourian sense as the tedious "work of progressive composition of a common world"[1] shared by humans and nonhumans. This leads us to account for the specific processes, concerns, moves and ways of knowing in conservation.

Awareness of Time(s)

Time is incredibly palpable in conservation. As an essential dimension of archiving, it appears in conservation in specific ways. The quest for durability is described by Karen as follows: "Our job here is to try to preserve the objects in the collection to make them last as long as possible."[2] Although a good long-term preservation scenario for physical and digital objects varies and aging has a different meaning in the physical and digital realm (see chapter 7), "lasting longer" is important for both types of objects. The friends at the CCA work, on a daily basis, in this battle against time and for duration. Time, though, is a wily foe. It is elastic and foldable, something that is constantly questioned; duration cannot be assumed. In contrast to the seemingly peaceful and eternal time of objects in exhibitions, here time is vengeful. It is a struggle—prolonged, projected forward, pushed back, extended in a protracted now and then projected again into the future. Rather than a single commonplace understanding of time, in archiving we encounter different modalities of "stretching" the duration of architectural objects. Karen explains: "We're used to saying to ourselves, okay, if we keep things [flat paper works] safe in acid-free folders in a vault, they can last for two hundred years. And we expect them to last at least that long or much longer. We expect them not to change."[3] The conservators anticipate the aging of objects, yet the information communicated by the objects is expected to remain the same. In fact, the lifetime expectancy of an archival object exceeds the one of architects (two or three times, even more). Lasting longer without changing significantly and outliving their creators is the modest ambition of these objects. This ambition is supported by other nonhumans. Acid-free folders, for instance, can ensure a safer environment for paper drawings and slow down aging; they aim to mitigate changes, allowing only for minor alterations of the objects' material properties, which will not hamper their capacity to "talk," to freely transmit information of relevance to Architectural History.

Time also folds in the conservation lab. There is an interesting tension between the temporary nature of design visuals that usually have a short life span (architectural working models, drawings on napkins, sketches on tracing paper) and the importance for conservators to preserve them for as long as possible. Since early twentieth century, most architects have tended to work on tracing paper. Although easy to use in design, it is extremely problematic for conservation. While architects do not necessarily think that sketches and drawings on tracing paper will need to be kept forever, when they end up in the archive, they pose a number of challenges for conservators. Tracing paper is moisture-sensitive. If it is humidified and dried, this leads to a change in scale—the paper might shrink in one direction or another—and scale is critical to architectural drawings. Karen explains, "Paper conservators will not worry about it. But we do. So, we will flatten things in different ways than other people will in order to avoid those kinds of problems."[4] Conservators of physical objects aim to prevent the literal shrinkage of time. Flattening things is a way to unfold time, to keep time flat. Perhaps we can blame this ignorance of time on the architects? There is a different "archival awareness" in the moment of design invention; in the midst of a design process, architects create on the spur of the moment and rarely think about whether a quickly made drawing will become valuable (as seen in observations of the practices of Foreign Office Architects [FOA], Moshe Safdie architects, or Siza's firm), or whether a model will have a social life (as seen in my ethnographic study of the Office for Metropolitan Architecture [OMA] or Eisenman's practice). They rarely consider them as having the potential to become collectable and to have a place in History. Most architects instead keep their drawings in storage because they might need to be able to refer to them for information or go back to some ideas developed in the past. Yet, even if they think a particular drawing could gain value and should be "kept beautiful," they would not alter the conditions of storage; the drawing might still linger in a damp place.[5] Architects have a different "awareness" of archiving their design process, one that is often without concern for Architectural History. They cannot estimate if and how working design materials will acquire meaning or historical value outside of the remits of their practices.

The same goes for working architectural models, which can be equally challenging in terms of conservation. The CCA's collection has a rather large number of models that designers have used to test ideas—experimental, rather than final, provisional, rather than presentational. These models are typically made very quickly, with poor materials, and thus are especially susceptible to the ravages of time. As when working with tracing paper, architects produce these models on the spur of the moment, "slapped together with the idea" or because they needed to try things out. Does this work? Do we like this option? The models are not made with the expectation that they would eventually be shown outside of the studio. Often assembled with poor craftsmanship, haphazardly, the models usually start to fall apart. That is how they end up in the conservation lab. Karen explains:

> Very often architects would use some rubber cement and will just stick things together. Rubber cement does not last. Things pop off. When collages arrive, some of the collaged pieces might come off after the exhibition, or something pops off. We will inform the owner if it is a loan and then we will attach them properly. The same happens with models. Architectural models were usually made because they [designers] were thinking through ideas and they grabbed a little of this glue and took these toothpicks. They were not made of good materials to last.[6]

The most recently received crates of Alessandro Poli I have inspected with CCA's conservation staff are full of pieces of wax that have melted or have fallen off. So, I witness indeed that the materials used by designers to "think through ideas" are usually "not meant to last," but are used for a quick fix. The spontaneous and ad-hoc nature of design thinking is best facilitated by materials that can be swiftly manipulated as witnessed also at the OMA, where the versatility of foam offers designers an excellent medium for speedy cognition. Then, the question of conservation shifts to how to fix rubber cement, wax, and toothpicks?[7] Here lies the challenge of architectural conservation: how to preserve products of instant creativity generated on the spur of the moment? How to make them endure?

Many practicing architects are not aware of the importance of safe storage, or simply lack the knowledge of all the hazards that can harm archival materials, or do not care about archive preservation. If, for instance, an archive has remained in a warehouse with a garage door for years, the material is most likely to get damp, and dampness poses critical risks for the stored architectural objects. Therefore, the task of spotting traces of dampness in poorly stored material is part of the routine of skillful conservators, who are like detectives of time. They inspect material in its original location, interview donors about the movement and storage of objects prior to the shipment, and report these facts. They also have a long checklist concerned with potential risks posed by a donation. Equipped with a flashlight, they inspect the boxes very carefully to see if "anything moves," and if a sign is detected, they warn the other friends at the CCA. Conservators are tasked with looking for signs of time, scars of time. Determining whether the objects have been poorly treated by time is, ultimately, a way to conserve them, to keep them alive. In fact, everyone at the CCA who deals with objects shares this responsibility, not just the conservators. All incoming staff get a handling course. Of course, dealing with risk factors requires more conservation attention to improve the safety of architectural objects and to increase their integrity. However, sometimes conservation is too late against the ceaseless beating of time, and in spite of the efforts of conservators, objects can perish. The key challenge in conservation remains how to keep something alive, to make it pass through time without transformation, to make it persist.

As Karen explains, if the objects are very moldy, they cannot be used for exhibitions or research. When time has left traces on them, and the hazards of environment have accelerated the process of aging, conservators have to find a way to preserve what is left of the architectural objects; they can copy the information held within the object, such as a drawing, and make a reproduction. The replica remains, and the moldy drawing can be de-accessioned if it is CCA-owned and there is a danger of putting other collection objects at risk. However, if the threat of contagion is not that high, the original will be kept, but perhaps separated, and this will be noted down in the database. For instance, a hand drawing might have value for the information it contains and for the artistic character of the drawing itself; but at a certain point, if it becomes a danger to human and object health, the conservators can decide to make a reproduction. Paradoxically, the duplicate becomes the only way to save the original and to grant it a new life.[8] The copies generated over the course of design are different than the surrogates produced during archiving and curating. The curator of photography Louise Désy clarifies the ontological difference between a copy and a surrogate: "A surrogate is an exact copy. A copy can be larger. It can be smaller. A copy is not exactly the same as the original."[9] She explains that when "the object is too fragile or the exhibition is for months and there are lighting or conservation issues, we cannot show the object, so then we would produce a surrogate of the CCA object."[10] Thus, the surrogate as the exact physical replica of the object replaces it in shows and helps the archival object to survive through time, minimizing the possible damages caused by lighting and temperature. The threats for physical architectural objects and the process of conservation problematize the original/copy dichotomy. Moreover, this problematization also leads us to questions concerning time. In the conversation lab, time becomes palpable and visible. We encounter it through two distinct processes: on the one hand, there is the effort to battle Time's arrow[11] and the aging process, the ceaseless movement forward; and, on the other hand, there is the attempt to confront various environmental hazards—air, water, dampness, changes in temperature and humidity, any of which can make archival objects age. While all objects are given equal attention in the lab, those with more precarious and "contagious" conditions, such as a moldy drawing or an infected collage, will be treated with priority. Conservation is not just the fight against time, but also the containment of objects as they relate to other objects.

Bugs, Containment, and the Aesthetics of Care

We continue our visit in the conservation lab, and while I expect conservators to talk about the amazing way architecture straddles the worlds of art and science, I witness active chemical reactions instead: "That pile of blueprints over there is a pile of chemical reactions, really," says Karen, "and so they're still active things and adhesives involving chemistry and you have to think about reactions. We're not doing scientific calculations particularly, but we still have to understand reactions between things."[12] Being in the midst of "active things," we can sometimes meet a number of strange creatures (such as insects and mold) or phenomena (like odor or oxidation), which are otherwise remote from our understanding of architectural objects and the very culture of valuing objects with exceptional aesthetic properties.[13] Although very rare at the CCA, pest problems in the collection are a major concern for the conservators.[14] Bugs, understandably, are ignorant of Architectural History. Like time, they eat into the object, speeding up its deterioration. The life of archival architectural objects is marked by all kinds of dangers related to organic matter; the more living matter a collection hosts, the more paper- and wood-eaters[15] it attracts, and the more the danger increases. Although an architecture collection is less abundant in organic matter than a textile or an ethnographic collection, the objects are still at risk.

Yesterday, a bug was found and quickly brought to the attention of the conservators; it was located upstairs on the third floor in the hallway and was taken to the lab for identification. David explains, "We encourage people to bring bugs to our attention,"[16] and in the last few years friends at the CCA have become more vigilant.[17] Since the architectural objects travel from around the globe, bugs can come to the CCA from anywhere: New York City, Delhi, Singapore. The first bug in recent years at the CCA traveled all the way from India.[18] The one found yesterday came from Italy with the drawings of Alessandro Poli, as part of this donation. To the surprise of the conservators, the shipper did not spot it earlier; it traveled unnoticed all the way to Montreal hidden in the crates. As the Poli drawings are meant to become part of the CCA archive, there is a risk of the bugs proliferating, and that is why the inspection is carried out in the lab.

As we are looking at the picture of the bug, Karen shares her anxiety: "I was all over the place when I found the bug."[19] They are indeed quite restless that afternoon in the lab. The bug found in Poli's crates is a new discovery for them. The conservators go through the list of bugs they have previously seen, and they examine a poster depicting the most common North American museum pests, they zoom in, observe and compare,[20] but they are unable to identify this particular bug. Amazed and surprised to see "such a bug at the CCA," both Karen and David do a lot of further research, consult books, make phone calls in Karen's office. The bug is submitted to meticulous inspection and identification procedures; on that afternoon of June 2015, no precious architectural object receives more attention and care than that bug. David takes a picture and prints it for further examination; scaled up, the bug appears as a giant, serious creature, enjoying the limelight of the microscope; placed in the middle of the table, the picture is surrounded by posters with other bugs, research materials, and various studies to allow comparisons.

David and Karen often attach the camera to the microscope to produce microscopic photographs of details and corners (see figure 12). Purchased to carry out treatments that need a lot of manual dexterity and precise manipulation, the microscope is a daily tool. Karen explains: "The microscope gives us another level of depth of insight that we wouldn't have otherwise."[21] It is a really useful tool for identifying insects and the media of the objects, as well as for checking small details on the images; the camera attached to the microscope extends the vision of conservators, multiplying their depth of insight. The careful microscope-and-camera-mediated identification is important to ensure that it is not a pest that will be harmful for the collection. With relief, Karen announces that the bug is not dangerous. The photographs themselves allow the bug to travel without spreading into the collection; once a good photograph of the original specimen is produced, the conservators send it to the Canadian Conservation Institute (CCI) whose staff have expertise in identifying pests and are interested in knowing more about different bugs found in collections. The shots produced by David are working pictures, similar to the pictures made by Alexandre in the shipping area; adding to the scripts generated in the conservation lab, they allow for further

FIGURE 12.   Karen looking through a microscope, CCA

consultations with more friends. As the bug pictures travel between institutions, knowledge is gained and exchanged: CCI experts learn from CCA conservators, who learn from the microscopic inspection of the bug. As images and scripts frantically circulate that day, the institutional working archive continues to grow.

Although the CCA collection is not particularly at risk of infestation caused by mold or insects, all friends remain vigilant and make sure that bugs do not have access to the collection; they are on guard. Usually, the museum technicians dealing with incoming material are the first to see the objects and to alert the conservators of any kind of issues. When upon opening the cases in the shipping area, if the museum technicians notice living bugs inside the case or in the wood cracks (in the case of a big wooden model for instance), they immediately close the case and repack it in order to contain the insects in the case. This is a means of creating quarantine around the objects, of placing them in a "state of enforced isolation," similar to the measures taken to contain contagious disease. Here again we find ourselves in a quasi-medical world. Dealing quickly with the bugs and placing them in quarantine are imperative to avoid putting many other objects at risk. A company that specializes in fumigation can be hired by the CCA. Thus, destruction bears many different faces in this lab: eliminating bugs or moldy edges so as to prevent collection objects from perishing. There is something puzzling in the environment, evoking the procedural technicality that the production of architectural models and drawings requires. What we witness under the microscope of the conservators, amongst the scalpels and chemicals, the magnifying glasses and the tracing paper, is a relationship between idolatry and iconoclasm, a finely balanced game of life and death.

Condition Reporting

Very often a large number of objects flock into the conservation lab, especially when there is a big exhibition planned at the CCA. Conservators can become surrounded by as many as three hundred objects at once. Some of them "call" immediately for treatment: as soon as the box, crate, or folder is opened, their odors or other chemical reactions fill the air. In order to transcribe these signs emitted by the objects, thorough and time-consuming reporting of their conditions is needed. Assisted by technician Anne (who works on a contract basis) and Emily (an intern), conservators spend time to carefully examine all of the objects individually and, if needed, look through the microscope to better identify their features if they cannot be guessed by the eye or other senses. This is the stage of "diagnosis," of scrutinizing the symptoms, discerning and detecting the flaws in an object: imperfections, tears, scratches, folds, insect damage, or stains. A simple and apparently static object, when examined by Anne, suddenly multiplies. A closer look at the condition report shows that an architectural drawing is decomposed into forty different features: surface, dirt, discoloration, and cracks, to name a few (see figure 13). Each object has a number, an inspection date, and a condition report. For instance, the photograph in figure 13, collection number ARCH 272898 (ARCH designates that it is a CCA object), was inspected on June 12, 2015, by Anne Gauthier, and has a note indicating that it was "passable" (or satisfactory). In the report, we read that "there are stains and cracks, a few creases"; we inspect the list of color coded features of the photograph, and lastly, look at the dimensions. For instance, "Stains" (number 6 on the list), is color coded with orange and appears as orange marks on the surface of the photograph's photocopy; while "detached areas" (number 30 on the list) is color coded with brown and appears as brown marks. The condition reports prepared in this meticulous way provide an in-depth view of the ontological granularity of the archival objects and indicate whether the objects are "safe to exhibit" or "need special consideration."

Conservators, as witnessed here, first produce a photocopy of the original photograph, then carefully inspect the original, identifying and measuring specific features, then, inscribe the traces of that inspection back on the photocopy while color coding and numbering each of the forty features of the photograph and tracing correspondence with the list of features in the report. This examination

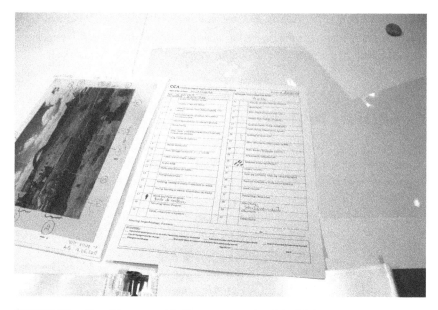

FIGURE 13.   Condition report in the conservation lab, CCA

does not aim to identify and value the objects' exceptional intrinsic properties, but rather to engage in practical work on the objects' material granularity and their effects. This process of condition reporting serves to help determine if a treatment is necessary and, if so, to plan that treatment.

When an object arrives at the CCA as a loan and has a few tears, Anne has to spot them and deal with them right away. It is dangerous for the object to go in the exhibition with a tear as it may worsen its condition. There is a protocol in this case: when Anne spots the tear, she notifies Karen and David, and they intervene after they receive permission from the owner. Anne shows a photo as an example. We read on a note that "the frame is wavy," and Anne explains that it was a bit wavy when it arrived. The note placed next to the object is important because it allows its trajectory to be traced. It is a way to account for the fact that the damage occurred not because the object was not exhibited well at the CCA or because of a temperature problem or other issues. Rather, the photo arrived in this state and its surface was wavy before. As we have seen, the architectural objects joining collections are never alone; they are complex multilayered beings composed of a material box, plus packages, plus dossiers, plus notes on the object's trajectory and previous travels, and reports that document their material condition (alterations, traces of restoration, and other interventions).

Here is Anne at the moment when she is engaging in condition reporting now that the show *The Other Architect* is over, and everything has been taken off the walls and out of the vitrines. The objects are back in the lab, and Anne needs to make sure their condition has not changed. She takes the hinges off the objects that they have been mounted—a process that takes hours and hours. As Karen explains, "If we have two hundred drawings mounted with hinges, that's eight hundred to a thousand hinges you've got to take off."[22] Focused, careful, and exacting, Anne is removing the hinges from the corners of each object, her hands cautiously manipulating its surface (see figure 14). Here is her binder of condition reports. A huge one. There are about five hundred and thirty objects that she must go through. In these binders we find the condition reports written by the conservators when the objects first arrived in the lab. These reports keep the traces of repair that some objects had to undergo before they could be shown, as well as the owners' permissions to do this repair work (as seen on figure 13). All these traces, actions, interventions, and everyone involved in them are documented and kept in the condition reports. Anne consults again the condition reports that were made when the objects had arrived and inspects the objects to make sure that their condition, reported back then, has not changed.

Anne recounts her process: "Sometimes the corners are very fragile. And even if we are very careful, we need to notify that we are putting on corners as sometimes there might be an alteration. I am just checking that everything is fine. If I see something that is falling off, I will notify Karen, and she needs to get permission from the owner."[23] As we follow Anne's inspection of the objects after the show, we witness the formation of a new crowd of concerned friends around them—conservators, curators, and owners, joined by hinges, corners, and scalpels. They all ensure that everything is done with care: repairing tiny changes such as a crack caused by a slight climatic variation or a small lifting of emulsion might help the object reach the needed state of stabilization. The owner is normally happy to have the object repaired and agrees with the small changes suggested by the CCA friends. Karen affirms that there has never been a drastic change after a show. Again, we have seen that the aim of conservators is to ensure "that nothing changes."

"Corners are always tricky," explains Anne. "When you take off paper corners, you have to be really careful. Sometimes even with being very careful, some pieces can come off."[24] I watch her while she removes the corners; however, before she begins, she always double-checks everything. Manipulating her tools extra carefully, especially when the very sharp metal scalpel reaches the surface of a photograph to cut a corner, Anne wears protection glasses and also covers the objects in protective sheets. There is something interesting in this symmetry of protecting bodies and objects. She removes "the sheet that protects" the object, and very cautiously cuts the corner to avoid bending the photograph instead of pulling it off the corners. This sequence of manipulations is performed so as to "free" the

FIGURE 14.   Anne removing hinges of photographs in the conservation lab, CCA

photograph from the mounting; she is able to remove the photograph much more easily than if she had kept them. She then puts it into a transparent folder. Anne follows the same sequence of operations for every object. It is a very repetitive task. Similar objects follow, and similar corners are to be cut. Anne remains very concentrated. The operations may seem easy, yet each of them requires a level of focus and dexterity. Anne knows she cannot afford to let her concentration go astray. Everything is important. All the little details, the fragility of the corners, removing the protection sheet, using the round and very sharp scalpel carefully, cutting according to the plan, applying weight onto the photo so the photo does not move. All these little details are significant. All of them. All in sequence.

Treatments and Stabilization

On another table in the lab, Karen carefully inspects the condition reports to consider on the specific treatments that the drawings and models might need: perhaps chemical treatment, or tear repair, or to be unfolded. Together, Karen and I look at a drawing and its condition report. However, I am not sure what signs she is looking for, and how they lead us to a particular kind of treatment. "Treatment" has a complex, multifaceted meaning. It stands, first, for handling and dealing with objects, using a chemical agent to preserve particular properties of the architectural drawings and models; but it also stands for the (quasi-medical) care given to the objects as "patients," for their "injuries," "illnesses," or the threat of dilapidation and destruction. Moreover, it also refers to the manner in which conservators, but also other members of the society of friends, deal with architectural works. Treatment is a part of the daily caretaking activities in a conservation lab. These are "not very glamorous treatments," the conservators often joke. They work in a tight timeframe to get the objects ready for exhibition without engaging in invasive treatments, such as washing works of art on paper or de-acidifying them. Their tasks are more modest, as Karen explains: "We are just doing the minimum to stabilize things. We may have to do surface cleaning. When the objects are ready, we will need to mount them, whether they go in mats or onto mount board. So, we have to think of a safe way for them to be exhibited."[25] The use of the term "stabilized" here is revealing. It points to the fact that architectural objects in the lab are in a state of decline, degradation, a process of fading, of aging—that is, a state of inevitable change. Yet, thanks to the conservators' work of caregiving, archival objects engage in a process of "concretization"[26]—that is, the tendency to become more resilient and less dependent on the environment and the support system of the lab. In the course of conservation, objects gradually become more stabilized—stabilization being a movement toward concretization.

Conservators are "not trying to make things look like new" as restorers would do; conservators rather "keep things from deteriorating, make them secure."[27] So volatility—rarefaction—is the mode of existence of architectural objects in the conservation lab. The drive to stabilize precariousness guides the work of conservators. Conservators stabilize objects when they are in a critical state, like doctors who stabilize patients in traumatic emergencies, in order that it becomes unlikely that they will give way, crumble, collapse, or fall apart. Thus, objects-in-conservation are far from being solid, motionless, or concrete; instead, they fight against themselves.[28] In contrast, stabilized architectural objects are not in conflict with themselves, and therefore do not need the artificial environment of the conservation lab; they are eloquent, performative. "Stabilization" tells a lot about archiving in a collecting institution like the CCA. Rather than enhancing the aesthetic value of architectural objects or cleaning them up to engage them in a new cycle of aesthetization as a museum would do, in the research logic of conservation at the CCA, it is important for objects to keep the traces of life, of experimentation, of deterioration, of decay. Stabilized, repaired objects are more autonomous and can exist without the artificial lab milieu; they are less reliant on it and the quasi-medical procedures there; and when their internal coherence increases, they can be released from the lab. Thus, when stabilizing objects, conservators think about the moment when these objects will leave the lab and about the conditions in which they will be exhibited: in the CCA shows upstairs, far from the vaults and labs on the ground, a drawing (and yes, it could be one of the Chandigarh drawings of Le Corbusier) will be exposed to more viewers. All these conditions matter because they could harm the object. Different options for exhibiting a given object are explored ("framed with Plexiglas glazing," "encapsulated between two pieces of shiny Mylar," or "showing it flat on the table"); these are not just three aesthetically different ways of showcasing the objects' value, but offer different ways of preserving their integrity, of stabilizing them to ensure that they have an effect. Curators think about the best way to make an object *speak* meaningfully to others, at the same time that they remain concerned about their preservation. Equally, while the conservators' key objective is to keep the objects "healthy" and safe, they remain concerned about the curatorial narrative, thinking together with other friends how to showcase the eloquence of objects.

For conservators it is essential that they provide equal care to all architectural objects; they often joke that they "have tape on the back of their fingers," transparent tape that does not discriminate—a democratic "touch." They are not expected to make "value judgments" of any sort. All objects need to "be given the same level of care," Karen clarifies. "But when you're here and you end up with thousands of objects, you are going to make some choices."[29] Like a good doctor, a good conservator sets priorities and gives patients different levels of care tailored to their conditions and specific needs. This morning, Anne's careful condition reports have resulted in her flagging all the photographs and collages that need urgent treatment: they are the ones that have loose pieces. Then, Karen, sitting at a computer, writes to the CCA associate director of collections explaining the proposed treatment and asking for approval. Once approved, she writes back to the institution that has requested a loan of that object, fills out another form, and signs the form that signifies that the CCA will approve the loan provided that treatment of the object is done first. The regime of treatment invites the architectural objects to enter a contractual relationship wherein materials and scripts, objects and friends with different expertise, all converse with and talk on behalf of the object-in-conservation. Signing forms refers to a juridical regime of responsibility and care; it also sends us into the practical regime of answering a number of questions: Who cares for what and for how long? Who is in charge of providing the care? Who speaks on behalf of what and where? Signing is an act that redistributes the care among bodies, instruments, and objects. Yet, caretaking is not meant to suddenly transform less autonomous and dependent drawings into more independent ones, so as to make them rapidly autonomous like humans, responsible and talking. Caretaking does not swing the object from one extremity to another—from dependence to emancipation, from objectivity to subjectivity, or vice versa. Conservators never naturalize the process of caregiving by saying "this is an old drawing; how do you expect us to make it talk?" Rather, as care providers, they assist the slow mutations of objects. Objects-in-conservation are continuously in the process of acquiring degrees of freedom; they exist in a collective effort of care, caught between dependence and autonomy; they transform in becoming. This points to another paradox throughout: to conserve is to change, to alter, without changing.

The decision to do a treatment is made after a discussion with other friends. It is in these discussions amongst friends who care about the objects in question that we can witness to what extent the architectural nature of the objects "matters in terms of doing well the job of conservation."[30] The "conservators are trained to know when it is important to ask something."[31] Thus, if there is an uncertainty about an intervention, a discussion with the curators and archivists helps clarify and take the matter further; they consult, discuss and finally make a decision about what to do. These discussions are always assisted by a set of guidelines that inform them about when a permission to do a given treatment is to be requested from the curators, and when they can do it without asking. Most of the time a consultation is needed. Even if a similar treatment of objects has been authorized in the past, they still send a note to the collection director, Martien de Vletter, outlining the treatment that is needed and asking for her approval. Karen's note might say: "I'm thinking that maybe I should take off this tape that's visible because it's dirty and not doing its function anymore, and yet it was put there by the architect."[32] Every treatment holds certain risks of slight content modifications, and that is why permission is needed. All treatments require discussions, and this consultation process is what tightens the collaborative network around the object;

its fragility and ephemeral nature are stabilized by the entire network of caretaking. Both the object, through time, and the collaborative network of friends seek and require stabilization.

This brings us back again to the quasi-medical mode of existence of conservation objects. In the painstaking process of conservation, friends deal with the delicate and unstable character of drawings and models; they detect fragility, overcome risks, treat, and intervene to stabilize the objects in a complex and lengthy process that bears remarkable resemblance to the medical regime of caregiving. A number of scripts accompany the travels of these objects. The condition report is an initial diagnosis, produced in the lab following a careful inspection; as the object travels with the condition report, other scripts accumulate—permissions, loan documents, photocopies, documentation, and signed forms—a paper trail. There is never an original, singular object whose quality can be revealed at once. A bunch of things travel together—the architecture object, *plus* all the traces of tears, decolorizations, cracks, *plus* the condition report that documents them, *plus* the signed permissions for repair and treatment, *plus* the exhibit documentation, *plus* the travel papers. The object is invariably surrounded by its "identity" papers and "medical" records, as passports that enable "passage" and allow it to travel further and to continue to receive care, but also keep traces of its travels and treatments.[33]

Tests, Instruments, and Tired Bodies

In the context of the conservation lab, tests are more reminiscent of treatment trials or experiments than, say, of blood tests in a doctor's office. When Karen explains that she does "tests" on the objects that she wants to mend, what she expects from the tests is, for example, "to find out what adhesive would work to make sure that water wouldn't cause anything to run."[34] As tempting as it might be to follow the medical analogy, here it does not seem apposite. Testing the object will not lead to the discovery of some inner parameter of its functioning. The "clinical" chemistry and "molecular" diagnostics that take place in the conservation lab aim to reveal how the object will react to possible strategies of mending, repair, and improvement with the help of various substances and instruments. The idea is to minimize the risk of worsening the object's condition.

A multitude of instruments and materials support the work of conservation: spatulas, blades, magnifying glasses, flashlights, sandpaper-type things, a tacking iron, erasers, and sponges. Moments ago, we saw the huge microscope placed on the table. We just witnessed Karen and David using it to inspect the bug. They often use it to carefully examine objects in order to "identify" them. "Identification," in their terms, means that sometimes features of architectural objects are not discernable to the naked eye, or through smell or touch, and the microscope is needed. This technically controlled and mediated form of observation of the architectural object points to the limitations of the other senses. The etymology of "identification" is revealing in this context. It is the process of making something recognizable as either the "same as" or "different from" previous knowledge; turning it into the category of "the same as," of something familiar, makes it treatable. They cannot treat the unknown. The architectural object, for the conservators, is thus more than what meets the senses. After careful inspection and identification, the conservators confirm whether a specific treatment is needed and define it. They also use the microscope to identify the medium or media used in the object in order to be able to describe it in the most accurate way. This information will be displayed on the object's label or in the publications, will enter the classification scheme, and will also help conservators better understand how to treat it. The medium identification is also important when an image has to be reproduced for an exhibition or a research publication. In all, what do we see? People testing, examining, discovering, identifying, and gaining knowledge about the architectural object—knowledge that in turn informs conservators and then, archivists and curatorial, research and publication teams. Under the microscope, or when submitted to tests, archival objects yield dazzling secrets.

Handling fragile architectural objects in the lab, conservators are very often exposed to risks. Thus, dealing with the fragility of objects and the fragility of humans are still part of the daily routines of conservation. Hence the symmetry of protection we saw earlier. Most people in conservation at least at one point in their career have had some kind of accident. For Anne, it happened when she was working with boxes. Boxes are seemingly harmless but can become the center of an accident: "For instance you hear a sudden noise from a box falling, you jump when you are doing something. I happen to work with a bigger knife, and I just cut myself."[35] The risk grows when the CCA puts on a major exhibition and the lab space fills with hundreds of objects. At moments like this, "there is a lot of activity," explains David, and, "dealing with that much stuff, you are under time pressure, and accidents can happen."[36] Karen adds that time is a crucial factor here; conservation requires time to do delicate manipulations with caution and dexterity. Any interruption, any distraction can increase the risk of failing to complete the tasks; failure makes the archival object concrete, tangible, real.[37] Even though the labor can appear mundane, conservation work is visually and intellectually demanding: the quantity of objects to be treated and the condition reports to be completed can become overwhelming. And in this process "your eyes do get tired," says Anne, "and you need to have the right tools." I stare at Anne's magnifying glasses as she looks through them (see figure 14). She is using them for protection and also to avoid straining her eyes. This type of glass is used extensively in conservation. As special prostheses of the conservators' bodies, extensions of their eyes, they enhance the capacity to see.

Damaging the eyes of the conservators or damaging objects—these two risks are equally considered in the lab. Some mistakes can lead to irreparable damages— "mistakes that cannot be undone."[38] Both Anne and David say that it is rare for them to damage an object; the risks for them, for their eyes, their health, are much greater. However, when it happens that the object gets damaged, David points out that "you hope it [the object] belongs to CCA."[39] "It is embarrassing either way,"[40] adds Anne. Karen compares conservation with driving a car in terms of the degree of concentration needed: "You drive a car, and every once in a while, your brain is not quite functioning properly, and you do something that's a mistake."[41] She also makes a comparison to a lapse in focus when one is skiing: "When you take the last run down the ski hill, and you're tired, . . . that's when you break your leg."[42] For Anne "often mistakes happen when you say, 'I'll stop in the next five minutes,' but you don't stop and you should have stopped."[43] These mistakes occur because one loses concentration and track of time, but they also require one to stop the flow of time; the conservator has to step back, get some distance. In case of a mistake the conservator has to prepare a report that documents the accident. She has to reflect on what has happened and decide on the next step in order to correct it in the best possible way, and start a treatment with the permission of directors, curators, and archivists (if it belongs to the CCA) and approval of the owner (if the object is on loan).

If the other friends make mistakes on computers, they can easily undo them. As Espeth Cowell, in charge of collection and program services at the CCA, said to Karen recently, "You know, I can make mistakes all day long and I just click 'undo.'"[44] In contrast, mistakes in conservation cannot be undone. They leave material traces on the object—the damage is there, and a new cycle of conservation has to begin: permissions for repair are requested, condition reports are made, discussions with archivists, curators, or owners are pursued, and approvals to treat and intervene on the objects are granted. As the mistake leads to the damaged object, comparable to the broken leg, it is irreversible, irreparable. It has happened: it stays in the past. The archive builds on this, retrieving the past without reversing it. The time of conservation begins again; it runs back, it restarts the cycle with a different speed.

Treatments and "Surgeries"

When administering a treatment—such as unsticking surfaces or treating a drawing that smells—the conservators resemble surgeons. Here is one such situation.

I observe Karen as she works with some drawings that are stuck together; she has to delicately pull each one off individually. While inspecting the drawings, she finds that many of them have added stickers, and the adhesive around the stickers had spread out from between the sheets. A quick and easy way to detach them would be to dust a bit of cellulose powder onto the drawings and then rub them with an eraser. This would dry and then remove the adhesive. However, Karen uses a different method. She takes up a Teflon spatula, which is used for mixing and spreading pastes in painting, or for pushing aside or lifting parts of the body in medical examinations. In art and architectural drawing conservation, its thin and flat surface allows for easy manipulation. Karen maneuvers the Teflon spatula to slide effortlessly between the drawings. Cautiously, she removes the adhesive little by little. What a spatula does, explains Karen, can sometimes be achieved with a solvent, but the drafting foam has a coating on it that might be solvent sensitive. That is why she chooses to remove it mechanically with the spatula. Karen's "surgery" on stuck-together paper surfaces does not happen in the objective world of instruments alone; nor is it the product of her personal evaluation of the drawing. What we witness as the procedure unfolds is the tangled dance of a number of entities—objects, instruments, bodies, and skills—that make conservation possible.

When the need for treatment is identified immediately—through smell, say, upon opening a box—conservators follow a different set of procedures. Here is another situation (see figure 15). Karen and I look at some plans that have arrived from New York City. They were done on drafting film: "Hang on, let me put my gloves on," she says.

> If you move them, you might get a whiff of something unpleasant. I think that's because the plastic is deteriorating. They're not too bad, but some people say they smell like fish. Anne is cutting this carbon paper, which has activated charcoal in it. We will put some of that in the folder to try to absorb some of the odor, which is probably caused by the acid that is coming off the paper or the plastic. We don't want that mixed with anything else in the collection either.[45]

A treatment that aims at eliminating odor involves the participation of another nonhuman actor in the conservation process: activated carbon paper. Carbon is commonly used to absorb small molecules such as benzene, toluene, ethylbenzene, and xylene and is recommended for water filtration and odor elimination. In the CCA conservation lab, it is used to deal with odors that come off boxes and folders that often present unpleasant surprises for the registrar staff. Karen divides the stack of drawings into much smaller folders. At the end there are forty folders on the table. Then she places a big sheet of carbon paper in each folder to

FIGURE 15.   Karen performing a treatment of an archival object in the conservation lab, CCA

absorb the acid. She explains, "This paper actually absorbs not just the odor, but the chemical causing the odor."[46] Worried that people will find the fishy smell irritating, she aims to prevent this from happening. Odor requires urgent treatment, not just because it is unpleasant, but because it can spread quickly. The ozone can damage the material further and will chemically catalyze reactions. Karen needs to make sure that the contaminated objects are not in contact with any other objects—just as patients with infectious ailments should not be in contact with healthy people—because the acid causing the smell could affect the rest of the collection. The process is complete when a reaction between the carbon and the acid eliminates the odor.

In the context of treatments, the choice of types of paper or adhesive is very carefully made.[47] Adhesives are important nonhuman actors in conservation. Several kinds are used, but Karen uses mostly a traditional paste made out of wheat starch and cooked in-house. It is water-based and can be strained. "It's very pure and it's never going to be too yellow and it remains removable after years."[48] The quality of adhesives is defined by the degree to which they react with other materials, but also by their capacity to remain invisible, without leaving traces of interventions. Conservators make sure the object is fully prepared to embrace a new life such as going into an exhibition or traveling; thus, a treatment should not leave any marks (spots, scratches, or wrinkles). The longer objects can live without being marked by preceding use or treatment, the longer they can be exhibited, viewed, and researched, and the longer they stay archival and able to contribute to Architectural History.

In addition to the CCA-cooked paste, the conservators also use "cellulose,"[49] or a cellulose derivative adhesive, which is a more modern adhesive that can be mixed with water or with ethanol and can be applied several times. But first, they test the object to make sure that it will not react with ethanol. Follow Karen take a tiny brush and apply a tiny, pin-sized dot of ethanol onto the object; carefully, she blots it to make sure it has contact, and she keeps testing until she is positive that she can use ethanol on it. Karen is observing how the object reacts to ethanol to decide which adhesive to use. Here she describes the process:

> In this case, and this is an architectural reproduction, we need to be very careful. There's a little dab of cellulose, because we have seen some reactions happen over the years where water-based adhesives were used, and we are trying to avoid that. If I were trying to take the hinge off, I could take ethanol, and go like this [she makes a movement with her hand], but the ethanol spreads out. I have no control over where it goes. It should show better on a dark piece of paper. Like if you look at this [she points toward the tiny drop]. If I put a drop of ethanol, look how fast it spreads. And I don't want that to happen because I don't want the ethanol to release the adhesive, to go any farther than exactly where I need it. So, I use the same adhesive now as a poultice because it's got ethanol in it. So, if this has been attached to here with cellulose and I wanted to remove it, I would brush cellulose right over the place where it was adhered. And I put enough ethanol, release it into there to soften the adhesive and then I pull it right off. So, I don't have to worry about the ethanol spreading because I've got it controlled in this gel.[50]

As Karen tests which adhesive to use, and we witness how the cellulose controls the spread of ethanol, preventing it from damaging the drawing, she also explores different alternatives to risk reduction, assessing the unpredictable behavior of ethanol and the different treatments that are at stake, carefully measuring the gestures to place a drop, to soften and release the adhesives, to avoid additional diffusion, using poultice to control its spread with the gel. We are again in the hospital, witnessing a quasi-medical way of treating objects. Even the use of poultice (that is as a soft, moist mass of material, typically consisting of bran, flour, and herbs, which is applied to the body to relieve soreness and inflammation and kept in place with a cloth) points to the procedures of alleviating the wounded body of the conservation object or calculating risks to avoid "inflammation."

In the same vein of risk reduction, conservators are cautious about attaching hinges. Minimum intervention is the rule; hinges, adhesives, they all can cause infinitesimal, miniscule modifications, which, with time, can accumulate and lead to bigger alterations of the object's fabric, structure, fibers. Every single chemical placed onto the objects interacts with them and changes with time. Every surgery happens in a concrete dispositive as a way of weaving connections between materials, techniques, skills, and people. The various scenarios for mitigating risks closely follow the objects' grain.

What the conservator does in the three situations of treatment just described is very different. While the "surgery" performed on the "stuck drawing" is highly mediated by instruments, the smell treatment and the adhesive test do not require instruments or the dexterity of precise and timely operations. In the case of the activated carbon paper, it facilitates the process of absorbing the chemical causing the odor; similarly, the ethanol acts and reacts quickly with cellulose to indicate which adhesive should be used. These treatments are less mediated than the spatula operations. If the risk in Karen's surgery on the stuck drawings is to damage the surface, and to some extent the drawing's quality, or to hurt herself in the process of cutting, the risk in other treatments could be much bigger—that is, to spread the odor over a larger number of objects or to spread ethanol over a bigger surface. As we follow how conservators use a variety of instruments and materials to manipulate objects, control chemical reactions, and perform treatments, we witness how mediated their engagement with the archival architectural objects is. This mediated nature of their work contrasts sharply with unmediated acts of contemplation, admiration, or touch, where knowledge can be achieved directly by the means of senses (vision, smell or touch). Yet, the conservation treatment of an architectural object is not performed through the lived experience or subjective appreciation of a conservator, mobilizing all her senses, nor does it happen in the objective world of instruments. Treatment is about activating different modalities of actions of the objects—by identifying the various media, understanding the behavior of solvents and adhesives, coordinating between different rhythms of manipulations, measuring the degree of risk, controlling reactions, carefully handling fragile surfaces, sharp tools, and strained eyes. Conservation links bodies, risks, tools, objects, time and space, solvents, instruments, and different architectural friends.

Knowing in Conservation

Sometimes Karen, David, and Anne need more information about the architect and the specific working methods of a practice to ensure that they will apply the "correct treatments" to the objects in the conservation lab. A few weeks ago, when they had to deal with the restoration of a scale model, they did some research to find out "if the architect wanted the building to face the other way"[51] so they can adjust the model. While conservators are not supposed to make value judgments and have to treat the objects equally, putting a drawing or a model into the context of the working habits of the architects helps them to make a good intervention in conservation. A dialogue between archival conservation and the current conditions of architectural practice emerges. Designing and archiving connect in conservation too.

Karen explains, "Sometimes when I ask myself years later, 'Did I work on this object?' I only know it when I turn it over and 'Oh I recognize the back' because I had it turned over for so long when I was repairing tears. I might not even recognize the image, but I will recognize the back."[52] The routine manipulation of architectural objects in the tedious rhythm of repair makes the conservators achieve a degree of familiarity with a specific facet of the objects that other friends or visitors rarely notice. Being able to recognize a drawing "by the back" denotes a distinctive skill of knowing the architectural object (its edges, surfaces, corners), which is quite dissimilar from the common regime of appreciation of drawings and sketches, all meant to be contemplated "face-front," as it were, as that is what remains visible, valued, and remembered; the "back-knowledge" is gained only in the regime of careful identification, treatment, mediated observation, and meticulous manipulation for the purpose of preservation. If the knowledge *about* is important at the start, what is gained in the process of conservation is knowledge "by the back." There is an outspoken epistemic dimension of this type of engagement; here again, the aesthetic judgement is suspended.[53]

Architectural knowledge in the lab is far from being an encyclopedic stock of information and recipes. The repertoires of knowledge vary: knowledge *about* the architect, the practice, the working technique, the media, and also *about* the storage conditions and the risks objects have been exposed to, could be useful at the start of a project; knowledge of *how* to handle details (back, corners, edges, media) is achieved in the process of skillful manipulation and meticulous treatment of objects-in-conservation; knowledge of *how* to use specific techniques (of flattening paper) or specific processes (blueprint, prototype) or *how* to handle huge quantities of objects is vital for maintaining the architectural specificity of the archival material. In the spatial arrangement of the conservation lab, all these ways of knowing interconnect and facilitate better treatment of the archival objects; conservators' knowledge emerges as dispositional and gradually grows within the reciprocal exchange between active things and people within the ecology of the lab.

Conclusions: Between Valuation and Effects

The preservation of architectural objects requires description, careful identification, knowledge of the collection, and knowledge of the behavior of materials over time. Objects are scrutinized in terms of analyzable properties rather than in terms of aesthetic effects. The architectural objects in the conservation lab are no more or less interpretable than they are knowable. Following Karen, Anne, and David, I witnessed at every moment the striking resemblance between the regime of treating architectural objects and that of medical treatment, for conservation balances the efficiency of healing and the risk of damaging a body (human or other). Solvents, adhesives, carbon papers are reminiscent of drugs in the way they exercise a therapeutic effect while also generating side effects. As pharmakons, they risk causing destruction while aiming to heal; both go hand in hand.

Conservation introduces a caregiving regime. As such it risks transforming the object into a passive "patient" submitted to active interventions and manipulations. However, at any moment in the process, we do not witness an active human (conservator) taking care, fully in control, providing treatment to a (passive) nonhuman (archival object). All treatments implicate humans and nonhumans in a symmetrical dance of agency. The caregiving process constantly adds to the objects-in-conservation agents who take care of them, as well as more objects and scrips that add to and support them in order to stabilize them. Conservators, bodies, instruments, and other types of beings are all mobilized in this process, which does not miraculously transform the object from damaged to less damaged, from dependent to less dependent. The object-in-conservation exists in all these states at once. Conservators accompany the object through all the trails and trials as it straddles the boundaries of autonomy and dependence. Objects converse with, talk back, react to, and can even strike back or damage the bodies of caretakers. Thus, treatments neither objectivize nor subjectivize the objects-in-conservation. Watch Karen, David, Anne, and you see a lively lab; hundreds of operations of handling scalpels, controlling reactions, taking a look through the microscope, releasing an adhesive, removing a hinge. A complex politics of care is at stake here. Yet, none of the experts involved can fix an object in a particular state; they only help the action slide from one mode to another so as to sustain the objects as archival.

If the speech of architectural objects flows smoothly throughout the other sites (galleries, study and lecture rooms), here, in the conservation lab, the speech is interrupted, hesitant, complemented, even amended by gestures pointing to the microscope, to objects, to screens, to codes, to chemical reactions, to hinges. Here, the friends replace what they want to say by a finger designating a certain phenomenon produced with the help of an instrument or via a certain mediation, a phenomenon that is hesitant in manifesting itself as it depends on the visibility of traces of humidity or infestation of the surface of a drawing that smells. If the speech in the galleries flows in an uninterrupted way, here, the friends have to cross the huge divides between the monsoons in India, the techniques for detecting the smell, the fragile surface of a deoxidation paper, and the human speech generated in an uncertain set of operations. Often interrupted by obstacles, such as a failed test, unintelligible results, surfaces difficult to treat, and interjections like "I found it! Here it is!," the speech is heterogeneous indeed. It is a speech mediated by scalpels, folders, binders, codes, reports, oxidation papers, and a microscope. Conservators handle objects through the wide window of a specific instrument, a discipline, and a specialization that they have spent years mastering.

If the shipping area was a quiet space where only Marie and Alexandre were working on packaging and requests, the vaults formed a vacant space, occasionally filled with life, and the offices of Mary and Giovanna were frequented by a few friends only, the conservation lab is the scene for the hectic and collective work of a number of conservators. They spend more time in the space of their lab, without traveling very often to other sites of archiving, and they rarely receive visitors from outside. Whereas at other sites of archiving, we witness people usually working alone, in the lab we are much more likely to see people gathered in a circle around a specific object or a specific test through which a certain phenomenon is being probed. Their discussions revolve around the enigma of that being—the insect or the monsoon climate in India—which they made capable of talking. Passionate about the fate of that insect or a moldy sketch, worried that it might contaminate other objects, cautious and careful, they are fully invested, fully there, "hands on"—or rather "gloves on." In this site of archiving, the instruments, the equipment, the controlled temperatures, the chemical products are not the final result of the activities. It is the treatment of the architectural objects that matters: oxidation, de-infestation, neutralization of smell, restoration, and cleaning. All these procedures go in tandem with the production of more working scripts, written protocols, reports, drafts, files, notes, and measurements. All these scripts circulate among the labs and facilitate the movement of architectural objects. Here, we witness objects constantly negotiating with the environment, battling uncertainty, the erosion of time, begging for care, demanding precaution and stabilization of the different climates.

However, the conservation lab does not submit the objects to the same kind of rigorous questioning and pressure to produce results that scientific labs do; that particular form of enunciation is not present here. Here, when an object "talks" about its condition after a test, a chemical procedure, or an instrument manipulation, the knowledge gained is mobilized to take better care of it and to repair it: knowing *how* and knowing *that* constantly interrelate and rarify. The result is the improvement and stabilization of the archival object, not the fabrication of a new fact; we are in the heart of a quasi-medical regime of treatment that has its own politics of care that cannot be witnessed at other sites of archiving.

The behavior of the friends here is different from what it is in the vaults, the registry, the offices of curators, directors, or cataloguers. The bodily posture of conservators, always leaning toward an object, differs from that of other friends. Touching the objects is more mediated, compared to in the registry, where Alexandre only changes different colored gloves, or the offices where the hands pointing to architectural drawings remain bare; in conservation, the equipment multiplies: gloves, pipettes, scalpels, microscopes, spatulas, knives, and sponges. The conservators have a distinct way of engaging with the objects, a highly mediated, slow, and precise way of caretaking, accompanied by specific techniques of documenting these procedures and inscribing the traces of interventions, which results in singular ways of knowing the objects-in-conservation. Here, as on other sites, new scripts continue to pile up and to escort archival objects.

It is impossible to detach archival objects from the ontological anxieties of conservation. Whatever secret life they have, or are imagined to have, in the world of aesthetic architectural values, this is not how they "live" on this site of archiving. Treating objects in conservation activates fine ontological distinctions, highlights material granularity and epistemic worries; it sets archival objects in full swing and galvanizes the circuits of time.

THE PLOT OF ARCHIVING

Log: 1:00 p.m. After franticly touring the streets of Porto on a warm August afternoon, my taxi stops in front of a white, imposingly modernist house on Rua do Aleixo. One might wonder why we are in Porto, far away from Montreal. It is because when unraveling archiving we need to visit different places, continents, and countries. Following how the archival material is selected and organized, how it travels and mutates from one site to another, we are led to engage in a multi-institutional, multi-actorial and multi-siting ethnographic study. To avoid generalizations about archiving, I will recount a very specific event, namely the arrival of Álvaro Siza's fonds at the CCA, where it is one of the most important recent acquisitions. As my ethnographic study is unfolding over the summer of 2015, I witness the big crates arriving in Montreal after a long journey from Portugal. These crates contain objects that range from the 1950s to the early 2010s; the material is being processed at the time of my observation. Rather than telling an extensive story of archival acquisition, in what follows, I will describe the negotiations for acquiring Siza's fonds, the logic behind the "split" of the archive, and the rationale for Siza to join the CCA. We will follow the process of organizing and archiving the material in Porto and the steps of processing and rehousing the archive in Montreal, as well as Siza's reflections on the trajectory of this fonds. Sketching the actions of archivists, curators, and architects involved in different situations of archiving allows us to dislodge archiving from the subjectivity of individual perspectives, of lone pairs of eyes or single voices. We thus place the enquiry *within the heart* of archiving and continue to trace its ontological granularity. Designing and archiving reconnect here again through the coming and going between the sites of archival production in Porto, where some specific mechanisms of generating archives in design practice can be witnessed, and the sites of archiving in Montreal. Thus, we follow the *becoming archival* of architectural objects and scrutinize the ways archiving matters for practicing architects.

The Arrival of Siza's Fonds in Montreal

Before tracing the work of the archivists processing Siza's archive, let us listen to the director of the CCA, the director of collections, the founder of the CCA, and the chief curator to understand how the archive reached the CCA. An acquisition follows the hierarchy of decision making at institutional level; it is not a mysterious act. The director of the CCA, Mirko Zardini, explains that the acquisition of Siza's archive was a little problematic because of the process. In the past, the CCA used to purchase archives. The founder of the CCA, Phyllis Lambert, also recalls that at the start they were dependent on the "market"[1] in the sense that the CCA would pay the owner of the archive: "In those days everything that came through was basically through auctions. And then, of course I suppose there were collections you could get in Europe if you found them."[2] Since Mirko has stepped in as the director, the CCA had begun acquiring material strictly by donation, and this was a big change. Siza's archive made its way to the CCA through a donor acquisition strategy.[3]

As a private research-oriented institution that is very deeply rooted in North American culture, the CCA, until a few years ago, concentrated primarily on the archives of North American and English architects (Peter Eisenman, James Stirling, Cedric Price, Ernest Cormier, and others). The sole exception was Aldo Rossi. As Mirko explains, though, "In light of the idea of CCA becoming a real international or global institution, it was really not acceptable that CCA policy on the archive was limited to the Anglo-Saxon postwar experience."[4] The CCA was interested in expanding and enriching this network of materials with contemporaneous archives that represent different opinions, strategies, and ways of thinking architecturally, as well as different cultures. That was the reason for acquiring the Siza archive, the Abalos & Herreros archive, the Alessandro Poli archive, among others. That was also the reason for acquiring some materials from Japan and India (related to the activities of the exhibitions). Siza's archive was also obtained as a part of the CCA strategy "to build a certain perspective on postwar architecture,"[5] and the acquisition of Spanish, Italian, and Portuguese material is part of the ambition "to make this perspective more culturally heterogeneous."[6] Thus, the arrival of Siza's archive was meant to contribute to the process of the de-

Americanization of the CCA. My investigation happened exactly at that moment, when the collection was opening up to more variety.

The acquisition of Siza's fonds was the result of a combination of opportunities, economic factors, and cultural politics. Siza himself recalls that when Zardini approached him for the donation, he was happy to accept: "I had already been in Montreal and visited the archives and I think they are the best in the world. They are very well organized, with much activity, both exhibitions and publications."[7] Nevertheless, when this decision was announced publicly, "the archive was considered very important for Portugal." Siza recollects, "I was seen as a kind of traitor, for my archives were about to be 'exported' from the country."[8] This happened, he explains, "because when you send a work of art outside Portugal you must communicate to the national department. I know they had never considered architecture as art but when the news came, and when we sent the obligatory documents to them, it appeared to be a problem. This was in the newspapers and the controversy broke."[9] In response, he had to write a note to explain why the archive was going to Canada by highlighting the lack of similar opportunities in Portugal, and how important it was to find a place for his drawings and to make them available for students and historians.[10] In order to mitigate the outcry in Portugal and to find a compromise, the CCA had diplomatically recommended splitting the works. As Mirko notes, "We suggested to Siza to divide the archive among different institutions. We considered that Siza is one of the architects whose contribution has been relevant for the creation of the political and symbolic identity of a country, especially after 1973–1974 with the revolution in Portugal. We suggested that the Portuguese projects stay in Portugal at the Serralves Museum of Contemporary Art in Porto and at the Fundação Calouste Gulbenkian in Lisbon, and that the international projects come to the CCA. And we proposed that the three institutions work together on the archive."[11] Thus, the CCA approached the two Portuguese institutions and negotiated with them. Siza agreed to the split; the works related to Lisbon and the south of Portugal remained in the Gulbenkian (there were also other works from other parts of eastern Portugal), and works from Porto and the north remained in Serralves; these collections included about forty projects each. The remainder of the materials, over two hundred projects, went to the CCA.

The Siza archive presents an interesting example of witnessing a network of institutions in action. Portugal had no archival institutions that could match the magnitude of the CCA, but the Serralves already had the know-how of a collecting institution, and the Gulbenkian had a nascent architectural component (though not yet an architectural department). The distribution of the archive among the three institutions placed it into a dynamic network capable of promoting a discourse about architecture that did not exist previously in Portugal. As Mirko says, "The collection is not only what you have but also what other institutions or people have. It is especially about what you do and what other institutions do."[12] The production of an exhibition on Siza requires that each of the institutions works together, sharing projects among them. The partnership of the three institutions has already proven to be very fruitful as they have managed to produce by now a number of successful exhibitions and publications.[13] We can see that an archive has the capacity to develop new relationships and instigate architectural discussions that were hitherto nonexistent. The decision to donate an archive is based on far more than a concern for individual legacy; it rather embraces a larger ambition for advancing new curatorial and architectural cultures that transcend the boundaries of single firms and single collecting institutions.

After many discussions between the CCA and the Siza practice on Skype, Zoom meetings, phone calls, and visits, the details of the split were sorted out. For Pamela Casey, a CCA archivist, sharing the archive with two other institutions has proven to be an interesting working arrangement, especially when it comes to agreeing on the project index. As the archive is project-based, the index is supposed to help researchers looking for specific materials find out which institution holds them. While there is no shared, universal search tool, "finding aid," or website—each of the three institutions has its own—there is shared documentation that guides scholars to the right place. That is, a shared "map" shows the distribution of Siza's archive based on consistent descriptions by the three institutions, which are required to follow the same international archival standards.

An archival institution, we witness here, does not possess anything; it simply has a respect for and a sense of accountability for the material. The idea of ownership "that institutions have incorporated, coming from the tradition of the private collectors," is misleading, posits Mirko, and has "to be substituted with the idea of responsibility," a shared responsibility. This is also a result of the move to a "donor-strategy" of acquisition. The copyrights and monetary aspects also play a role. Archives are challenging, repeats Espeth Cowell, responsible for collection and program services, because when an archive is acquired, often the copyrights are not from a single source. Also, "if it is an old practice, they will grant the copyright, while with the archives of active firms generally the copyright remains with the creator. Also, the copyright of an architectural drawing is different from the copyright of a photo as the creator of photographs makes money from their reproduction, whereas an architectural drawing, especially a technical one as opposed to a presentation one, is not actually a money-making thing in itself. It's a product of a process."[14] Thus, money-making and copyright arrangements are also to be taken into account in the processes of acquisition or donation. Moreover, as architectural practice becomes more and more distributed across various geographical and institutional contexts, the legacy of an architectural firm ends up being distributed within a network of institutions taking care of these resources, facilitating digital access, and sharing research.

Splitting archives, however, is not new; it is an established practice. Distributing and sharing the legacy of an architect is the model, not an exception. Phyllis Lambert remembers: "When the family of Léon Vaudoyer decided to sell the archive, I was adamant that nobody in North America should buy anything from his archive. . . . And so, I guess that's an interesting question about whether you have to split archives in different places. To a certain extent you can say, if that's coherent, it can work. The way we are working on the Siza archive follows this logic."[15] Phyllis also warns of the danger of dispersal: splitting a collection can disrupt connections within a coherent whole. That is why the split of the Siza archive requires the institutions to find a way to build stronger synergies to maintain the whole. The distributed archive calls for a specific way of crafting the architectural legacy.

According to Giovanna Borasi, the chief curator at the CCA, the split is logical from a curatorial perspective. She recounts how the CCA started with a small show on Siza,[16] which was timely as it was before the Portuguese Pavilion was presented at the 2016 Biennale,[17] and included his first two European projects outside of Portugal, which were both social housing projects.[18] When the CCA began processing, they decided to set priorities about where to start. In the past, an archive like this had to be "closed" for five years for processing purposes, and no pieces for research were released in the meantime. In the Siza case, however, a general overview was completed, and a selection of early projects made. By doing the processing in stages, the CCA was able to open up the archive part by part so that researchers could access the different parts. The "whole" is purposely missing at this point. When the entire distributed archive is processed, all its parts become accessible. With live archives, it is important, argues Giovanna, "not to create an overall catalogue or to follow a monographic approach."[19] While receiving relevant archives is important from a historical point of view, dealing with living, practicing architects could be challenging, and the archive remains open. Thus, nothing is stored passively; it is redistributed, put into dialogue, open for interpretation and for different types of access; it is networked and renetworked many times.

Accessibility is an important dimension of an archive for Siza. "Siza was very conscious of the value of having his archive represented in an international institution, and to be described in English,"[20] explains Pamela. This ensures a much wider reach. Yet, another reason for architects of his caliber to donate to the CCA, elaborates Giovanna, is that he trusts the institution. Siza confirms, happy "to see that all my work will be maintained well at the CCA."[21] Moreover, he knows that he will not be isolated, and his legacy will be seen within the context of other materials. "The researcher will be able to do a time cut transversally."[22] Architects do not want to be a lonely voice in an echo chamber. Their archives are often processed and catalogued alongside those of other architects.[23] To be part of a "mingling of people" is important for Siza, repeats Giovanna. "When he was working in a certain period, Aldo Rossi, James Stirling were there too, and their archives are now at the CCA as well."[24] The physical proximity of archives facilitates a dialogue among all these architects and their oeuvres. The relational space of the collection enables transversal reading, juxtaposition, and comparison of architectural works connected in time. While commenting on the "good company" his archive has at the CCA, Siza exclaims, "All important architects. I learned so much from them!"[25] and he recalls going to the CCA to see "the sketchbooks and documents of great architects, American, European, and so on; the architects that I appreciate." Being in "good company" is also very important for the first international architect acquired by the CCA, Peter Eisenman. He explains: "I think Phyllis Lambert has a really interesting archive which represents to me the avant-guard of architecture of the 1960s and the 1970s; she has John Hejduk, Aldo Rossi, James Stirling, she has me; she has a lot of the avant-guard, which is quite nice. She is trying to have a significant collection of the people from the sixties and the seventies. And that is a good idea. It is nice not to be alone in Canada. . . . That's the value of it, to have five or six of the important figures at the time."[26] In this archival space-time, the comparison between various architects from the same generation emerges naturally; the heterogeneous material in the folders that showcase the way that design has been elaborated in each practice relates to other worlds of practice, thus accelerating a comparative research endeavor—a skeleton for historiographic reasoning.

Porto: "Mountains of Paper"

The story of Álvaro Siza's archive started in his design practice a couple of decades before it reached Montreal. Archiving is neither an unfamiliar nor a recent activity for his firm, which is still active and producing archives.[27] This raises the question, If an archive reflects the thinking of architectural practitioners, what exactly is the connection between this thinking and the debris that collects in an office? How does the archive reflect also the collaborative working dynamics in a creative practice? And how does it bridge the gap between designing and archiving? Attempting to answer these questions, we will have a glimpse at the design work of Siza's firm and its ongoing love affair with archiving.

Explaining how archiving began, Siza says, "I started my practice in '54, and by the nineties, there was a mountain of documents accumulated, and I felt the need to organize because there were a lot of drawings."[28] Chiara, an architect working at his practice at the time, volunteered to start arranging the archive and has now been doing this for over twenty years. What prompted Chiara to become an architectural archivist was the fact that back at the end of 1990s, she was often asked to look for materials for exhibitions and books.[29] There were a number of influential projects in the practice, including the Faculty of Architecture at the University of Porto (1993), the Toren van Siza (1999), and others, and as the number of projects grew, and the more paper accumulated in the office, the more difficult it became to search for materials in the piles. Chiara "appointed herself as an archivist," recalls Siza. The first projects she started arranging were the Marés pool (1961–1966) and the Chiado neighborhood rebuild (1988–1989), which contained thousands of drawings. Thus, the reason for starting a structured archive was "to organize the works in progress,"[30] and Chiara gathered materials, assembled all the new drawings, and began classifying them according to the date of each work.[31] Here, the archivist and the working architect deal with two competitive temporalities: the incentive to catalogue the completed projects, not to lock them in the drawers of History, but to organize them in a way that they can better serve the practice. Moreover, since some projects can be ongoing for fifteen, even forty years, the working architects may need to revisit and re-invite them into the current design work. Hence, there is a folding, sliding time running with different speeds, depending on the type of the project and the context, which, in turn, requires the architect to go back and reopen an archive for different reasons: maintenance of the building, renovation, completion, a project put on hold and never finished. There is also another temporal dimension: the incentive to capture and order the ongoing course of design, intensified even more by the introduction of the computers into the office and by the increasing geometric complexity of the buildings.[32] In spite of his "bad relationship with machines," as Siza likes to say, designing with computers became a routine, and while this resulted in the proliferation of digital files, it also raised awareness of the value of paper documents and drawings and had a major impact on the decision to begin an archive.

"Mountains of paper," as Siza loves to call them, piled up in the office on the second floor, and when moved into the "kingdom" of Chiara, on the ground floor, they were ordered and filled the large cavernous space. Here again, we see that archival "fever" is linked to the messiness of design and the desire to "clean the office." As paper piles up, there is a need to look back in time and put them in order. Like Walter Benjamin's Angel of History, whose face is turned towards the past while his wings are caught by the storm of the future, propelling him irresistibly to turn back to the debris of the past, the "Angel" of a working archive requires constant thinking of how to arrange the past in a way that allows it to continue in the present and organize different paths into a future. The lack of an archiving institution in Portugal at the time also had an impact on Siza's personal decision to begin organizing his practice's past. In the 1990s, the archive of the National Monuments in Portugal had begun to assemble an archive and collect the works of modern architects, but the project was interrupted. As a result, there was no institution in Portugal that could accommodate Siza's archive in a place where his works could be viewed and consulted by students, historians, and theorists of architecture. With the exception of a private collector from London, who bought some drawings of the Piscinas de Marés and Beires House, and the Centre Pompidou in Paris, which purchased a number of drawings and models for its collection after the 1990 exhibition "Álvaro Siza. Architecture 1980–1990,"[33] the bulk of the archive remained on the ground floor of the office on Rua do Aleixo in Porto.

Regarding his archive, Siza states modestly, "Even I did not think about it until the 1990s."[34] Until then, most of the drawings were done by hand, but the computer changed the practice, and curators and publishers started requesting digital files rather than original drawings. The 1993 Pritzker Prize recognition for his entire oeuvre led to more projects and commissions, and as more "mountains of paper" piled up, the need for archiving became even more pressing. That glorious moment of achievement, along with the increasing demand for digital files, coincided with the practical need of storage space. Thus, at the moment when the digital began taking hold, Siza started organizing a systematic archive of paper[35] and began attaching more importance to the legacy of his own practice.

Two Houses, Many Worlds

It is a long process, an arduous journey, for an archive to arrive at the CCA: a whole assembly of institutions, people, skills, negotiations, contractual and informal agreements need to be in place. This brings us back to Montreal. The process starts with trust, according to director of collections, Martien de Vletter. Drawing from her own experience as a publisher, Martien believes that just as the work of authors and publishers, which is "all about trust,"[36] the acquisition of an archive requires stable relations grounded in trust, in an obligation to one another, and a "shared responsibility" for the work archived. Both the donors' and collection directors' activities are far from the mode of salespeople and buyers, who rely on elusive schemes to convince. Instead, acquiring an archive begins with building mutual confidence between the parties, which is a long process of back-and-forth conversations that aim to develop a common ground. Martien often explains to donors that they have to decide if the CCA is "the right fit" for them. She expounds, "That is why it took a while before Siza gave his confidence and trust to the CCA, and the other way around."[37] It took a year before a conclusion was reached and a contract drafted. The archive finally had a firm foundation upon which to travel to Montreal.

Picture the two scenes. Scene one—Porto, a large office on Rua do Aleixo, a man in his eighties, drawings, models, letters; an archive; smoke, cigarette butts snubbed out, dispersed sketches, and ashes menacing the fragile paper, floating through the air like dust (see figure 16); this is architect Siza, his archive, his past piling up and subsequently ordered, on his premises, in his possession.[38] Scene two—Montreal, big boxes in the immaculately clean vault spaces, pristine shiny floors, silence; the archivist Adria Seccareccia wearing gloves to manipulate some drawings. An older man visits the vaults, inspecting the boxes; a pack of cigarettes, drawings, yet a lack of smoke. It is Álvaro Siza on the premises of the CCA. Martien explains that as soon as the archive arrives at the CCA, "It achieves an archival standard, not a museum standard. . . . It's not his [Siza's] anymore. So, there is a change from an intellectual point of view and from a physical point of view."[39] We have to wonder what happens to the archive between these two scenes. The route from office to collection has an effect on the materials themselves; they

FIGURE 16. Architect Siza in his office in Porto; next to him, his archivist, Chiara

undergo some alteration, a process of transubstantiation; they are materially and intellectually reorganized: processed, rehoused, catalogued, and rearranged according to the CCA standards, and thus acquire a collection mode of existence. At the CCA Siza is not allowed to smoke. But it is important also to reflect on Martien's distinction between the archive and the museum. The archival standard differs from the museum's because archives are read primarily as groups of research objects consulted by individuals, while museum objects are treated individually and need to be in a pristine state as they are publicly accessible. Problems with folded or cracked drawings in an archive are important only when the objects are selected for an exhibition or publication, and this requires that they be treated individually at an object level, whereas commonly in the archive, objects are stabilized, not cleaned or embellished (as seen in the work of conservators in chapter 5).[40] While the CCA descriptive standards had previously contained a mix of museum cataloguing and Canadian archival standards, the CCA has recently reviewed and adjusted them in their attempt to be consistent. Thus, "instead of the objects being described very specifically, more attention is to be paid to the big picture."[41] The multiplicity of the archive is endorsed and maintained as such at every ontological level in the practices of a collecting institution.

Archivists at Work: Ordering, Reordering

A number of archivists work on the Siza fonds. In Montreal, in 2016, we meet Pamela, who is supervising Adria, who is processing the material that has already made its journey to the CCA. Both of them have expertise in working with archives. If we cross the Atlantic, in distant Porto, we meet the architects (and archivists) Chiara Porcu and Magda Seifert in their archival "kingdom," which opens up a different archival world than the CCA. Trained as architects, neither Chiara nor Magda has a special training in archiving. Magda remembers the intensity of the work when they had to prepare the first shipment of materials for the CCA back in 2014, but as of 2018, there is less material to process. When the boxes of Siza arrived at the CCA, they already had a layer of order introduced by Chiara (helped by Magda during the final stretch of preparations).

To grasp the original order of things in an architectural archive, some knowledge of the architectural practice is needed.[42] We witnessed a disorder when opening the boxes of Cedric Price with Giovanna (see chapter 3). Yet, through the analysis of this archive it appeared that there were layers of order in this apparent disorder. And if this was indeed the case, how were the different layers interrelated? How and where were they produced? How did they make the shifting dynamics of architectural practice resonate? The Siza archive tells us a different story of layering "order" over an archive and illustrates a strategy of archiving that is distinct from that of Cedric Price, for the dynamic relationship between archiving and designing is in full swing here.

As the archivist works, she acquires knowledge of the working practice, and she starts intellectually arranging the material in order, in series, and subseries (see also chapter 4). The archives of the practices of living architects are composed of drawings, lecture slides, letters, binders, communications with clients, among other materials; in the classification scheme they are all described at a series' level as groupings of material that reflect different activities. Siza's fonds has three series: first, the projects, which reflect the professional practice (and each of the projects has its subseries within that series), second, the sketchbooks, which are a constant reflection of Siza's working life.[43] The two types of documents were also located physically in different places; the projects were in the office and the sketchbooks in his house. This provided the archivists with another indication that the materials bear traces of different activities and they are to be catalogued within their own series, not integrated into one whole. The third series contains materials from Siza's lectures, teaching materials, conferences, events, presentations, and published work. The classification scheme also includes specific CCA guidance on how to title the series, how to express the title and the information given, and how to describe the material. Identifying the different types of activities and arranging the material related to them logically are important moves of archiving.

When the material was at Siza's practice the correspondence was arranged vertically and placed on the shelves, and the drawings were placed horizontally and arranged in the drawers.[44] White stickers were place on the boxes to indicate material that was to stay, red stickers to point to material that would travel. All of the materials were grouped into projects and therein arranged into sets (ten drawings or so could form a set whose temporal and epistemic boundaries reflect the working design dynamics within an architectural project); the projects were numbered sequentially and by year, so that for example, "16/80" meant the sixteenth project in the 1980s. Although the CCA renumbered the archives, the order still reflects the decade of the project.[45] At all levels of archival organization, the multiplicity is maintained and continues in the process of rehousing and reordering the material.

The arrangement of this material closely mirrors Chiara's knowledge of Siza's practice and her experience of working for the firm. As an architect, she had an understanding of the specific projects that she had worked on, although she did not have an in-depth understanding of the other projects and drawings. Thus, if the knowledge of the practicing architect is partial, grounded within the world of a specific project, the archiving process provides an opportunity to broaden it. Siza endorsed a horizontal arrangement, rather than vertical, and Chiara organized the archive "as if it were an architectural project," separating the drawings from correspondences, clustering the different projects. The profound knowledge of the different phases of architectural projects gained through design experience helped her to develop a plan for the archival organization; this understanding of architectural practice informed her archival work. As Chiara says, "I do not work on the archive as an archivist because I have the soul of an architect."[46] In conversations with archivists from Italy, Chiara had learned that all schemes are possible and that the most important rule is to start and finish a scheme even if it is not the best one. This attitude is for her reminiscent of the logic of architectural work; when the scheme or skeleton is there, the details can be added, reworked, and refined afterward.

Chiara gradually developed knowledge of where the things stood in the archive: "on that shelf" or "in that drawer." "Knowing where" is a variation on knowing how. It differs from all the factual and propositional knowledge she has about architectural processes in general, and Siza's work specifically. It is a specific mechanical knowledge of the inherent organization of the archive. It is through inserting, inspecting, memorizing and, placing as a repetitive series of operations that Chiara acquired the "where" knowledge. The minute skill of "knowing where" is often compared to the grandiose ambition of "knowing all about Siza." Both Chiara and Magda portray how encyclopedic his work is and at the same time how impossible it is to have knowledge about all its aspects. An oeuvre that crosses many different fields outside architecture implies various collaborations and spreads out of the confined boundaries of the Rua da Aleixo office, to sculpture, painting, exhibitions, writing, fashion, and even the design of eyeglasses, and thus it can hardly be fitted into a single category. "I know only part of Siza," explains Chiara. "There's absolutely nobody who could know the overall dimensions of his work."[47] Archiving confronts the archivist with the partial character of human knowledge and the impossibility of gaining an in-depth, panoramic, panoptic, all-encompassing comprehension of the work of an architectural practice. It also reveals how architecture is part of a broader network of entangled fields, arts, and industries, never an isolated bubble. After two decades an archivist can gain knowledge about only a very small part of the complex universe of Siza's practice. Archiving is not about knowing all, of developing a bird's eye view; it is about knowing a little, but knowing it well, and knowing where to find more.

Although all projects were meticulously organized by Chiara, another level of organization of the material had to be added in order to prepare it for the CCA. This was prompted by the need to present the archive to the National Archive in Portugal to receive the required licenses and the official approval to send it abroad. It resulted in extensive work "from morning to dawn." Chiara and Magda "had to list, prepare, count, photograph and organize everything. . . . That is also why the archive came to the CCA in such an organized way."[48] Sometimes forty folders or dossiers had to be recounted. Counting may look like a simple activity; Siza teased them on a number of occasions: "It is not that difficult to count!" Yet Chiara counted, Magda counted again, and then they checked and rechecked to ensure that they had the correct number. Counting here involved more than just arithmetic. That is, the numbers were not merely passive abstractions, but the result of a series of actions that were necessary to identify, locate, and distinguish material archival units. Everything had to be taken from the shelves, put on the floor to photograph, then arranged into labeled boxes, with smaller labeled boxes going inside the larger ones (see figure 17). Everything was nested into another series of "forms" to hold the materials together. This all took a long time. The Porto archivists prepared a huge working document for the CCA to help them organize their work. Still in use, it contains information on the name of the project, the year, the location, the number that Chiara has given it, and a list of what the archive contains: folders, copies, dossiers, photographs. Magda recalls, "When we started doing it [that work] we didn't exactly know how we were supposed to do it. It was trial and error, trial and error until we got here."[49] Archiving is, we witness, not simply about ordering everything at once, but a slow, iterative process that goes step-by-step, back and forth, trial and error, piece by piece, thus gradually turning physical material into numbers and signs.

Repetition and Trash

An archive comes to the CCA in different states. Sometimes it arrives after being left for many years in a storage room, the boxes and materials in disarray. However, no matter the state, it is difficult to determine what to throw away: "When it comes to eliminating material, typically you wouldn't eliminate a lot,"[50] says Pamela. Instead of performing a selective appraisal of material, archivists keep numerous versions of the same document, copies of copies, a proliferation of documents. We could compare the "versions" of drawings to the "versions" of a manuscript; it is interesting to hold onto the early drafts because they hold traces of the major structural and editorial changes, the flux of the decision making of the author(s). Likewise, multiple versions of annotated drawings reveal the evolution of the drawing and the architects' thinking. This creates a nonhierarchical assembly of materials, a condensation of coexistences, a simultaneity of events. The task of the archivists is not to make selections, to adjudicate or evaluate what is the correct or the original version, but to "guide people through all these versions and when they were made."[51] They provide the signposts through the stream

FIGURE 17. Boxes in the archive of Siza in Porto

of the copies so that the thinking and experimentation design process emerges from the drawings. Archives, we witness here, exemplify the intensive internal life of architectural projects that can be traced on the basis of their many different reiterations and successive mutations. Archivists witness all versions of when and how an architectural product might have been created, including the involvement of other people. They grasp this arrangement of the archive as a reflection of the inherent dynamics of design process and strive to explain "the logic of the order to the researchers so that they can find their way through it."[52] In this vein of work, Chiara selected all materials that are not architecture-relevant in Porto before they traveled to Montreal; these included personal documents (receipts, photographs). She also helped Siza prepare the sketchbooks: one day Siza brought them to the office, and they went through all pages and took out the personal information; the torn pages were either kept by him or given to some collaborators—for instance, to his long-term collaborator, Souto Moura. As some pages containing personal information had to be destroyed, the office bought a shredding machine; both Chiara and Magda remember that "terrifying moment" when the daunting noise of shredding accompanied their work. Still, the archival "fever" remained: even the shredded paper was kept.

Chiara never throws anything away. She takes her time to look and inspect the material. Even a copy of Siza's drawing cannot be discarded. Instead, she secures it in a folder titled "Copies to be trashed," which is also, and paradoxically, part of the archive. The copies are never thrown away as "you are never sure if it is a copy of a copy," explains Chiara, so she "puts it into the process."[53] Time passes, and then she goes through the folder again, reorders things, and sometimes she finds out that the copy could fit in another folder. She removes it from its status as "to be trashed," and places it back within the archive proper. The "trashing it later" policy allows her to gain time, to go back and compare, to wait until a difference is discovered; more time is needed for the archivist to detect such differences in the drawings. In these archival exercises of analysis, of "finding the difference," time plays a critical part; it folds differently due to the proliferation of copies. Archivists do not take a Platonic perspective, comparing iconic images with replicas, distinguishing between copies and originals, differentiating good and bad reproductions, but rather maintain *all* these differences as having their own merits. We are in the realm of reiterations here, which refute the logic of model and reproduction, essence and appearance; such distinctions operate only in the world of representation. Within a series of repetitive drawings with variations, a kind of internal reverberation is produced, a resonance that induces a movement that overflows the series itself. Raising up these series of images, to assert their rights over originals or copies, the archivist operates "the vertigo of simulacrum"[54] wherein hierarchy, fixity of distribution, and the determination of value all become impossible. When both similarity and resemblance are now based on the condition of being simulated, selection is no longer possible.

In the dance of proliferating versions and the difficulty of getting rid of materials over the course of archiving, we find out again that there is no *one* correct, original, single version, but rather a stream of reiterations that suggest that there are many possible variations produced and tested at each phase of the design process, yet tend overall in one direction. The condensation of coexistences in this realm of reiterations generates a positive power that entirely negates the supremacy of the original in the creative process of design. Following the moves of archiving, we witness that the archive does not outline the beginning or the end, the precious first or last idea, the one author behind it or the one force above it; both linearity and transcendence are overthrown. Instead, archiving foregrounds the entire dynamic trajectory of a project, the flitting direction of travel, the stream of tested options and the branches of explored scenarios, the endless iterations. The archivist's techniques function as reversible, foldable devices through the sliding of which many infinitesimal "differences" slowly emerge. That is, the diagram of forces of an evolving design concept is captured in its multiplicity, a multiplicity that is not ordered from above, but organized from within, an archive.

Foldable Times

The life on the second floor of Siza's practice where design unfolds in full swing is overflowing with surprises. However, a project travels downstairs only when it is stopped, put on hold, or completed. In a way, this reflects yet inverts what we witnessed earlier at the CCA: as the objects move between floors, a transformation of their form and modality of action occurs as layers are added to them, as they enter new sets of relations and expectations. While objects at the CCA are stabilized as they move up from the vaults and the labs to the galleries, here, they are stabilized as they move down from Siza's office to Chiara's ground floor. There is a transformation taking place as the objects travel and enter into new sets of relations. Take a look at the spatial rapport between the two floors of the house on Rua da Alexo, the practice and the archive. Siza and Chiara communicate daily. Designing and archiving reconnect. During my visit, Chiara is supposed to prepare a drawing for Siza, and he is waiting; he calls her many times; then he calls her again to join the interview in his office. Both the sites of the practice and the archive are in constant communication. Chiara knows about the ongoing projects in the practice, but begins to work on them only when they enter the archival space on the ground floor. Listen to Chiara. I overhear her speaking Portuguese;

she makes a joke that she resembles a "surgeon," "cutting pieces of the drawing." The archivist, like the surgeon, intervenes into the materials, like the conservators who perform surgeries in the lab (see chapter 5). In another moment, I inspect some materials that Siza had just given her (see figure 18), it is not a selection, but a bunch of things that contains a little bit of everything. It is a hodgepodge, a mess of stuff. A note on the front page reads, "from arch Siza to Chiara." The folder contains a representative collection of what is on his desk, and the desk is full of everything: sketches, maps, correspondence. It is now Chiara's job to organize it. In other cases, the collaborators on specific projects organize the material and send it downstairs, or Chiara goes upstairs to "rescue the material" and bring it down into the archive. Going back and forth between ongoing design practice and ongoing archiving, up and down, in and out, both Chiara and Siza make and maintain a living archive.

With time Chiara has cultivated an ability to recognize Siza's hand drawings and handwriting in their different variations and from different moments in time. Siza has a very specific and unique way of drawing. His collaborators often try to mimic the way he draws, and the differences in the drawings are hard to detect by an architecturally untrained eye. Yet, with time, Chiara gradually learned to distinguish these small differences: what the work is and who has completed it and how. The hardly noticeable variations kept in the archive can in fact reveal

FIGURE 18.   Chiara with materials to process, Siza's archive, Porto

the hidden workings and inherent collaborative dynamics in an architectural practice. A drawing has many layers of information that only an archivist can grasp
and decipher, many signs. Signs are enigmas, "hieroglyphs" that resist ready de-
coding. "Signs are the object of a temporal apprenticeship, not of an abstract
knowledge."[55] And Chiara is the best example of such a temporal apprenticeship.
She is far from acting as a detective going after the "mystery" of some "original
works," striving to unravel the "truth" on the basis of all traces available, driven
by the question of "what has happened?," mobilizing a past so immediate and a
future so near. Instead, she performs a reading of all signs on the surface. These
"hieroglyphs" both reveal and conceal; they deny immediate comprehension and
induce a process of indirect decipherment. To archive is therefore to think through
these "hieroglyphs," to interpret, to translate.

Some archival documents remain puzzling; it is not easy to interpret them and
place them in a folder or match them with other pieces. Inspecting a drawing of
the Porto School of Architecture, we find out that while Siza was working on this
major project, he also worked simultaneously on other projects together with his
collaborators. When interrupted by them, he would switch to the other project
that required immediate attention and address their questions or concerns by
drawing on the surface of a drawing from the Porto School of Architecture: a
sketch, a calculation, a detail from a completely different project "landed" on the
drawings of that other building. The drawings bear traces of that "jump" from
one project to another and the ability of the master architect to think simultaneously about two different projects. The drawings speak about this coinciding
design engagement with two (or sometimes more) different worlds, and the related collective arrangements. Recollecting these traces, Chiara tries to retrace the
dynamics of design, the specifics of the projects, the interventions of the collaborators, and thus her work is reminiscent to that of the "Egyptologist" described
by Deleuze,[56] unfolding visible traces, reading them like "hieroglyphs" and reconnecting events, people, things, and sequences, indulging in traceability. The
archival materials bear all these traces of overlapping temporalities, multi-actorial
dynamics, and levels of intervention; as fusions, they cannot be easily placed in
one isolated folder; it is impossible to disassociate their various strata, the entangled worlds. Here again, the archive conveys the contingency of the design process and the collective nature of architecture making; in its entangled network
there is far more than one single unique idea and one single voice.

For years, Chiara relied on her "soul of an architect" as she contemplated various archival materials, and as she organized these, they began to train her, too.
The archive gained an agency that surpassed its maker. With time, Siza also
changed his ways of doing things—drawing and handwriting techniques evolved
and morphed. Nothing stayed the same. His drawings in the 1970s vary from his

work in the 1960s; just as Chiara had developed her skills to evaluate the archival differences, Siza developed his own handwriting and drawing techniques. This is a challenge of completing an archive alongside an architect who continues to work and to develop new skills or evolve existing ones. The tiny modifications in his approach can only be noticed by someone working continuously with the practice. Recently some drawings from the 1950s were found, and Chiara had doubts about them. They had Siza's handwriting but did not look like his drawings. However, after some time, indulging further in the "Egyptology" of archiving, Chiara understood that these were collaborators' drawings; she imagined Siza looking at them and providing feedback by adding some measurements, scribbling notes. Thus, archival materials also allow for a reading of the process of design collaboration or mentorship; the different layers of text and image bear witness to a collective process of design, and a multilayered and composite design venture. "Design is not linear," Chiara and Magda contend. "It's not always the same. It changes over time."[57] The process never stops: "You have to move forward then backward to understand it." The new information obtained is, as Chiara beautifully says, "put into the process again."[58] Here, the series of drawings gain importance again; archivists are always sorting out "bunches of things" and organizing them in sets; we never see *one* initial or final iconic sketch of *one* master only. And once again, we witness the fallacy of the established belief in the original sketch, the first idea, or the single creator. What is foregrounded in archiving is rather the multiplicity; the many layers of a drawing or handwritten page and the ways that many dispersed sketches are brought together with other materials and deciphered to understand how a design concept emerges in the relational dynamic world of a practice, and in dialogue with different technologies, bodies, skills, and spatial practices. As archivists perform a reading of all signs on the surface, the power of the heterogeneous series is reaffirmed again; it is what stays on the surface and dilutes the binary of original and copy; the collective, multitemporal, pluriverse course of designing comes to the fore again to defy some beloved myths of creativity.

The archive "started training me," repeats Chiara, and it does so, as we witness ethnographically, by emitting signs. Every act of learning from archiving is an interpretation of the "hieroglyphs" of Siza's drawings and other design materials. That is precisely why Chiara's work is reminiscent of that of the "Egyptologist." Becoming an archivist is not based on memorized exposition, but rather grounded in an apprenticeship to signs. Just as one becomes a carpenter only by becoming sensitive to the signs of wood, a physician by becoming sensitive to the signs of disease, one becomes an archivist, we see here, by becoming sensitive to the signs of the drawings' infinitesimal differences and the multiple layers and overlapping temporalities of a design process. In archiving there are only "hieroglyphs" and thinking through them; reading the surface that confirms the power of all series, the archivist unfolds the compressed signs and explicates them.

Just like the archivist, who moves back and forth to grasp the dynamics of design process, the architects at work also go back and forth through the sliding timeline of their own projects. Siza often comes downstairs to the archive to ask for a specific drawing that he needs for ongoing projects; he remembers exactly what he has drawn, or rather his hand "remembers." Let us watch him coming downstairs and hear him saying, "Chiara, I want you to find this specific door handle that I drew. It's like this [gestures]. Please find it!"[59] Then he draws exactly the same sketch that he made years ago; he needs that drawing to go back to this specific detail from the 1970s to be able to reuse it in a current project. Siza confirms he often goes back to the archives to find specific materials: "There is a work I made in the seventies, the bank, the Borges & Irmao. They contacted my office because they wanted to make an intervention in the building . . . so I had to consult the drawings."[60] Thus, the archive becomes an important mediator between the building and the architect. Siza often responds to requests for modifications or renovations of buildings even from the 1960s; a current project for the restoration of a 1962 swimming pool makes him revisit old drawings again. This is a feature of design we also find in Peter Eisenman's practice in New York. Records are also kept there (such as files, correspondence, models, current projects) because the architect takes care of the living building. Eisenman explains, "The Holocaust memorial in Berlin was built ten years ago, but we are still negotiating, like some stones have cracks, and things like that. So, these are the records that you are legally required to keep."[61] The archive thus allows both Siza and Eisenman to reexamine old projects and intervene. Working practices hold "a library of things" that could be mobilized in new projects. That is another reason Chiara never throws anything away, even when it is a copy of a copy, and she "keeps it in that order because it means that it was made for a purpose."[62]

Copies of copies, series of repetitive drawings with variations, all of them accumulated through decades, all produce reverberations within the practice that spans decades, inducing a bigger movement that overflows the large series themselves. The living archive allows practicing architects to browse the ever expanding "library of things" that contains the accumulation of all series. Both archivists and architects run back and forth in time to find, interpret, and reactivate design from the past. Buildings, too, age, and need interventions that take designers back to previous phases of their lives. Operating as an "apprenticeship to signs," archiving recaptures the recent past and integrates it in an ongoing design present. The well-organized archive maximizes reuse and enables design to happen seamlessly; as all actors go back to the past to reactivate it through the present, more design elements are reclaimed, and a particular practice style emerges.

The archive, we witness here again, is a much more complex entity than the mere reflection of the "mind of an architect." The *"plus, plus, plus . . ."* formula continues here. The archive, we see, as we trace the trajectory of the Siza fonds, includes drawings *as* reiterations/versions/reproductions, *plus* the many participants in architecture making that contributed to these versions, *plus* different but simultaneous projects, *plus* various collaborative dynamics. It captures design-in-connection *to* many other professionals, *to* the multiple lives of the buildings, *to* the conditions of production and consumption of architecture, *to* the technologies that made them possible and that makes them possible now. The multiple traces of collaborations between archivists and architects, the inner dialogues between designing and archiving are also to be *added* to the archive. Here, again society and design form hybrids whose layers are difficult to disengage, hybrids that talk back, surprise, educate and fascinate their makers.

Making Connections

Chiara learns a lot about Siza's practice through the years: at the start, for instance, she thought that the Malagueira project in Evora, in the south of Portugal, was a little different from the rest of the projects. It was unclear where to situate this work within the entire network of Siza's practice. The meticulous work in the archive helped her gain a more profound understanding of some of the early projects of social housing and to connect all those projects in order to be able to better understand the way Siza's practice worked. By placing these projects in relation to others, by situating them within a historical net, Chiara began thinking through their specific interrelated "hieroglyphs." Since the contents of signs are enfolded within them, rolled up, compressed, disguised, to interpret them is to unfold them. Explicating different sets of "hieroglyphs," tracing new relations between projects allows Chiara to perform a skeletal epistemological structuring of the works that will eventually become imprinted in the classification scheme of the archive. It is this initial epistemological work of the archivist that prepares the ground for the later work of the researcher and thus forms a basis for Architectural History.

The CCA respects the internal organization and epistemological structuring of the archive established by Chiara. Archivists at the CCA continue the arrangement of the Siza fonds in close proximity with the working practice of Siza to "code, collate or correlate, and create connections between materials within the fonds,"[63] so that they can further guide researchers toward other relevant material and help them to make sense of the correlations. It is their job to establish the connections between different archival series and between the various materials in a series (for instance, connections between the projects and the sketchbooks). At the CCA, Pamela and Adria delve further into and add onto Chiara's work by tracing supplementary connections between the materials and reading layers of the "hieroglyphs" left by Chiara. For instance, if they notice a connection between a series of lectures that Siza gave in 2003 on a theme that is also present in the sketchbooks where he explored it first, the archivists connect the dots. They indicate the availability of relevant material and where it can be found; however, they do not mention the specific content. By so doing, the archivists set up again a distinction, in the archive, between a "where" knowledge, which, through their work, accumulates, and a knowledge "that/about" left for historians and architectural scholars. Yet, it is the "where" type of knowledge that leads the scholars to generate more knowledge "about." Defying appearance, archival work is not just about counting folders and sorting sets of drawings; it involves a meticulous sequence of practices of identifying, resituating, and reconnecting epistemologically various groups of materials that were hitherto unrelated, thereby preparing the grounds for scholarship.

Making connections guides the work of Adria.[64] She has a lot of previous archival experience, and while she is not an expert in Siza's architecture, as she states with modesty, she is an expert in the materials for the archive. At the start of this project she spent the first two weeks reading about Siza and watching interviews in order to better understand the architect, his practice, and his major projects; as we have seen, this knowledge "that/about" is very useful for processing the archive as it informs the knowledge "how." Adria has been working on Siza's fonds since January 2016, and in June she still has over two hundred projects to go through, some smaller than others. Her work usually takes place in the Centre des Collections (CDC) building, where the drawings and the textual records are housed, but today she is in the vaults where the photographic collection and the sketchbooks are kept. As she has already rehoused the drawings, she is now working on rehousing the projects. Rehousing involves the physical activity of housing the material in different boxes. It is part of the processing of an archive in addition to the intellectual arrangement of the material. If the correspondence materials around projects come in boxes that are very acidic, the CCA archivists have to move that material into acid-free folders and boxes; this is a physical displacement of the documents. When considering rehousing, archivists often have to assess the materials and the conditions that they come in, judge if it is safe for them to stay in the current folders, and plan how to classify the archive. While the physical objects change "houses" and move to different "containers," the content and the original order remain the same. Materials talk back to the archivist. As the head archivist Robert Desaulniers describes this process, "You open every box, and you open the crate, to have a feel, because it plays a part; it's an art to

FIGURE 19.   Adria processing the archive of Siza in Monteral, at the CCA

catalogue and organize things properly. You have to know what you have before you begin the work."[65] And Adria does (see figure 19). This afternoon in the vaults I watch her go through the photographic materials; she opens the boxes, gets a feel for the objects, then she surveys the slides and the photographs carefully, and if they happen to be in plastic sleeves that are highly acidic and yellowing, and thus are at risk of disintegrating, she has to make a quick assessment to decide whether or not to rehouse the material and place them into new folders. Surveying, assessing, and rehousing often happen simultaneously. After that she starts working on the description of the objects. Let us follow her more closely for a moment.

Adria is going through the material to "identify some projects in high demand."[66] This includes projects such as Bonjour Tristesse in Berlin and the Punt en Komma project in The Hague (part of the CCA exhibit *Corner, Block, Neighborhood, Cities. Álvaro Siza in Berlin and the Hague* [September 24, 2015—May 22, 2016] and that is why they are given priority).[67] She is processing this material. Adria notes how Chiara has described everything nicely and categorized and numbered the contents in a way that is easy to follow. Here we can see how the trail of activities from Portugal is taken up again in Montreal, how the route that the archive takes continues. The documents are placed in folders and packages, and the material is very well arranged. Although some of the material is about to be rehoused, "The information is clear," Adria notes. "Intellectually, it is really easy for me to understand the materials," she adds.[68] As Chiara has identified and indicated clearly the archival material, reconnecting all signs, Adria follows her guidance.

Before rehousing the material, Adria catalogues all the information. She keeps a large Excel spreadsheet on her big computer screen, a script in the making reminiscent of the file produced by Chiara and Magda, where she has created an access database for herself to intellectually and physically connect all of the materials within the Siza archive. It is her workflow, allowing her to keep track of the progress of her work. Excel files are easier to edit and to look over; each project is inputted in Excel before being placed in The Museum System (TMS) catalogue. Adria is performing a "file-level" description for all materials. As shown in previous examples, cataloguing at item level is rarely performed; even the sketchbooks are not described at file level, and the drawings are not inspected one by one but rather as sets. Thus, the multiplicity of the archive continues here as well. Adria is looking at the photographs at file level, careful to preserve the original order that Chiara imposed; after inspecting the content of the files, she provides a description of each file with photographs.

The CCA identification scheme is clear: a number, the title of the file, translated in English, a creator, a date, followed by an administrative label, and then the information on the content, which includes a general overall description at the file level. Sometimes, Adria includes specific information that does not come out in the title of the file but might be useful for the researchers. We look at the files of Bonjour Tristesse (1980–1984) and she explains, "Essentially, here I'm going to write that the file includes drawings for the seniors' club and it also includes drawings for the kindergarten, so that people know."[69] In fact, Siza's practice designed not only the corner apartment building (Bonjour Tristesse) in East Kreuzberg next to Schlesisches Tor, but also the overall concept of Block 121, as well as two additional buildings situated in the same block, a kindergarten and a seniors' club. Thus, Adria's "note" attached to the file, another script, mentions that it also contains drawings for the two additional buildings; this note explains Adria's reading and translation of the "hieroglyphs" of this project and is supposed to help researchers find the relevant documents, make the connections, and engage in further interpretations. In the Excel file, we also see information on the size of the drawings and a credit line. Some details on the physical description can be added, such as "the drawing has been folded," followed by the location in the CCA holdings where the file can be found. This information goes to TMS, where Adria has to insert a very brief information supplied at the file level: "Berlin, August," and so on." It is at the "project level," which comes next in the sequence of actions, that the text will go into a greater description; that is where archivists "flesh out most of the collection."[70] As we witness here, a basic Excel file can contain various orders of heterogeneous types of information, which reconcile the worlds of the conservators (the folded drawing), the researchers (location of the material and finding hidden connections), the archivists (reading of signs and translations), the archival systems (TMS and the hierarchical structure of files), and Architectural History.

While browsing the photographic material, Adria sometimes stumbles on things she does not fully understand. If the issue is of archival nature, she can get in touch with the office of Siza in Porto and arrange to talk with his archivists over Skype.[71] Going through the materials together, the CCA archivists learn a lot, explains Robert.[72] As the archive travels across the Atlantic, some aspects are lost in translation. For Adria "it is an archivist's dream" to have the possibility to reenact this dialogue between the "map" made by Chiara in Porto and the CCA "map" in Montreal, to recover what could have been lost. Caught between the two interpretations, she can question the order: "Why is this document here?" and if Chiara cannot answer, the question will go back to architect Siza and his collaborators.[73] A simple question like this reveals both Chiara's reading of Siza's practice (seen through the structure she imposed on the archive) as well as Siza's own thinking on how his work is to be archived, structured, and understood in connection to his practice. Adria expounds, "I am trying to get this view of how he understood his work process, and then while looking at the sketchbooks and the drawings and the photographs, I'm also understanding his work process at the same time."[74] Caught in an interesting chain of interpretations of interpretations, of "hieroglyphs" of "hieroglyphs," which involve different temporalities, people, practices and locations, in the process of rehousing and cataloguing, Adria gains knowledge about Siza's work process and his firm. Trapped in this explanatory loop of "maps" (Chiara's map of Siza's practice and Siza's own map of the process in his firm), Adria's work is far from being dull and repetitive, Rather, it is cognitively rich,[75] multiplying even more the readings of "hieroglyphs" at different levels, and leading toward the production of a shared CCA map of Siza's fonds.

Conclusions: Deciphering the Signs of Design

In this chapter, we have spent a longer time unraveling the plot of archiving— "plot" meaning both a small piece of ground where an object or a building is placed and a specific chain of events that unfold as an interrelated sequence of actions. This plot of archiving, in both senses, presented through the Siza case enfolded before our eyes as a hectic storyline involving multiple actors traveling between Porto and Montreal, archivists and boxes, architects and folders, different sets of enfolded "hieroglyphs," spreadsheets, and sketchbooks, all crossing the ocean. It involved different humans and nonhumans, practices and sets of skills, and led them to find their own place within the process of architectural archiving, and for Siza's fonds, its plot within different collecting institutions, and ultimately in the "golden books" of Architectural History. Archiving appears here to be a very different activity than the ones we have ethnographically sketched before. Whereas registrar activities take place in the registrar's office and the shipping area, and conservation occurs within the confined boundaries of the lab, archiving crosses many sites, lands and countries; it is multi-ontic and multi-siting. It is by meandering through all these sites of archiving—from the architectural practice, to the firm archive, to the archiving sites at the CCA, and to archived-based History, that archiving happens. Architectural archivists never work in isolation, in a secluded space; they constantly straddle the boundary between an active architectural practice generating archives and the sites of archiving, traveling between the hectic collaborative dynamics and conflicting temporalities in the design process and the classification logic of an organized archive. The most challenging issues are often decided in discussion with working architects.

Archiving continues the regime of hesitant objects' speech complemented by gestures pointing to classification schemes, series and subseries, folder numbering, Excel files, undeciphered doodles, "hieroglyphs," a perplexing speech reminiscent of the one of objects-in-conservation and very different from the fluent one in galleries and lectures. Here, we witness objects constantly negotiating with the unknown rhythms of design practices, demanding clarity and precision. Archiving is about deciphering the signs of designing. Here, the friends replace what they want to say by a finger designating a "where" type of knowledge that will then lead to knowledge of "that/about." To be able to talk, an object-in-archiving crosses many times the fissures between the foldable rhythms of practice and the steady linearity of History. The speech of an object-in-archiving is less mediated than an object-in-conservation; here, folders, numbers, boxes, series, drawers and sleeves replace the scalpels, oxides, and microscopes. If conservators have specialties for handling objects, archivists develop specialties as they engage in archiving objects from the same design world (Chiara learns to distinguish the Siza from the 1960s from the Siza from the 1980s and Adria learns to decipher Bonjour Tristesse). As the relational set up of archiving unfolds, they become apprentices of specific signs, skillful "Egyptologists," not masters of abstract and encyclopedic knowledge.

Whereas at the other sites at the CCA, we witnessed people working alone or gathered in a circle around a specific object or phenomenon, archiving combines both solitary and group work. Archivists mobilize their knowledge of "that/about" to further develop the strata of the "the knowing where" that is finely overlapped by establishing connections between documents and series and producing written notes with additional guidance of "where to find things." In addition, the modalities of "knowing where" create new possibilities of "knowing that." It is the reconnecting, repositioning, rehousing, reorganizing, and resituating of the material, always plural (as groups of objects, series, sets of drawings) and always in new configurations, that matters here, rather than the specific intervention in a single architectural object. Moving beyond the dichotomy of "knowledge that"/"knowledge how," a dispositional way of knowing emerges in the web of archiving. The new dispositions of knowns and unknowns ignite fresh epistemic potential for history making. Archiving is script generating, yet the making of the big Script (the classification scheme) is accompanied by the production of more working scripts, more written protocols, spreadsheets, and notes. Like the scripts coming from the other sites of archiving, they circulate and facilitate the movements and the gradual concretization of archival objects.

Whereas at the other sites—the vaults, the registry, the offices of curators, directors, or cataloguers, the conservation or photo labs—we rarely meet the architects, the creators of the archives, here we meet them often, very often. Either directly or metaphorically, we are confronted, just like the archivists, with a specific architectural practice that has generated, and is still producing, the archive. The bodily postures of archivists differ from those of the other friends of architectural objects that always lean toward an object or assemble around it. Archivists are rather surrounded, invaded, and overwhelmed by the crowds of objects that they are to arrange; the archivist's work happens within these objects' nettings. The touch of objects here is still mediated (more than in a gallery room and much less than in a conservation lab); if in conservation the esoteric equipment multiplies (pipettes, scalpers, microscopes, spatulas, knives), in archiving the me-diation occurs in the company of a mixture of both esoteric (scalpels, cutters) and ordinary objects (office equipment objects such as folders, boxes, drawers). If con-servators have a precise, skilled, and highly mediated way of engaging with the objects, archivists have a slow, mundane, and investigatory way of engaging with the "hieroglyphs" and the layers of an archival object as it relates to design practice. Documenting and inscribing the traces of their investigation by adding notes, cor-relating and repositioning material, they superimpose a layer of "where" guidance, directions, indications, and inscriptions. If conservators stabilize objects to make them resilient and eloquent, archivists attempt to structure the information about "where to find more about the object," to enable the eloquence of both archival objects and their spokespersons—researchers and curators.

Here, we also caught a glimpse of the specific archiving practices developed in the past twenty to thirty years, as a way of mastering the fear of endless accumu-lation of things and amorphous amassing of paper in design practice. An archi-tectural archive, we witnessed, is more than what "collects the dust of statements that have become inert"[76]; it is rather the active system of the statements' func-tioning; it is at once the thing to be translated and the translation itself, the sign and the meaning. Far from being purely aesthetic artefacts, archival architectural objects appear as epistemic objects that speak on behalf of a practice. Archiving is performed in connection with the current dynamics of design practice; ar-chiving it is a way of thinking through the "hieroglyphs" of designing, to inter-pret and translate them. Far from simply storing, arranging, and numbering boxes with things, the archivist is the first to reach out to the finer ontological granu-larity of architectural objects in their journey to become archival. While conser-vators are preoccupied with the architectural objects to be able to take better care of them, archivists engage with the objecthood of the collection on its structur-ing epistemological level, to enable further conceptual readings to be developed. It is another layer to the beginnings of Architectural History. While Álvaro Siza's name is engraved in this History, no one has ever heard of Chiara, the archivist who spent twenty years working alongside him to organize the archive of the prac-tice, or Adria, the archivist who spent three years processing the Siza's fonds for the CCA holdings, and we can continue the list. Retracing the moves of archiving al-lows us to witness the usually invisible work of a great variety of silent actors (in this particular instance, mainly women), who generally remain outside the lime-light of mainstream architectural historiography. When we track the *becoming ar-chival* of architectural objects and dive into the ontological granularity of paper archiving, we suddenly realize with surprise and total bewilderment, how limited, complex, local, and unpredictable architectural objects can be, and how circum-stantial, contingent, and partial the production of Architectural History is.

THE LIFE OF AN OLD FLOPPY DISK

Log: 5:00 p.m. On a late June afternoon of 2016, tired by a day full of interviews and ethnographic observations at the CCA, I end up in the serene space of the gallery room for the exhibition *Archaeology of the Digital: Complexity and Convention* with the conservator David Stevenson.[1] He is an expert in the preservation of digital heritage, which sets him apart from the other "preservers" at the CCA. As we walk through the exhibition, we stop at the different projects, and instead of discussing the content of the show, he shares surprising stories about models, software, computer-aided design (CAD) files, and polymers, tips on how to assemble a model, open a file, receive the right instructions on time, and account for the aging of materials. As we stop at one of the models, David recounts its intricacies and complications:

> D: This is the Carbon Tower by Testa & Weiser. So the highly complex 3D model was printed back in 2001. It's very fragile, and it's very hard to put together. The instructions for how to assemble it were very important. These horizontal structures here that are interlaced are really fragile, and they hang off the side and they have to connect at certain points. There are vertical cores there. They all stick together, and there are five different levels here that assemble together. It's very new and there is a question of where it belongs in the collection or whether it will go to the collection after the exhibition.
>
> A: What material is this?
>
> D: It's a type of 3D polymer used for printing. The printer provides a structural weakness. It ages over time.[2]

The gallery room (see figure 20) contains many stories like the one about the Carbon Tower, stories in which synthetic creatures composed of 3D polymer talk about buildings, where CAD files and digital printers unfold the design process, and where the structural weakness of the printer and the interlaced fragile materials of the model expose for us the precarious nature of an archive, where the digital and the physical remain inherently entangled. Archiving the digital is apparent as the shadow of the various operations of archiving discussed in the previous chapters and is persistently present at the different sites of archiving. Throughout my observations, the friends of the architectural objects refer to the difficulties and challenges that the digital age has set for them and reflect on the changing nature of archiving.

Before we continue into the world of archiving the digital, however, it is important to distinguish between the digitization of existing archives and born-digital archives.[3] The differences can be shown through the CCA's varying approaches to them. *Digitization* refers to the process of converting information into a computer-readable digital format, in which the information is organized into bits, and the outcome is the digital representation of objects, documents, and images. The digitization of existing physical material is done selectively, Mirko Zardini explains, as the CCA curators and conservators do not "consider [it] reasonable to digitize an

FIGURE 20.   Visit to the exhibition *Archaeology of the Digital: Complexity and Convention* with the conservator David

entire archive."[4] He points out that the "intention is to have a curatorial strategy for each selection."[5] Thus, only a part of the physical material that is of particular curatorial or research importance undergoes digitization. In contrast, the challenges are different for the born-digital archives, and their preservation sets new obstacles.[6]

During my ethnographic study, a few friends of architectural objects are engaged in completing work on the CCA's third exhibition on born-digital archives entitled *Archaeology of the Digital: Complexity and Convention.*[7] Exhibition and acquisition happen at the same time; in response to this exhibit and as part of a larger strategy, the CCA is actively seeking and incorporating digital material into its collection. The *Archaeology of the Digital* multi-year research project launched by the CCA in 2013 investigates a particular historical moment between the mid-1980s and the early to mid-2000s, when architects began experimenting with computer design, using and rewriting "a lot of nonstandard software and working on nonstandard computing equipment."[8] It is a moment when the computer started to radically change architectural practice and design thinking.[9] The encounter between the computer, the new design and communication tools it affords, and architectural practice resulted in a significant change in this brief period of time. In response, the curator for the exhibition, Greg Lynn, had identified twenty-five projects that were exemplary for this moment when design practice and technology actively impacted each other. For the CCA, this exhibition was also a means for acquiring a lot of new material, especially from firms and architects whose archives are exclusively digital. The show thus functions as a catalyst for obtaining digital material outside the remit of the projects selected for it—to continue to accumulate and grow the collection at the CCA. It keeps both the archivists and the digital conservators busy.

The digital is almost synonymous with this show. The Kolatan/Mac Donald Studio project records represent one of these twenty-five projects. As the collection director, Martien de Vletter, explains, "It's physical material; It's a couple of drawings; It's a couple of prototypes and a lot of disks that they [the architects] are not able to open anymore and we have to figure out how to open those files."[10] The CCA show not only exhibits these projects, but also provides an occasion to better understand them and to preserve the born-digital materials; to define the protocol for preservation and description of digital material; to consider the software and the structuring of the archive where they deposit the originals. The exhibition is again not a final outcome, but a conceptual vehicle for generating a novel reading of architectural projects and processes, a practical tool for reflecting on the existing tactics and methods of archiving at the CCA, and a strategy for rethinking topical issues of digital preservation.[11]

As I write these lines, many architectural institutions around the world are facing the same problem: namely, they are receiving old floppy disks or other digital-born material that can no longer be readily accessed. Digital archives in architecture have been the focus of recent discussions in the field of archiving.[12] Yet, only a few institutions are tackling the problem and searching for solutions. As Martien indicated above, when receiving materials that cannot be accessed, CCA technicians have to "figure out how to open them." They need to find the key to unlock the information inscribed in the material. Instead of embracing a technocratic perspective, the CCA's strategy is twofold, enabling access to these archives ("how to open the files"), while also solving key preservation issues ("how to preserve them for the years to come"). Tim Walsh is the first digital archivist appointed to help the CCA friends understand these archives. He explains that "there is a lot of overlap. None of the archives are purely physical or purely digital"[13]; exceptions are very few.[14] Martien also pointed this out earlier when the boxes from the Kolatan/Mac Donald Studio containing a mixture of drawings, disks and prototypes arrived. Tim deals with two types of materials: the digitized material, which includes an analogue version, and the born-digital material that has never existed in any other form. Thus, the archivist's role is dual: organizing this hybrid collection of physical and digital material by maintaining the network of contextual relationships and taking care of the long-term preservation of the digital material. The current challenge for Tim, and for the CCA, is to be able to safeguard the born-digital projects. Learning from this, they can transfer the knowledge to other cases; for instance, they can safeguard the hard drives that contain standardized AutoCAD computer drawings from the practices of Abalos & Herreros, Siza, and Eisenman, among others. The CCA approach to the digital is very distinctive. "Within the bubble of architectural institutions we are at the forefront at the moment," Tim proudly affirms.[15] While many firms that donate digital archives to the CCA still prefer to bequeath the final products (the finalized renderings and drawings), the CCA finds this material the least interesting, even when the building is constructed and even if the final products are "as-built drawings." At the level of the digital, they continue to collect according to their specific philosophy of acquiring material related to the process rather than the finished products. As in the paper archive, so in the digital one, it is multiplicity that is valued and maintained; it is the series of reiterations that has a power here, not the first or the last iconic specimen.

Fear of the Digital

Speaking of the emerging practices of archiving the digital, Tim points out that "there can be this kind of paralyzing fear that, because you don't know how to do things perfectly, you don't do anything at all."[16] Moreover, Tim says, his job "would be a lot easier if [he was] not in an architectural archive, and that work-ing with digital material, in architecture specifically, poses additional challenges.[17] For one thing, the files are much more complex than those being created in a lot of other fields, hence, archiving digital materials in architecture involves a con stant struggle around opening a file, being able to describe it, and being able to provide access quickly. This struggle is exacerbated by the fact that it needs to oc-cur on an ongoing basis. Tim's fear draws us into the specificity of archiving digital materials in architectural archives, inviting us to reflect on several ques-tions: What is the nature of the digital archival objects that are capable of trig-gering such a "paralyzing fear"? How do they get to the CCA, and how are they treated upon arrival? What makes them so fearsome? How do we grasp their tech-nological and access-related complexity?

Digital files usually arrive at the CCA through "network transfers" or via ob-solete types of media that are often used with software that is no longer available or no longer functions on current computer operating systems, which themselves are rapidly changing. Sometimes, when the registrar's office receives material, it is secured in numbered folders, which may not be accessible for a certain period of time. As a result, archivists have to confront layers of obsolescence from the very arrival of the digital objects. Nevertheless, the first step for them is to iden-tify all of the digital materials, then transfer and back them up on servers. The processing of digital archival objects often follows a method of arrangement and description similar to that of the physical archive. While organizing the material, archivists also do appraisal and a "weeding out" of the materials, but it is never very selective; again, we can see the commonalities with the physical objects. Yet any digital file, Tim states, is "essentially a recipe. It's coded in a particular form so that a software system knows how to interpret it and create the thing that you see on your screen."[18] This creates dependencies: specific files are dependent on specific software that can render it and lives within a particular operating system that functions within specific computer hardware. It is in the same way that spo-ken languages are dependent on those who can speak and understand them. Thus, what is distinctive for the digital is that working with design material like that created in CAD, Illustrator, and InDesign generates numerous dependencies; groups of drawings can be linked through a group of different folders and can all connect back to one title block (which contains all the information necessary to identify the material and to verify its validity). All these dependences rapidly change and are not always reversible or compatible, and any archival arrangement has the potential to "break" them.

The born-digital material also arrives with a large army. Its scale can be much larger than a physical archive; and the scope of work required needs to be much more meticulous than the labor of the digitization of existing physical material.

Because of the colossal scale of the archive, the processing is done at an aggregate level—a standard archival practice that we have also witnessed with physical archives where the inventory and the description are performed on a group rather than an object level. As Tim confirms, "It is just one of many media that are coming in the archives that are getting aggregate descriptions."[19] The multiplicity of the digital archive is essential: there are thousands of files, of which many have their own description; there is a huge quantity of metadata to be extracted, file formats to be standardized, and machines to be used in order to go through and process the material.

Let us return to the example of the Carbon Tower. The material for the Carbon Tower arrived at the CCA in two folders, and the original order of its contents was preserved. They contained a couple of projects from the firm Testa & Weiser. When the archivists went down to the actual inventory listing, they noticed that the material was composed as an aggregate and that the archival description was made at the aggregate level. Some aggregates contained a small and reasonable number of files, but others had over three thousand, depending on the original order of the archive. In the case of the Foreign Office Architects (FOA) archive (which contains another project from the show *Archaeology of the Digital: Complexity and Convention*), it comprised up to 350,000 digital files that were primarily on CDs and floppy disks. Thus, whereas in the conservation lab, Anne was dealing with tens and sometimes hundreds of photos, here Tim is dealing with thousands of files, as well as a number of machines, automated systems, and types of software that can help him process this large army of objects.

Like paper archives, digital archives arrive in different states: "messy" or "sanitized." Usually, when the archive has been organized by one of the firm principals prior to its arrival at the CCA, it is well-ordered and neat; and if the original order is navigable, it is often kept in its original state. In other cases, the CCA receives an existing stack of disks that had been stored in the back corner of a design firm, probably forgotten; the architects neither know the specific content of the disks nor have the drives to read them anymore. In this case, they simply let the CCA know which projects they relate to,[20] and the CCA does the entire organization from scratch. And if the material is not navigable, which is often the case with messy archives, the archivists have to take care of it, accessing, processing, "weeding out," and arranging the material. "Ideally," Tim explains, "you should be able to go into some browser-based thing, and in one tab it's the original and another tab it's the archivist's arrangement; in another tab you can make your own order and save it."[21] Thus, the advantage of the digital is that various arrangements can be overlaid on one another, and the dialogue between these alternative arrangements can shed light on the material.

The next step in the work of archivists is to think about the preservation qualities of the digital files—that is, their "renderability" and their relative obsolescence. The archiving of digital materials is inherently entangled with preservation concerns as time is an active agent here, even more vigorous than in the world of paper, insects, acids, and mold (see chapter 5); it rolls, flies, precipitates, and makes archivists constantly wonder whether there is "another fifteen-year window before that tape is unreadable."[22] The concern for the archivists is "how can we demonstrate that when somebody is looking at this thing twenty years later it will be functionally the same as the thing that was created and originally used?"[23] Here we can get a sense of the fear Tim was talking about. The difficulty to open and read the material can happen either because the software has changed, or because the file formats are dependent on a particular company and bound by licenses. A curator can decide if a project or a specific material deserves some extra focus and "discoverability"—the possibility for the material to be easily found in a database search, accessed, and used. Moreover, a different effort is needed to identify projects and materials in physical from and to digitize them. Digitization is supposed to save the physical material from the destructive influence of time, or at least, to slow it down, and to ensure that the material will be readable for a certain period of time—however, digital archives are even more susceptible to time and are not forever. The additional work results in additional description of the digital, audio-visual, and video material in the collection. At that point the archivist produces object descriptions of the selected material to "make it discoverable"; and the specific object is being signaled out of the aggregate. This is similar to the operations of flagging documents in the folders of Cedric Price's fonds, which we saw Giovanna doing during our morning visit in the vaults (see chapter 3). The curatorial or research attention can often take objects out of groupings, sets, and aggregates and confer on them a distinctive status.

Preservation of born-digital material poses distinctive challenges. What makes the archiving of digital materials unique is the existence of a technological environment in which the digital material was initially generated; it is often accompanied by some unresolved technological troubles that have to be addressed at a higher level (i.e. the migration of files between formats, copyrights, licenses, and so on). To tackle them, the CCA follows the UNESCO Persist project,[24] in collaboration with companies such as Microsoft and Autodesk; they also follow ISEAD(G)[25] to describe material. Together, these institutions and projects form a network that takes care of the licensing framework for legacy software for non-profit research uses and attempts to "collectively figure out," as a broad international community, issues of preservation and access. However, architecture poses further problems for the preservation of digital materials as many institutions involved in large-scale, born-digital archiving, which are comfortable working with word-processing file formats, do not work with CAD files and 3D models.[26] These are highly complex, highly proprietary tools with a very competitive software market. The software companies attempt to convince their clients to upgrade every few years, and it is not in their interest to make things completely compatible. Preserving digital files differs from the operation of singling out specific objects in order to digitize them because it requires the gathering of the digital preservation community; it is a shared practice that demands the networked efforts of many different actors, skills, technologies, and institutional bodies.

Time and the Cycles of Obsolescence

The awareness of the importance of archives is only a recent phenomenon in the realm of the digital and varies from firm to firm. Thirty years ago, practicing architects had no or very little interest in archiving their work. Even the architects who were included in the *Archaeology of the Digital* exhibition as pioneers in digital technology and methods in architecture did not seriously consider issues of archiving digital materials. In the busy and messy world of design firms, matters of archiving and preservation are difficult and overwhelming for practitioners and can easily be put aside. Recently, however, there is more archival awareness among practices that use software integrated into their workflows, and there are more reflections about the systems of work, data integrity, and long-term preservation.[27] Larger firms, for instance, have begun to appoint specialist staff to work on the archiving of digital materials, indicating a growing consciousness about their own legacies; if the firm working culture is such that going back to refer to legacy projects is important for continuity, inspiration, or reusing certain design elements, archiving becomes crucial for their daily design work. In these practices, the archive is alive, effective—a self-referential catalytic power activating design solutions from the recent past (as we have seen it in the case of Siza's practice). In other firms, however, it is enough for architects to "just burn things to a disk and never look back at it again."[28] Depending on these two modalities of firms' engagement with the archive—an active or passive archive—the work of digital archivists and conservators vary too.

An awareness of archives is always a reflection on time. However, time translates differently in the physical and in the digital realms. Picture the following: disks received in the 1990s in the registrar's office at the CCA were given a folder title, numbered, and then eventually put aside. Had the registrar flagged that particular folder at the time for its specific content, the archivists could have saved it by taking care of the old disks at the moment of arrival; now, however, it might be too late. Twenty years is a short span of time for a human and even shorter in the life of a built structure; but, in the world of archiving digital materials, a twenty-year span plays an important role. Archivists operate with a twenty-year delay as firms need to keep their records in-house for a certain period of time according to specific statutes. The demands of the day-to-day practice mean that these materials usually sit dormant, until somebody like the archivist Robert Desaulniers comes along and appraises the material to decide if it is an appropriate fit for the CCA collection.

Meanwhile, time flies in the world of archiving the digital, and software obsolescence and file-format obsolescence quickly become obstacles to the readability of the material, which is further complicated by the proprietary nature of these formats. Materials can arrive in "legacy media" (from floppy disks to CDs, ZIP disks, and digital-audio tapes [DATs]), which over time, becomes less relevant to design. Moreover, hardware ages and requires cycles of updates. As a result, Tim notes, "We can't often reasonably expect that the original format will still be useable in twenty years. So, in that case, we try to give another option, something that is as close to the original as possible but is in an openly documented file format or more widely used."[29] A special digital preservation software called "Archivematica" is used to automate a lot of these processes and supports many kinds of file formats. The processing is also run at the aggregate level: a folder of one thousand files is processed as a group. The folder is given a unique identifier and is digitally fingerprinted so as to ensure that the files will not be corrupted over time. Some of them might require manual work and are thus flagged. CAD files, for instance, have no perfectly suitable preservation format. Instead, the preservation format is a copy that will hold the original for as long as possible to ensure it is readable. Thus, "instead of working on every individual file," explains Tim, "you can alternatively keep the files exactly what they are and work on a handful of emulated environments that match the original computers that they were created on to use the files."[30] In a digital world, the objects, as files, multiply in number even more. The pressure of time, the fear of losing information, forces a multiplication of files, of series of copies. If paper archives contain groups of drawings, sets of a selected few (as seen in chapter 6), here, an archive can contain 100,000 files. As a result, it is even more difficult than in paper archiving to treat them all at an object-level; digital files exist as aggregated groups, always among others; never just one. Moreover, compared to the physical groups of objects, the digital aggregates entirely depend on the highly complex and rapidly evolving computerized design environment. Thus, we are again in the realm of reiterations, or reverberating repetitions, inducing the movement of series facilitated by technology. The "vertigo of simulacrum" continues its route, raising up the multiplication of copies to a level where strict hierarchy, fixity of distribution, and the determination of value all become impossible. If the files were created on specific operating systems such as Windows NT or Apple OS 8, customized software can be created and installed in virtual machines as emulations of computer systems (based on computer architectures and providing functionality of a physical computer), into which the files can be fed. Here is another multiplication, not simply of numbers, but in terms of an ontological thickening of the digital: the thousands of files, *plus* the emulated environment that closely resembles the environment they were created in, *plus* the copies. Digital preservation, hence, does not simply end with the preservation of an object, the treatment of a "patient," the survival of a shrunken tracing paper drawing, but rather starts with the aggregated object, adding layers on top of it, multiplying it further: files, software environment, technological procedures. This multilayered aggregate (files, *plus, plus, plus . . .*) will travel in time and will allow a digital archive to be read, understood and interpreted as a material of architectural historiography.

Moreover, the digital world presupposes a certain skillset of the researcher that may be surprising. Can we say that any architectural researcher today knows how to interact with Maya software or a variant of Maya from twenty years ago? Even the researchers who had been using it at the time could have forgotten the commands, which, in any case, have changed over time—as has the researcher, whose expertise shifts with the software, and her computer, which also goes through series of updates. To the difficulty of access, we should add the difficulty of learning new skills and gaining technical expertise. To the aging of humans and buildings, we must add the aging of software and technologies. However, if the researcher is intrigued by the interplay between software, files, and technological environments, this composite assemblage will continue to travel in time and mutate as an epistemic object on its own, to be interpreted as well, along with the information it holds for architectural scholarship. It becomes impossible to separate the researcher-software-hardware assemblage from the modalities of architectural knowledge that it enables.

Creating copies, emulating the software environment or any other modes of reproduction, and duplicating digital files allow the archive to engage in a forward time travel, extending into the future. This is precisely where it poses specific legal challenges: copyrights and license agreements are but some of the issues with old software.[31] Traveling into the future requires a legal framework related to changes in operating systems, drivers, and software. According to Canadian copyright law, CCA archivists can create a digital preservation copy of software. Yet, using that software to provide access to researchers from outside the institution requires the CCA to negotiate directly with various software companies. Since some may no longer exist, they have to deal with orphan copyright issues. Here, the UNESCO legal framework—PERSIST—can help archiving institutions with such challenges by developing a joint platform for facilitating digital preservation.

If a surrogate of the physical archival object is done in specific cases for exhibitions and produced in the conservation or the photo lab, digital preservation copies have a different raison d'être: to extend the life of the object and make its preservation traceable. CCA archivists always keep two copies of all digital material, one in the state in which it arrived, the other, in the processed and preservation-friendly versions. They are always twins. Given that digital preservation practice is still relatively in its youth, Tim reminds us that "it may be that our practices make sense now, but in twenty years, people will wish that we hadn't done what we did. I think it's really important to have a back-up, a fresh slate."[32] The twenty-year time span appears again; the interventions of digital conservators are also susceptible to time just like old floppy disks. The concern with the future is far from abstract. The digital archivist is, then, invested just as much in the future as the past. History is constrained by the limitations and uncertainties posed by the future (of technology). We can see that archiving time runs on a sliding scale, rushing back and forth, always leaping ahead or backward, with the same measuring unit of twenty years, and thus altering the role of both the archivists in architectural firms and the work of architectural researchers.[33]

Archiving the digital thus implies care for and foresight in regard to digital media, software, legal requirements, copyrights and licenses, the overall technical environment, and instructions for how to open, access, and use digital content. It is essentially a form of thinking about the architectural objects as being entangled in their wider legal and technological networks in order to ensure that they remain archival in time, maintain continuity, and are able to talk to wider architectural communities. Layers of technical and legal instructions pile up and mediate the researcher's dialogue with the aggregates of archival objects. Traces from digital preservation processes are also kept as a part of the composite whole of the digital archive. Now we can better understand Tim's "paralyzing" fear. In their daily practices, digital archivists anxiously slide back and forth in twenty-year chunks, questioning themselves: Is that the right move or decision? How do we facilitate access? How do we ensure relevance? If we ignore *this*, will Architectural History still have materials in twenty years, or will these materials be lost, shut out from its annals? That is a daunting fear, indeed.

Paper Overtakes Bytes

For the *Archaeology of the Digital: Complexity and Convention* (2016) exhibition, the CCA received both digital and paper records. Yet, the temporalities of paper and floppy disks that share the collective space of an archive differ radically. The paper material is often placed in a box and stored in an attic or basement for a long time before it reaches the CCA or is donated to a library or another archive. This common storage practice invites time to pass and implies a sort of "benign neglect";[34] in conservation, library, and archival science literature, it implies non-interference, a "letting-be." It refers to the fact that for traditional paper archives, time is typically not acting against the archivist. Time is rather "complotting" with him; thus, if twenty or fifty years later the material arrives at the CCA, there is a good chance that it will be in the same shape, provided it was safely stored and barring exceptional problems, such as flooding or severe mold. Paper is generally resilient and durable. Time is a "friend" in this archival configuration of duration. It allows more flexibility for conservators to intervene if needed, and a larger "time gap" before they start working on the documents after acquisition.

In contrast, digital material is more fragile and has to be solicited from donors much earlier to ensure that the files are not corrupt and that they are stored on storage media that is readable. Time acts against the archivist here, and every minute in this configuration of archival duration is important. In contrast with the conservators in the lab, who deal with the effects of time—the crinkles, the shrinking, the traces of mold, all that is left after time has worked on it—digital conservators run ahead of time to set up ways to slow it down, attempting to predict its folds, its working, and its future consequences. Competing with time, sprinting along it, as they do, digital conservators attempt to forecast damages, counterforces, and possible offsets. While at the level of the physical material, time moves with a slower pace, obsolescence happens very quickly in the digital.

An example can help us unfold this dynamic. The ZIP disks received from the Kolatan/Mac Donald Studio for the *Archaeology of the Digital: Complexity and Convention* are seventeen to eighteen years old, and already the physical disks as well as many of the file formats of the archive package have become obsolete. As a result, in order to make them useable in modern computing systems, digital conservators require extra knowledge about these formats and need to do more archaeological work. Sometimes, it might be too late to save the files, as not all media have the longevity that ZIP disks usually have. In the same way that there are potential hazards in basements—mold and humidity can destroy paper records—accidents can also infect and corrupt a server. It is paradoxical and surprising: a seventeenth-century drawing escapes obsolescence, appearing more youthful and stable than a seventeen-year-old disk. We encounter two different time scales. Oddly, the timely and trendy digital material ages with greater speed, risking disappearance, obsolescence and death, while the traditional material, the physical and "old fashioned," ages more slowly.

Archival time is also measured in the life spans of software, files, file formats, buildings, models, paper drawings and architects. Tim draws a comparison to explain these time dynamics: "If you are building something like a 747 jet, you know, the lifetime of the software that might have created the model might be ten years old, the file format as a whole might be twenty years old, if it's something like an AutoCAD DWG format, maybe longer, because it's just so widely used. Then this plane might be produced, modified, in service for seventy or eighty years. Similarly, the lifetime of a building or project can greatly outlive the software and files used to create it."[35] When the digital source is no longer there, this creates problems for the engineer or the architect who would like to return to this data to be consistent or for inspiration or to comply with the regulations in the digital industry, which is of growing concern to architects at the time of extensive use of digital technologies in design. Against all odds, it is neither the solid building nor the mutable digital material that lasts, but like the stubborn fern plant, it is paper that persists. Thin, fragile, crumpled paper: the paper on which these words are written, the paper that perilously sits next to Siza's cigarette ends, that risks mold and floods in basements, that piles up in architects' offices before being secured in the archives. Paper appears to be more resistant to the fluxes of time.

Processing Digital Materials

The typical trajectory of a digital object in terms of how it comes into the museum collections and travels to other places is in some ways similar to any other object. While in the past, the CCA had received digital archives (disks, videos, CDs, and so on) by courier services, now it is common for the registrar to receive the digital material through a file transfer protocol (FTP) or another secure portal. Alexandre and Marie accept the delivery of the digital archive and then register the materials. While the physical material can remain in the shipping space, where time is its friend, the digital material instead goes directly to the digital archivist in the race against time. It is placed into "the virtual shipping space," which is a folder that is intended to serve as a temporary holding spot for digital files. The original data is kept in this secure storage space that is regularly audited to ensure that nothing has changed. As the digital material comes into the CCA, it is run through a virus check, put in the shipping space, and backed up right away. The digital archivist then describes the material on the box level, counting and numbering the virtual boxes.

The virtual shipping space is analogous to a physical shipping space. David, the digital conservator at the CCA, explains: "We wanted to have that sort of concept in mind as much as possible as we work with the digital, to try to remember that there are similar processes and similar restraints and ways of thinking about digital."[36] As we have already encountered the way in which physical objects arrive at the CCA, we can see the similarities: the processing, the treatment, the cataloging, and the storing of digital objects are comparable to the treatment of the physical ones. Just as physical objects are at risk of being infested and contaminated, so digital files are also at risk and have to be submitted to a scrutiny of tests to avoid viruses spreading throughout the digital collection. Once the material is in the shipping space, it is run through the "file normalization system," which is a migration and metadata extraction and metadata-compiling tool.[37] Each individual file is outputted to an archival package and an access package. Then, it is placed into a virtual vault (at one time called a "dark archive"), where it can be accessed by researchers and staff.

From the moment the material enters the virtual vault, digital preservation becomes an important concern. David points out that "we are so used to thinking about digital files as just things we throw around here and there. We cannot have that kind of looseness from a preservation perspective. These things are bound by agreements in the same way that physical objects are."[38] The intertwined dependencies between software, operating systems, computer hardware, technologies, copyrights and licensing described earlier, whose longevity is often out of human control, makes digital objects more difficult to preserve. To preserve the digital material, Tim, as seen earlier, creates duplicates, twins of the file— "preservation" and "access" versions; the digital archival objects multiply from the start. As opposed to the conservation of physical objects, where the material has to be stabilized to last as long as possible, in digital conservation what matters is preserving long-term access. That is, anything from email to word processing files to CAD drawings, animations, or 3D models need to be preserved in a way that in twenty, thirty, or fifty years they will still be accessible. Ensuring accessibility, rather than stabilization, is thus the aim of digital preservation. As time leaps in twenty-year spans, preservers are constantly trying to keep up.

Collected Wholes

The most recently acquired digital material arrived in the CCA collection in the form of files. However, with the exception of "file transfers," digital archives are rarely purely "digital." They often reside on some sort of physical medium, which is how they are commonly acquired by collecting institutions. Thus, the digital collection also contains a rich variety of physical materials, including floppy disks, audio tapes, video tapes, films, and more recently optical discs such as CDs and

DVDs. As physical supports of digital material, these objects have a limited shelf life and wear away quickly and can become obsolete. This, added to a huge archive of paper drawings, prints, and physical models, forms a materially heteroclite ensemble of things sharing vaults, shelves, and boxes.

The archivist incorporates the digital material into the rest of the archive so that it can better serve the researchers. All documents should be kept in the same place "intellectually" (paper drawings, electronic files, CAD drawings, and 3D models) so that researchers can easily find information on a firm or a particular project. That is, the CCA takes a holistic approach to digital and physical material, such that neither is fundamentally different. The archivist who is processing the material works simultaneously on the audio-visual and the paper material and treats one project at a time, looking at the CAD drawings, paper drawings, and the models, describing them all together. Delving into the archive is important in terms of establishing connections and epistemically rearranging the material in a way that will make sense to the researchers. Here again, the work of the digital archivist is reminiscent of the work of the "Egyptologist," who is working with signs and unfolding their meaning. The project remains the main archival unit; it encapsulates the specificity of architectural archives without discriminating any material form. Hence, archivists try to ensure that researchers "have the same access point and they can understand it as a collected whole with those contextual relationships to each other."[39] Here again, as with the paper archives of Siza's fonds, the archivist is the first to rearrange the material, make connections, and epistemologically sift and reshuffle the "collected whole" of the archive with its inner relational design dynamics so that it can guide research purposes. The digital archivists also have to imagine the researchers working with this material and can provide guidance on how to interact with the digital (in the form of instructions, video aids, and others).

At the moment of my observation, the CCA receives such material for the *Archaeology of the Digital: Complexity and Convention* show; I watch the digital archivists go through an inventory of material in the vaults (locked in boxes some time ago, it was described in an inventory when it arrived). While the content is extracted from the physical media, the disks themselves may also have a "collection value" as a physical artifact if there are annotations or indications inscribed on them. Here again the archivist reads the "hieroglyphs" carefully, traces connections with other materials, and documents them so that the researchers who use this material will be able to see the physical disk and a "flag" that stands out to say that "if you want to see the digital files that are on this disk, this is the process."[40] Like the paper archivist, the digital archivist deals with the ontological granularity of the material and performs an epistemological restructuring; moreover, he acts as important facilitator who foresees the technical difficulties of opening a file twenty years from now and thus adds layers of instructions, licenses, and technological adjustments that make it possible for a file to talk. For instance, Peter Eisenman's archive includes a couple of boxes that contain hard drives received from his practice, which have been processed and form part of the digital archive now. Series 1, for instance, contains five hundred traditionally archived CDs. Yet, if we flip through the paper archives, in every fourth or fifth folder we find a floppy disk "buried" alongside the original paper documentation. All these materials have a shelf life of another ten or fifteen years in the best-case scenario. We witness that sometimes the digital material can hardly be disentangled from the hybrid archive placed in a box. As the box materials vary in terms of longevity and relevance, some of them can continue to talk while others risk morphing to "pieces of round plastic," mute and incapable of speaking on behalf of an architectural practice, a project, or a building.

The arrangement and description of the digital material are often done in collaboration with donors. That is a unique aspect of archiving the digital. It provides more opportunities for incorporating the actual creators' input. Archivists and creators go through the material via Skype (mainly used to understand the born-digital archives), share a screen, inspect the file directory with all of the folders and files, check if there are any linked dependent files, title blocks, or fonts hiding behind other files. Skype allows for these collaborations. Designing and archiving connect again. Even if the donors are across the world, they share a screen with the archivists, who can ask them, "What is this?," "What did you use to design it?," or "Who worked on it?" Further interrogating and investigating the order of the material imposed by the archivists in the firm, the collaborative working dynamics of the practice, the constraints of the media, and the choices for selecting and organizing the material, the archivists are able to acquire the contextual knowledge that they can refer back to and to make decisions informed by these discussions. These conversations with the records' creators form a unique resource for the archivists processing the material. Hence, the Skype discussions between Chiara, Siza, and Magda in Porto and Mirko, Giovanna, Martien, Adria, and Pamela in Montreal were crucial for the processing of Siza's donation. If archivists were not able to engage in direct discussion with the donors, arranging and describing the material would become an extremely difficult task, given the huge volume of digital archives. These discussions often facilitate the archivists' way of making sense of an archive. Archiving needs the interaction with designing in order to be relevant. Moreover, the freshness of the material (although sometimes decades old) makes it easier for the creators to remember the process and to offer insights into the operating system and the software used, the file name conventions and the folder organization conventions. In the realm of digital archiving, we witness again the dynamic interplay between knowledge "that" and knowledge "how." When archivists gain firsthand knowledge of the working process of a practice, the material, and the digital software used, this knowledge "how" is added to the collected archive to contribute to the knowledge "that/about."

Speeds of Aging, Angles of Conservation

The different materials in a "collected whole" require different politics of care. The conservation of a video tape, of a film, of a paper drawing, or of a CAD file, to name just a few in the typology of things collected, has an entirely different set of requirements. Moreover, what the "digital" is can have different meanings. For instance, it can be videotapes or cassette tapes that contain digital information on the magnetic tape.[41] The preservation of the cassette as a physical object requires different efforts than the preservation of files that have arrived on a hard drive; the drive is simply a carrier of information and does not always need to be preserved the way a cassette does. Whereas cassettes, floppy disks, and CDs can have some value, only "a very small number of digital objects have some kind of artefactual value, but most of them really don't."[42] A safe environment and good "care" for a physical object and a digital one vary enormously. "Digital objects," says the digital conservator David, "are even more vulnerable than most physical objects."[43]

As witnessed earlier, the aging of paper drawings can be slow downed by conservators so as to allow only minor alterations in the objects' material properties (for example, with acid-free folders and boxes that ensure a safer environment). Aging has a different meaning for digital archives. If we were to treat the digital materials as physical objects ensuring they are safely stored in the vaults, at a certain point in time they will cease to be relevant, and curators and researchers will be unable to make sense of them. A floppy disk or a CD will become "a piece of round flat plastic,"[44] the conservator Karen Potje stated ironically. The life of a disk is perilous indeed; it requires a certain amount of care and treatment upon arrival, as it will not be able to transmit information. The material object will become mute, a form without meaning. If preservation of physical material strives to minimize change, preservation of the digital implies making changes in order to defy time; time is measured in information bits, degrees of aging, and relevance. Conservators find themselves "forced to move something over time"[45] due to the fear of the obsolescence of software and hardware. Moving things forward through time involves migrating to different formats or updating formats in the existing software. David explains that "preservation has a different angle in the digital world because you're forced to change. You have to ask yourself what is essential to this to preserve, to keep it authentic for researchers. And if you can't keep it authentic, how do you know what you've lost and how do you document what you've lost so researchers can contextualize it? So, it's really a paralyzing complex in practice."[46] As a result of the necessity to swiftly change the digital objects, the series of copies proliferate even more; there is no original record to go back to. Here again, as in the archiving of physical materials, the proliferation of copies and emulated environments kills the idea of the original and overthrows entirely the model/reproduction dichotomy. Altering in the world of archiving the digital is a way of preserving; in order to maintain the digital material, the format, the hardware, the software must change. Preservation happens in connection with what is lost in the modification and the further contextualization of this relation of lost-and-preserved; preserving means varying by keeping track of the changes and the methods applied. As the question is not simply about keeping the integrity of the objects that contain original data (files and disks), but also about access to them over time and in future digital formats, adapting and converting the material are essential for making it readable and relevant.

Thus, just as paper material is stabilized in conservation (becoming more resilient and less dependent on the environment), digital files are altered to achieve some stabilization and keep the material readable. Yet, conservators of digital files face a number of new problems. Digital conservation is evolving quickly—so quickly that, as Karen notes: "I don't find myself able to keep up with it."[47] We must note that conservation of physical objects is evolving as well: things are done differently now than they were ten years ago. Whereas the conservation of physical objects takes place in the highly mediated quasi-medical environment of the conservation lab, digital preservation does not take place in rooms, in labs, under a microscope, but on David's or Tim's computers, in frequent meetings with archivists, cataloguers, information-technology specialists, through collaborative platforms and work software (such as Basecamp), and with external experts. A lot of research is needed for "setting up a real infrastructure flow"[48] and to run it seamlessly.

Conclusions: Archiving the Digital as "Object-Centric"

Archiving implies an "object-centric practice," the digital archivists David and Tim repeated many times. Yet the object driving this practice is elusive, always moving fast and forward in time, ahead of time, ahead of everyone else involved, multiplying, and encompassing a vast number of layers: software, preservation copies, technological environments, legal implications, copyrights, access, instructions for how to read the material. This implies a different politics of care. Digital archivists think creatively about the lifecycle of an archival object that travels forward through time and the number of mediations that will hold it together, make it relevant and eloquent in twenty years. While in the work of other friends, the architectural nature of archival objects does not always make a difference, in the work of digital archivists and conservators, it matters a lot. The typical abundance of audio-visual files, videos, audio files, photographs, text documents is fairly standard. However, CAD and Building Information Modelling (BIM) files are unique to architecture and thus present distinct challenges to the digital archivists at the CCA. Although all archives are important, architectural drawings, represented through CAD as digital material, are some of the most important documents, according David and Tim. The multilayered nature of the object that travels and the architecture-specific media make the task of archiving the digital very demanding, as well as distinct from the work of other friends witnessed at other sites of archiving earlier.

I have spent some time unraveling the various challenges of archiving digital materials, attempting to understand the nature of Tim's "paralyzing fear" and how it led to my own fear of writing this chapter—hence the reason I left it for the end. Previously, we have witnessed the plot of archiving in Siza's case unfolding as a hectic storyline involving multiple actors traveling between cities and continents, boxes and folders, institutions, design dynamics, skillsets and practices, where this interrelated sequence of actions resulted in Siza's fonds finding a plot in the CCA collection and a place in Architectural History. Here, we witness that archiving the digital implies a radically different set of practices and understandings of the objects of archiving. Although both digital and paper archiving are multi-sited and there is a similarity in the processes of registration, conservation, and cataloguing of digital and physical objects, paper archiving occurs in specifically confined physical locales of material practice, whereas digital archiving crosses many sites and global networks in the digital realm. To these many sites, we need to add the multilayered nature of the digital aggregates that travel and the multitemporal dynamics of archive processing. It is in the meandering through all these sites, through sliding twenty-year timespans that move back and forth, while handling all the composite layers of an object, that the archiving of the digital takes place. Just like paper archivists are in dialogue with design practitioners (when the firm is still active), digital archivists are simultaneously in active dialogue with designers as creators of archives, but also with computer specialists, copyright experts, software companies, digital heritage institutions, and affiliated industries. The collective and multi-actorial scope of architecture reaches its peak here. A problem is always solved with the help of a much wider network of collaborators and institutions relevant to the profession of digital preservation.

Archiving the digital moreover continues the regime of hesitant speech of archival objects complemented by gestures that we saw earlier. Yet, if in paper archiving, the hands were pointing to classification schemes and folder numbering, or the "body" of-an-object-in-conservation, in digital preservation hands are pointing to the air, to digital clouds and unknown technological hurdles, or down to the scratched surface of an old floppy disk or obsolete technology. If, in paper archiving, we witnessed objects negotiating with the unknowns of design practices, digital archival objects are in negotiation with the unknowns of software environments and technological change. If the friends of Siza's fonds replaced what they wanted to say by a finger designating a "knowledge where," the friends of the *Archaeology of the Digital* project replace it with "knowledge forward"— that is, knowing and speculating on what design will be in twenty years, and how an object will be accessed and read by researchers. To be able to talk, an object-in-digital-archiving should cross, many times, the fissures between the foldable rhythms of now and the unpredictable, technologically different tomorrow. The speech of an object–in-digital-archiving is heavily mediated; yet, some of these mediations remain invisible. Rather than the folders, boxes, series and drawers in paper archiving, we find another set of mediators: copyright licenses, software, file formats, emulated environments, and digital preservation copies. If conservators handle objects according to their expertise, and paper archivists develop their expertise in dialogue with a design practice, digital archivists acquire their expertise in part through Skype-walkthroughs with creators, and like software, this expertise is regularly updated.

Archiving combines both solitary and group work. Yet, if "the knowing where" of paper archivists, establishing connections and producing additional guidance of "where to find things" is primarily solitary, albeit also extended by group collaborations, the "knowing forward" in archiving of the digital is predominantly group-driven work. However, what "group" means here is not just archivists talking in person and over Skype, but hundreds of experts and professionals whose knowledge is mobilized for these discussions to occur. As we saw in Siza's case, archiving generates scripts (written protocols, spreadsheets, and notes). The work of Tim and David also generates a huge number of scripts, imprinting traces from activities such as coordinating people (minutes, decision notes, network drives for CCA departments), discussing with other friends such as information-technology experts, cataloguers, and archivists processing specific fonds (memos, instructions, minutes), writing CCA's policies of internal communication, which also multiply with digitization (storage of emails and files on CCA servers, digitization protocols), tackling digital presentation issues of the CCA's institutional archives, and working with standard-setting bodies in the field of digital archiving. The digital storage of all these scripts and "how they all live" together is one of the key concerns of digital archivists. While digitally processing the archive of an architectural archival institution, they cannot "keep everything that's produced as not everything is actually worth keeping" but rather retain only documents "showing the big decisions"[49] as well as the material that records the process. Script-production happens at a much larger scale and resurfaces on a meta-institutional level.

If, at the other sites of archiving (the shipping area, the conservation and the photo labs, the vaults), we rarely meet the architects as creators of archives, on the sites of archiving physical and digital materials we meet them all the time either directly or through Skype walkthroughs, and sometimes also their archivists and record managers (like in Siza's case). This dialogue with design and records' creators is crucial; designing reconnects with archiving. If paper archivists happen to be surrounded by a large crowd of objects, digital archivists are even more crowded by countless, and hardly controllable, swarms of digital objects orbiting in larger technological and legal networks. If, in the realm of paper archiving, hands can still touch the delicate surface of objects, in the realm of the digital, touching an object is unimaginable, hands are virtual, bodies are abstract, and access is the only realistic possibility. If all paper archivists can do is to add a layer of an infrastructure of knowledge regarding "where to find" the object that leads to more propositional knowledge about the object and to more connections to enable the eloquence of both objects and researchers, digital archivists add many layers of infrastructural knowledge of "how" (technological and legal mediations) to produce that type of "knowing forward" that will make the researchers capable of speech, and will ultimately generate more knowledge of "that/about." Speaking on behalf of a design practice, digital archival objects are even more epistemically puzzling than paper objects; acting in larger dispositional settings, they remain far from the regime of aesthetic eloquence. In addition to storing and rearranging, repositioning and reconnecting aggregates of objects, digital archivists reach out to the finer pixel granularity of architectural archives. Decomposed to bits, preservation copies, emulated environments, software updates, in the active and reciprocal struggle of archiving, the digital collection gains a sparkling epistemological thickness for decades to come.

CONCLUSION
Collections as Sites of Epistemological Reshuffle

Architectural collections are unique in character in that they contain individual archives, sets of sketches, models, drawings, prints, photographs, letters, and documents, while also holding traces from various sites of design production as well as of the broader institutional and sociotechnical contexts of architecture. Yet, little is done to shed light on the formation of architectural collections: how they are put together and maintained and how they happen to produce epistemic effects. Architectural objects often vanish in the dusty repository of Architectural History. Only a small fraction enjoy the occasional limelight of public attention as part of architectural exhibitions and publications. Their social biography, troubles and victories, deserve to be made visible and accountable for they form the basis of Architectural History.

Drawing close attention to the practices of creating and maintaining the integrity of an architectural collection as a material ensemble of distinct epistemological value and political outreach, I have argued for the importance of studying the secret life of archival objects. The process-oriented character of the CCA's collection and the institution's specific interest in the experimental nature of architecture make it a fertile site for the observation of this secret life; it has offered material for the understanding of the evolution of design thinking. We have been able to trace how inanimate architectural objects take on life through their interpretation as epistemic objects as they are acquired and integrated into the CCA collection: numbered, registered, described, documented, submitted to procedures of conservation and restoration, digitization and digital preservation. Following the daily practices of record-keeping, collecting, preserving, and cataloguing objects has provided insights on the know-how and tactics of archiving. It has also shed light on the mechanics of the formation of the "societies of friends" who interpret architectural objects and speak on their behalf, as well as on the scope of material and intellectual resources that have to be deployed to continue a design project beyond the life of any individual creator. Through this, we have been able to trace how the nature of architectural archives reflects design as a collective endeavor in which archivists, librarians, editors, curators, digital humanists, and conservators all play a role. More voices are welcomed into Architecture. Ethnographic sketches of various archival practices have allowed us to account for how the disorderly collections of working design materials are assembled and organized as Archives, and gathered in Collections that form the basis of Architectural History. The specific practices of arranging and caretaking of objects have illustrated the various mechanisms of the production of structuring effects in an architectural collection, and more importantly, how these effects in turn reshuffle existing knowledge and generate meaning.

Archives as Additions

Tracing archiving as a practice has led us to rethink the epistemic and ontological boundaries of the archive as a coated relational aggregate of working materials that document the thinking process of designers and the social and cultural issues entangled with architecture. At that moment in the vaults, as we gathered around the architectural drawings of Chandigarh and a distinct and collective "NO!" resonated in the space, we witnessed to what extent Le Corbusier as an architect, his practice and these particular drawings coexist and co-define themselves. Coexistence implies simultaneity. Drawings and architects are related to each other in the sense that they exist and have meaning insofar as they are intertwined; multiple reiterations of drawings are added, series join series. This removes them from a Platonic regime of image and prototype, copy and original, and closer to an Aristotelian world of things as "what they are . . . in relation to something else."[1] In all instances of archiving (and in many cases discussed in this book, including Cedric Price and Michael Wilford, Álvaro Siza, Peter Eisenman, Studio Mumbai/Bijoy Jain, Ernest Cormier, Alessandro Poli, Foreign Office Architects (FOA), Testa and Weiser and other architects and firms collected at the CCA) we witnessed to what extent the architect and the practice are co-existent with and correlated to the archival materials (images, models, sketches, drawings, letters). We can say that the architects can be defined only *in relation to* those materials. In the CCA vaults, Le Corbusier is present in these images (and vice versa); Siza is present in these drawings and sketchbooks (and vice versa);

Testa and Weiser are present in these digital models (and vice versa). The archival materials are not random renderings of architects' work, but rather partake in their very being. Likewise, architects are not understood by the mere presence of these images, models, and sketchbooks. Nor are drawings signs of a great architectural talent (they are much more complex and multi-layered); they cannot be reducible to any understanding of the architect. Yet, we need to see Le Corbusier's drawings to define his presence in the CCA collection and understand his place in the History of Architecture. But we cannot do this merely through his drawings, models or buildings. There is "more" to Le Corbusier than that. We are far from the pure regime of incarnation. Instead, Le Corbusier *and* these drawings *and* Chandigarh coexist; the extension of Le Corbusier includes his archival appearance. In other words, Le Corbusier exists not only as an architect or as a set of drawings, models, and buildings, but also in the way he manifests, persists, and mutates through time in the architectural collections. Archives, therefore, do not come to replace architects; they are *an additive part* of an architectural oeuvre. Coexistence and addition are at the heart of archiving.

The whole CCA collection is indeed a major additive aggregate. Once an architect or a firm finds itself in the CCA collection, he or she or it will not be isolated. There is a joint architectural legacy that is being produced when one archive *adds* to another: when eight boxes of Cedric Price and Michael Wilford's fonds join twelve boxes of Aldo Rossi's fonds and five boxes of Peter Eisenman's fonds. In the archives the work of an architect is "seen with other materials from other architects. The person who works with the archives will be able to do a time cut transversally."[2] Therefore, when an architect or a practice "enters" the CCA collection, he or she or it does not exist as a lonely voice, but rather enjoys the company of other architects and firms from that period. A "mingling of people and works," the collection operates as a contextual machine providing a broader relational space where new dialogues and transversal readings of works become possible. In this nonhierarchical assembly, the condensation of coexistences is amplified, new juxtapositions of, comparisons with, and connections among people, objects, space-times, and design processes can be established. As an assembly of added things, of proliferating reiterations, series of series, a multiverse, each archive that is part of the collection sheds light on architectural production and furthers the demystification of beliefs in the power of the single author or the iconic first/final sketch; there, the multiple overthrows the one.

In this regime of addition, archival objects are submitted to various procedures that aim at enhancing their archival appearance, making them talk, and extending their agency. The work of conservators does not end with treatment, the work of cataloguers does not end when all of the codes are added, and the work of archivists does not stop when objects are rehoused in new folders and described. Instead, friends continue to follow the objects to installations, shows, publications, and in their travels beyond the premises of the CCA. Focused primarily on "what those objects are doing,"[3] they organize their activities "from the object's point of view." Continuing to care for stabilized objects *extends* the work of many friends. Watch Anne go up into the galleries every two weeks to dust the models there; if she happens to notice that a hinge has popped out or a model has been picked up or touched by visitors' hands, she signals it promptly. Watch Bill, the vigilant guard, tour the gallery spaces: if he happens to spot irregularities of real concern, he brings them to the attention of others. Conservators react instantly and repair and stabilize the objects again. Thus, the care and cautionary work never stops; far from being site-specific to the conservation lab or the shipping area, care accompanies all phases of the archival objects' lives and is amplified by the vigilance of all friends, who never stop "paying attention and making sure that objects are doing what they are supposed to do."[4] Sites of archiving are far from being ivory towers of cold expertise; friends reach out to each of the places where objects deploy their eloquence to ensure that the conditions are right for the eloquent objects to remain stable, sustain their regime of agency, and successfully communicate curatorial visions. Both archival objects and friends constantly circulate back and forth between sites of archiving and display; they breathe, live, experience; things happen to them, and they meet again. This mobility points to an important feature of archiving: its multiple regimes of temporality and spacing.

Spacing and Timing

Everything in archiving is dependent on the speed of circulation: paper is used and reused; scripts circulate frantically; scalpels and folders follow their paths; objects remain *en attente*, leave the sites, and come back; entire exhibits travel outside the CCA and return again. How do we take account of these circulations? What are the specific time and space coordinates of archiving?

The ethnographic log in this book may have created the impression that time is linear; yet, as soon as we are in a specific moment of that log, we witness that time in archiving is far from being linear, progressive, united, and mono-layered. Time is in fact never straight here; it moves forward and backward; it jumps, it loops, and it restarts. Objects' and friends' trajectories intersect in a vibrant choreography. There is not one time, one moment of conservation, cataloguing, or registering, but many moments, many space-times. Very often when we follow archiving operations, we witness foldable and reversible times (rather than irreversible, linear ones). Time is symmetrical as archiving often matches designing. In Siza's archive, we found competing reversible temporalities: the times of the aging buildings, the aging architect, and the vibrant archive as a living library of ideas that extends the technical memory of the design practice. Moreover, we witnessed numerous disjunctions and jumps in time, rather than a step-by-step, steady course of action. We saw the digital archivist Tim jumping forward in time to preserve the entire technological ecosystem that allows a disk to be opened and read twenty years from now. Time happens to also be synchronic (versus diachronic). In the conservation lab, we encountered a crowded space, full of drawings, photographs, and models begging for care and attention at the same time, competing for Karen's surgeries or David's interventions. Time is polychronic (versus a single, unified sequential time). Photographs depart from the registrar's office, one after the other, battling deadlines, waiting on Marie's cart, reaching out to many different people both within and outside the CCA, while at the same time Alexandre is updating their codes in The Museum System (TMS) database. These polychronic times of the CCA are also multidirectional time flows (versus the unidirectional arrow of time). Watch the wonders that come out Cedric Price's box opened by Giovanna in the vaults and how they reconcile the many directions of travel and the multiple times of design exploration. Thus, what sounds like a broad repertoire of archival time is far from being extensive; these examples nevertheless suggest its rich, variable and multi-layered nature.

The various temporalities relate to multiple spaces. As the group of friends all work *in* the CCA, time also does things to them; tracing the flows, the speeds, the paces, the reversibility, the recurrence of routines, we inevitably end up with a complex and refreshing idea of space. Yet, the CCA is not just a space. As we trace archiving, we follow different operations and repetitions and numerous trajectories that produce distinctive variations and accumulations (and related types of expertise) as well as sites (as the result of spacing and site-ing these activities). However, this work of spacing is triggered by the intensity of time: it is because we trace the flows, the foldability of time, and its multilayered and disorderly course that we can witness the work of spacing (versus space as a simple, static container). Not one time and not one space, but many time-spaces resurface here, where we follow the various trajectories of humans and nonhumans; none of their practices could be measured through Euclidean geometry or through a tactile spatial apprehension; they can only be apprehended as a complex and dramatic relational entanglement of works. Thus, to the multiplicity of archival time we add the coordinates of spacing, traced through the multi-siting ethnographic inquiry, and an archival institution emerges.

Archival Ways of Knowing

Situated in the flux of time-space dynamics, the architectural archive can hardly be described in its totality. It emerges in various fragments and at various levels, and with varying degrees of sharpness. Yet, in all its shapes, the archive is not set apart from current architectural processes. If asked, an architect or a firm is often unable to describe her or his or its own archives since it is from within the archival immediacy of a practice that an archive emerges and gains eloquence. The ethnographic log of moves and sites of archiving recounted here in the present tense has allowed us to dive into a pool of analogies with designing. Ethnographically tracing the situated practices of archiving, a responsive gesturing (both indicative and mimetic) to various sites of designing (such as the Office of Metropolitan Architecture [OMA] or Eisenman's or Siza's firms, among other practices currently producing archives) emerged. The meaning of Giovanna's work, of Mirko's words, of the archival operations of Adria sorting out Siza's folders, and many others lay in the gaps and tensions between words and movements, humans and nonhumans, and in the OMA and the CCA dialoguing backstage. It is in this total movement of doing ethnography, tracing the moves of archiving in connection to different logics of designing, that analytics of significance began to travel and repattern the light around the well-ingrained myths of architectural creativity, authorship, and autonomy.

The ethnographic moments accounted here do not allow for any generalizations. Picture Mary, Giovanna, Adria, or David for a moment: Giovanna is not defined by her mission and her job as a chief curator, Adria is not defined by her role as a Siza archivist at the CCA, David is not defined by his role of conservator; they are instead all defined by what they do in specific situations of archiving depicted in this book. These actions, like many others, the events, the molecular interactions, and the moves are what make the CCA specific. The CCA appears here not as an institutional milieu, framing and structuring every action, devising and shaping all situations of archiving in a similar way, whereby the specificity of archiving is reduced to its key features. It is the other way around: the molecular actions of archiving transform the situations, which by extension, all together in their dance, make archiving achieve its goals and make the CCA work.

Taking a look at the backstage of an archival institution provided us with a unique entry into the important quasi-corporal work of intertextuality and intermateriality that is indispensable for archiving. We have thus been able to address archival knowing as a practical and continuous activity that contributes to the multiplicity and the inclusive sense of what is considered to be architectural knowledge. As the work of the friends of architectural objects followed here is "largely object-centric," as David frames it, and "there is only a very small part of . . . [the] brain that is paying attention to what it [the object] *is* in terms of its concept,"[5] these friends constantly develop and improve their learning *from* the objects so as to maximize the potential of learning *about* architecture. In fact, most of them have not been trained as architects or architectural scholars. Coming either from museum or library practice, digital preservation or art history, they had limited knowledge about architecture from the start. But as they have worked on the specific sites of archiving, they have learned from each project and from each other; every drawing inspected under the microscope and every object catalogued in new acid-free folders has led to new knowledge *about* an architectural practice, a building, a style, or a period. Friends learn by doing—by inspecting, identifying, diagnosing, treating, cataloguing, and rehousing archival objects— and from the specific curatorial and publication projects at the CCA. Sharing a concern with not harming the archival materials and with making them last longer, they gave priority to "doing the right thing with the objects"[6] instead of jumping into value judgment. Thus has Karen learned about Poli's buildings, Adria about Siza's projects, Tim about new file systems, and David about new digital preservation strategies. The knowledge piles up with the years. But, what kind of knowledge is this? While looking after the objects, friends manage to acquire a very distinctive object-centric infinitesimal type of knowledge that comes from the ontological granularity of archival materials; conservators gain "knowledge by the back" of drawings, diving into the grainy textures of paper, into corners and hinges; registry technicians learn to identify objects "by the smell" that testifies to travels from various climates; paper archivists fine-tune their "knowledge where" within the structured universe of collections and organized archives; while digital archivists perfect their "knowledge forward," juggling with decades of time spans sliding back and forth. All these precise ways of knowing emerge in an intensive, symmetric and intimate dialogue with the objects, enhance their archival presence, add to the archive, and place the friends within the wider sociomaterial networks of archiving.

Through archiving the friends extend and perfect their expertise and the architectural objects reveal epistemic qualities they have not manifested before. In this archiving regime, the "knowledge that/about" as propositional explicit knowledge (theoretical or factual) about architecture and the "knowledge how" as a skill, craft, and way to put something into action, which is situated, implicit, performative, and nonpropositional, coexist and define each other in a relational way. Knowledge piles up. As archivist Robert says, "After three days, after one week, the archivist becomes more knowledgeable about some architectural objects than other specialists at the CCA and more knowledgeable than the architects themselves, because you start to see things in a different way."[7] The distinct ways of "knowing how" developed on the sites of archiving as "knowing by/where/

forward" first overlap with, then rarify, and then eventually lead to the production of new propositional knowledge (and ultimately, to a new History of Architecture, of "knowledge THAT"). Thus, moving beyond the dichotomy of "that/how,"[8] a dispositional way of knowing emerges in the web of archiving. In this versatile web, the modalities of the "knowing how/where/by/forward" of some actors condition the "knowing that" of others, and vice versa. For instance, "knowing where" to find a drawing of Siza and creating an arrangement in which others can find it, see it, and know it, too, leads toward the extraction of new propositional knowledge that aggregates and gradually steers a new understanding of Siza's architecture. Disposition includes the particular arrangement of objects and friends of objects as well as the situation at hand. It points to the fact that the expertise that is required to put an archive together does not reside in any of the practitioners involved. It is collective and distributed, effective and renewable; it is flexible in terms of improvising new relationships between knowns and unknowns, between the "practical competence" of designers and the "technical artistry" of archivists. Crafting new arrangements, strategic set-ups of objects and distances, viewing and tactile positions, archiving, as witnessed in this book, generates a "potential born of disposition"[9] as a configuration of new relations in which knowing becomes possible. That is how it actively spawns new epistemic dispositions, and an architectural collection emerges as a vibrant site of epistemological reshuffle, rather than as a silent place for storing enduring historical evidence.

As busy as they are taking care of objects—archiving, repairing, coding, and cataloguing them—most of the friends rarely have the time for a "WOW!" moment—a moment to really engage with the objects with the degree of admiration and epistemological rigor that an architectural scholar would. While architectural collections bear similarities with art collections,[10] we don't generally hear friends of architectural objects say, "Oh my god, this is a Frank Lloyd Wright, or Cedric Price, or Le Corbusier!" The aesthetic judgment is suspended. You do not need to pronounce a "NO" to stop them from reaching toward a drawing with their bare hands. Rare are the moments of shared aesthetic admiration. Here are some of them: Magda remembers the enthusiasm of going through the first archives of Siza together with Chiara, who would say, "Come and see this," and they would share a "WOW!" together and indulge in contemplating some drawings. Only when dealing with a request for an image reprint or for a reference does Marie, from the registrar's office, get to see a drawing. Usually, she spends her days accompanying the objects in their travels; rarely does she have a moment to appreciate them as "architectural." Many other friends follow suit. Their extensively mediated contact with the objects is an additional obstacle for aesthetic engagement. The friends often glance at the objects to make sure they are in good order, but rarely take the time to contemplate them. Alexandre explains: "We manipulate a lot of the objects; we see them a lot, more than the architects do."[11] Yet, seeing the objects does not allow time for engagement. At a certain point the crowds of objects are so present that friends stop noticing their architectural specificity; they cease being "amazed by the objects."[12] Here lies an important difference between me, the ethnographer, in the vaults, mesmerized by the drawings of Le Corbusier in that sudden encounter, and all these friends of architectural objects. In the dexterous work of archiving, they continuously maintain the suspension of aesthetic judgment and skillfully produce detachment.[13]

Tracing the modalities of knowing and regulating attachments to architectural objects, this study contributes to discussions in anthropology of knowledge by moving both beyond the cognitivist, rationalist perspective that situates brain processing in the center of knowing and beyond the phenomenological perspective that situates the body and the senses in the center of knowing. Exploring the "archival ways of knowing" in terms of moves, of tedious work, of experience,[14] of timing and spacing, of intercorporeal and intertextual activities, the study suggests a symmetrical ecological approach to knowing that emerges from the relational dispositions of humans and nonhumans, in their dynamic timing and spacing, and captured both in specific sites and larger networks. Repetition contributes to and amplifies the dispositions. Robert explains, "We are so aware that the same archives will be visited and revisited hundreds of times by hundreds of people. It's never dry and someone will see things differently."[15] Archiving emphasizes the active and reciprocal nature of knowing, appraising, and preserving architectural objects in relation to what is already known about them and to many different participants in knowing; this emphasis, in return, influences how architecture and its world are understood.

The Work of Interpretation

Far from the regime of evaluation of aesthetic effects, archiving requires careful identification, description, and scrutiny in terms of analyzable properties. The architectural objects we witnessed in labs, folders, and databases are no more or less interpretable than they are knowable. Unlike rocks or trees or other things found in "nature," architectural drawings are things made, outputs of practice, the extensions of the worlds of design: a drawing is a witness to the versatile collaborative dynamics in Siza's practice; a CAD file illustrates Testa & Weiser's computing experiments. The tendency of all friends involved in archiving to interpret the phenomenal world of drawings and models gives architectural objects not only a life but also a society. An entire "society of architectural friends" gathers around these objects on different sites of archiving to converse with them, to decipher their "hieroglyphs," to unfold compressed meanings, to interpret them, and to witness how a drawing *adds* to another drawing, and how all together, they *add* to an architectural practice and *extend* our understanding of its oeuvre. Interpretation is understood here as a set of complex actions performed with reference to an assortment of related objects, rather than as an attempt to make contact with their intrinsic properties; as "Egyptologists," archivists remain experts in reading the surfaces of signs. Inspired by Dominic Boyer's understanding of the experts, we can argue that what defines an archivist is that special "skill in semiotic-epistemic competence for, and attentional concern with"[16] the practical activity of identifying, deciphering, sorting, arranging, and caretaking of archival objects. Handling objects in archiving activates the consideration of the finer ontological distinctions that exist between those objects. Indeed, it sets them in full swing. Thus, archival operations gradually turn into an elaborate exercise designed to make commonly mute architectural objects speak. Archiving activates stories about designing. It is a way for friends to come to terms with various aspects of architectural practice and different architectural worlds, to apprehend them anew and afresh, to generate new knowledge about them. When curators and archivists say that the drawings of Le Corbusier, the files of Cedric Price, or the sketches of Álvaro Siza are interpretable, this means they matter to them; they have an intimate knowledge of their material variability; their "hieroglyphs" makes sense to them in a recognizable way. Friends are in a position such that they can understand the archival objects and are, juridically, capable of representing them, as their friends. Therefore, they can make them speak by further rearranging epistemologically the order of things, by activating the ontological variability of the collection, and reconnecting people and things according to new curatorial arrangements.

This idea that collections perform actions and architectural objects talk is not strange after this ethnographic log has taken us to visit labs and vaults, workshops and offices. And yet, to talk about chatting architectural plans, traveling models, communicative drawings, and flying files makes sense only in an archiving context where the ontological variability of architecture is not simply sustained but greatly enhanced across the moves of archiving. There, the characterization of architectural objects is made on the basis of their specific differences and modalities of action, and not through a quick reference to the nature of a medium or a technique, or to the diversity of architectural cultures, styles, and movements. Archiving becomes embroiled in a planetary diplomacy of its own kind, wherein the virtues of objectivity are maintained as the actions of all friends remain predominantly object-centric; accordingly, in attempting to constantly create and negotiate different conditions for the objects, friends never rely on established knowledge and sentiments but continuously redefine both content and meaning. Without knowing it, friends follow "the principle of irreduction"[17] by distrusting all set definitions of aesthetics, judgment, valuation, functionality, creativity, genius, state culture of preservation, thus resisting all temptations to explain architecture, a temptation that continues to blind Architecture studies today.[18]

Architectural Collections as Accelerators

The active modality of engagement with objects does not occur in an institution that passively holds archives; rather, it is the archiving moves that sustain the institution. Record keeping permeates all activities of archiving. Every move generates traces: Alexandre's camera, Marie's cart, Giovanna's post-its, Mary's coding, Adria's rehousing, Tim's digital preservation, and the many curatorial discussions. More traces of objects' lives, all traces forming records, pile up *in addition* to what is already officially archive-able. Record keeping adds mediations, folders, boxes, colored gloves, all used to handle the objects with care; new scripts emerge. What kind of alchemy is it that takes us from the multitude of details of measurements, scripts, and condition reports to the question of archival value?

Tracing the spatial and material coordinates of the moves of archiving, identifying, classifying, conserving, repairing, selecting, and arranging objects helps us to produce a better understanding of architectural collections. Here, information from different sources, instruments, and scripts come together to form a unified vision where every type of data is connected to the world of architecture. Some of them are clearly related and compatible; others—associated to things "seemingly" unconnected—forge new relations hitherto unimaginable, producing new knowledge. While buildings cannot be brought into an architectural collection, we can instead bring all the mediators that have contributed to the production of buildings (models, diagrams, sketches, drawings, visuals, photos, quotes, letters, renderings), and we can exercise control over them. However, very often in architectural scholarship we fail to acknowledge the role of all these mediators—from the fragile concept model to the nasty letter from the client—and the set of instrumental practices that makes a building possible. As vehicles of knowledge, the mediators circulate through the archival sites and are mobilized in networks of transformation; that is how the buildings also circulate through all these networks. These networks, *qua* processes of archiving, function like accelerators dislocating the features of the buildings, redistributing space-times, and contributing to the capitalization of knowledge far from all the places where the buildings were designed and the places where they were built, yet still interconnected through the scripts gathered in archiving. That is a very different operation than the circulation of images and signs that aim to represent an architect's idea. What an absurd idea to think that only one image of a building, the one we saw in Cedric Price's book, is able to represent his work and serve as a point of orientation in an autonomous system, delimiting what we can think about Price's practice. What an implausible scenario, indeed. Instead, archival institutions are reminiscent of accelerators: they renegotiate and redistribute objects' proprieties and thus amplify and prepare the ground for the capitalization of architectural knowledge.[19]

Thus, instead of being static repositories that contain the stable bedrock of Architectural History, archival institutions actively contribute to and compose the phenomenon of the built that has an existence only because of its spreading through a series of transformations. When we stare at a picture of a building in the published text, the building is neither "outside" the picture and the networks that represent it, nor is it "inside," in the very nature of the sign; it is the archiving network that connects the image to the building and to a certain type of architecture and turns matter into signs. It is not enough to explore the world of the building or to contemplate its image only, as a "reference" that corresponds to it. To understand it, we need to witness how it travels through the archival network of models, renderings, and letters as mediators; and how these mediators *add* to it. Thus, a building resides in a certain manner of displacement, which optimizes the connections in spite of the diversity of the experts involved. The knowledge gained in archiving does not derive from the superimposition of a visual and a built world, but from the constantly expanding network of archiving, and the larger network of collecting institutions. That is how, within the acceleration of frantic moves of archiving, acting as a *dispatcher* that regulates the multiple relations between the work of reduction and the work of amplification, an archive becomes the accumulation of "drawings, *plus, plus*," a collection becomes an additive assembly of archives, and Architectural History emerges as ontologically grounded on cumulative series of "collections, *plus, plus*."

As a place where the circulation of mediators contributes to the production of knowledge, the architectural collection bears a resemblance to laboratories and to natural science collections.[20] It is the practical network of knowledge production, transformation, and capitalization that constitutes it. It is defined through a very specific and material relationship established between places, sites of archiving, and architectural firms, and the inscriptions that circulate between them to negotiate what will be given and the precise form of power that can be exercised from a distance. Far from being an isolated fortress, a collecting institution is rather a node in the large network of architectural knowledge production. Not a temple, but a regulator of flows and trends, bending space and time around it, an accelerator,[21] a transformer.

Architectural Wonders

When we follow Giovanna in the vaults as she opens a box of Cedric Price, or Chiara and Adria as they process Siza's archive, or Mary as she inserts new catalogue codes, we do not witness simple design or cultural or social objects. These are rather hybrids, where design and society merge with one another. Made out of irreconcilable parts of the architectural past, heterogeneous, relational arrangements intensifying the multiplicity of copies and amplifying the condensation of coexistences, their juxtaposition and comparison, the architectural collection might appear as a cabinet of wonders, stuffed with design "rarities."[22] Yet, it is far from being an encyclopedic inventory of architectural objects, intended to represent the entire architectural heritage (it does not have the aim of the Borgesian library: to contain every archive ever produced by all of the great architects and firms). The objects here are not samples of architectural style or patterns of creativity. What we have is a variety, "a microcosm," not an attempt at universality. It bears resemblance to the cabinets only because the categorical boundaries of its objects are not completely defined: here, architectural objects and social processes first rarify and ultimately merge; here, architecture does not usurp or reflect society, but rather extends, completes, and assists society; here, the mutual imitation of design and culture is wonderous; here, context becomes part of architecture—it is *within* the archival boxes of Cedric Price, never outside the boxes, the vaults, the catalogues. Rather than flowing from the fantasia of one architect, the marvels in an archive emerge from the society's anticipation of architectural design; they inspire new orderings of things that transform the ontological categories of design and society. As a result, the very opposition design/society in which architecture is commonly reduced to a reflective surface mirroring societal forces collapses. This calls for further, and urgent, rethinking of the conceptual apparatus of design theory and invites a different, fresh, pragmatist way of writing Architectural History.

In a collecting institution, as we have seen, no one believes in the "imaginary museum" of Malraux,[23] deeming, as he does, that the coherence of the fragments of the museum can be achieved only as a function of human imagination. If the purpose of a museum is to educate, glorifying a certain number of objects, a collecting institution pulls objects out of the dusty tranquility of storage and puts them on trial, challenging and reactivating them. Preoccupied with taking care of archival objects and sustaining their integrity and with creating relational archival assemblies that make sense, all friends sensibly engage with the practical and epistemological application of the collection, rather than trying to overcome it, in leaps of imagination. Far from a regime of valuing objects for their exemplary properties in a state-performed culture of preservation, what we witness here is a different regime of engagement with the modalities of action of these archival wonders: behind closed doors all friends are concerned with the ephemeral and transitive nature of architectural objects as material and epistemic entities; they engage in an elaborate exercise designed to make these silent objects eloquent. That is what defines the collection as a site of epistemological reshuffle. Archivable meaning is not determined in advance by the structure of the archives; instead, structure and meaning negotiate with each other in the minute operations of archiving. Far from reaching out to audiences or lauding the durability of expressive forms, the ideals of eternity, and by extension, Architectural History, friends converse with objects, decipher their signs, rearrange them, stabilize them, and prepare them to *speak*.

Minor Architecture

If the architectural collection is not the grand finale of architects' careers, marking gloriously their entrance into a memorable History of Architecture, what does archiving do to architectural scholarship and practice? Following the ethnographic log, we witness *archiving* rather than archives; we grasp that archiving is never about a specific object or about one man leading one show, but always about dealing with a multiplicity of architectural materials of larger social and cognitive importance for the discipline. Archiving is about *adding* to History *now*—adding new knowledge and interpretations, new types of relations among various visuals, creators, technologies, and contexts; it is about testing more possibilities of design in the present, and thus correcting it occasionally. That is how a more refined understanding of architecture can be produced, one that functions only when all judgments are suspended.[24] As a concept that opens up new avenues of research, *archiving* allows us to better scrutinize the current conditions of both architectural practice and architectural research without weighing them down with the old categories of styles, types, movements, genius, context, and social forces. Archiving thus generates what we can term "minor architecture," following Deleuze and Guattari's analysis of "minor literature" in relation to Kafka's work.[25] Just like minor literature challenges the official language, minor architecture escapes codification; it allows challenging the codified, official language of practice and theory and the dominant interpretations. We witness a reversal:

instead of relating architecture to some preexistent category or architectural style and movement, instead of "expressing" or "representing" architecture, archiving rather serves as a method of propelling the most diverse contents on the basis of ruptures and intertwinings of the most heterogeneous orders of signs, of hieroglyphs. It provides a rallying point for architecture to produce its own epistemic arrangements and expressions, its own speeds and movements. As an engine of minor architecture archiving helps us overcome dualistic, dialectical, or structural correspondence between design, on the one hand, and society and culture, on the other. It points also to the turbulent and secret life of architectural objects in collections, where, torn away from their own design rhythm and language, small, fragile ephemeral objects end up challenging the official Language of History making in Architecture. Archiving activates a *machine of expressions and interpretations* that can better grasp the deterritorialization of architectural discourse, its lines of escape, silences, and interruptions. It is a semantic machine that is essentially fluid, constantly infusing architectural objects, bodies and scripts, continually developing the meaning and the future of architecture.

As an engine of the machine of minor architecture, archiving generates an active *diagram* that puts into action a number of forces that grow the collection: practicing architects are "invited to look at archives and to make sense of them"[26]; researchers travel great distances to consult the collection objects; and entire curatorial teams are mobilized to rethink and reappraise the CCA materials to produce more interpretations. Instead of reproducing an immutable History of architectural forms, a collecting institution, one might say, *makes* Architectural History by dismantling existing interpretations, and by creating many instances of emergence and creativity, of unexpected conjunctions of events occurring at the same time, of improbable continuums. Activating the multiplicity of architecture, archiving feeds this machine in connection to the various logics and rhythms of designing. Constantly brewing new forms, technologies and inscriptions "to constitute mutations,"[27] architectural collections evolve. And so does Architectural History. Always in becoming, generating new realities, archiving is how Architecture *makes* History.

Acknowledgments

The idea for this project emerged on an early November morning in 2014, after a visit to the vaults of the Canadian Centre of Architecture (CCA) in Montreal. I was the first anthropologist of "The Moderns" (as my mentor Bruno Latour terms this type of enquiry) to embark on the "island" of archival expertise. And the CCA is the dream island for an architectural anthropologist! I am greatly indebted to everyone there who made this journey possible and moreover, truly enjoyable, and especially to Giovanna Borasi, Mirko Zardini, Phyllis Lambert, Martien de Vletter, Karen Potje, David Stevenson, Louise Désy, Tim Walsh, Mary Louise Gordon, Albert Ferré, Alexandre Phaneuf, Marie Gouret, Robert Desaulniers, Elspeth Cowell, Sébastien Larivière, Adria Seccareccia, Anne Gauthier, Pamela Casey, Kimberly Davies, and Caroline Dagbert. Special thanks to Martien de Vletter for careful reading and generous professional comments on two versions of this manuscript. For their time and support on the project, I am also grateful to Peter Eisenmann and Álvaro Siza, as well as the archivists in Siza's practice in Porto, Chiara Porcu and Magda Seifert.

Visits to other cities and other archives provided inspiration and food for thought and comparison with the CCA. I am thankful to Regina Bittner and Monika Markgraf from the Bauhaus Archive, Michel Richard from the La Fondation Le Corbuser, and Andres Lepik form Architekturmuseum der Technischen Universität München, as well as to Marta Mancini and Aimaro Isola from Isola's practice in Turin for sharing ideas on their archives and archiving practices. For their encouragement and comments on different stages of this work, I would like to thank Antoine Picon, Caroline A. Jones, Beatriz Colomina, Eeva-Liisa Pelkonen, Mark Wigley, Hélène Frichot, Matthias Kärrholm, Gunnar Sandin, Sandra Kopljar, Isabelle Doucet, Jennifer Mack, Gareth Doherty, Setha Low, Ola Oduku, Richard Brook, Michael Guggenheim, Andrew Moon, Vivian van Saaze, Lesley Mcfadyen, Adolfo Estallela, Michael L. Benedikt, Alessandro Armando, and Giovanni Durbiano.

In 2017 I was awarded the Lise Meitner Visiting Chair at Lund University, Sweden, which allowed me to spend more time on research and provided a generous and supportive intellectual milieu for discussions with scholars in architecture. Subsequent academic visits at the Politecnico di Torino, Dipartimento di Architettura e Design, Italy, and at Columbia University, New York, also offered further opportunities for research and discussions. A number of other institutions where

I presented my work on this project in the last three years, supported indirectly its successful outcome—Harvard University, Radcliffe Institute for Advanced Studies, Yale School of Architecture, Princeton School of Architecture, Kunstakademie Düsseldorf, Bauhaus Dessau Foundation, University of Edinburgh, Bartlett School of Architecture, University College London, Danish Building Research Institute, Aalborg University, the Nordic Research Network for Architectural Anthropology, and the European Association of Architectural Education, among others. They were all wonderful intellectual hosts and helped me improve the work through discussions.

The Manchester Architecture Research Group (MARG) at the University of Manchester Urban Institute provided a stimulating environment for conversations and writing. I am indebted to my colleagues from MARG for their support throughout the work on the book: Stephen Walker, Łukasz Stanek, Leandro Minuchin, Alan Lewis, Léa-Catherine Szacka, Deljana Iossifova, Kim Förster, Amy Hanley, and Angela Connelly. Léa and Łukasz in particular provided insightful comments on drafts. My PhD students—Brett Mommersteeg, Demetra Kourri, Benjamin Blackwell, Fadi Shayya, Alexandra Arènes, and Simon Mitchell—were the first to witness both the exciting and the difficult moments in this project. Brett was also my research assistant, and his intelligent work provided for efficient use of my time.

Jim Lance, acquisition editor at Cornell University Press, was the most wonderful editor one could dream of, especially in interdisciplinary projects. His continuous encouragement and intellectual finesse made the long journey of producing the book truly enjoyable. Two anonymous, but very generous reviewers provided invaluable feedback, and confirmed my hopes for the future of symmetric anthropology. Dominic Boyer, editor in chief of the Expertise: Cultures and Technologies of Knowledge series, offered precious editorial advice.

At home I had all the support I needed. My parents always helped in hectic moments of fieldwork and travel. My sons, Martin and Christian, inspired me to continue thinking between languages and writing in a language that is theirs but will never be truly mine. My friend Suzanne Shilton helped generously on numerous occasions with the boys. As usual, my husband, Svet, was there for me—his enormous patience is hard to thank. I dedicate this book to him, and to our way of archiving history.

Notes

INTRODUCTION

1. Forgey 1989.
2. The climate at the end of the 1970s was conductive to the emergence of the first architectural museums. Although the term "museum of architecture" is an old one, the 1970s and 1980s were when we witnessed the museumification of architecture, which was related to the growing currency of architectural sketches and the emergence of an art market for architectural drawings. It was precisely at that time that architecture "stormed" the field of culture as drawings became a "cultural merchandise." Institutions founded in this period in addition to the CCA include: Les Archives d'Architecture Moderne of Maurice Culot in Brussels (1968), the Royal Institute of British Architecture's (RIBA) Drawings Collection of John Harris in London (1972), the Centre de Création Industrielle (CCI) (1969), as integrated in the project of Centre Georges Pompidou in 1972), l'Institut Français d'Architecture (1980) in Paris, the Deutsches Architekturmuseum of Heinrich Klotz in Frankfurt (1984), and the Nederlands Architectuurinstituut in Rotterdam (1988). For a detailed account of this museumification of architecture, see Chabard 2011 and Côme 2013.

The growing awareness of the importance of architectural collections for the profession brought a number of diverse institutions together, and the International Confederation of Architectural Museums (ICAM) was founded in 1979. As an organization of architectural museums, centers, and collections, ICAM is dedicated to fostering links between all institutions interested in promoting a better understanding of architecture (see https://www.icam-web.org). Phyllis Lambert recalls that a number of people and institutions met in Finland to decide if "an organization for architectural drawings could be founded." John Harris became the first president; Phyllis Lambert was the second. Joining forces, they started thinking about "making inventories, compiling a joint system of cataloguing, marking, describing, and building a hierarchical system" (Phyllis Lambert, interview with the author, June 29, 2015).

3. The term "fonds" is used to name an archive. "A fonds is like a collecting unit. Usually you collect fonds. For the architects who worked before the year 2000, because of the presence of the physical documents of the drawings, and the great quantities of reproductions, the work of a firm is so huge. If the architects have worked in the 1920s and 1930s, you would want to acquire the whole fonds. But for someone who has worked later in the 1980s or 1990s, you may want to select some projects" (Robert Desaulniers, interview with the author, June 17, 2015).

In 1987, when Robert Desaulniers became head archivist of the CCA, the CCA was collecting complete fonds, and there were four or five; in 2015 there were 185 fonds, according to Robert.

4. See Canadian Centre for Architecture (n.d.)
5. Mirko Zardini, interview with the author, June 15, 2015.
6. Foucault 1972, 129.
7. Sébastien Larivière, interview with the author, June 18, 2015.
8. Previous ethnographies of architectural practice include Cuff 1992; Houdart and Minato 2009; Yaneva 2009a, 2009b; Jacobs and Merriman 2011; Loukissas 2012; Yarrow 2019.

9. The institutional settings of archives vary: some are connected to museums and galleries, others not; some are housed in academic institutions, others not. And these institutional settings matter. In the CCA case, the dialogue between collection and museum events (exhibits, publications, research programs, and so on) provides a very special setting for the dialogue of archival objects and various publics of academics, professionals and amateurs.

10. I refer here to Miguel Tamen's (2001) expression and adapt it to my fieldwork to designate a number of people taking care of architectural objects, making them speak, and being affected by them—that is, a "society of friends" of architectural objects.

11. On issues of iconoclasm, see Tamen 2001 and Latour and Weibel 2002.

12. Albert Ferré, interview with the author, June 16, 2015.

13. Phyllis Lambert began buying drawings in 1953, then more drawings and books, and in the 1960s she started a private collection of photographs. Lambert donated her private collection to the CCA in the summer of 1982. This included, at the time, 15,000 photographs, 30,000 books, 4,000 drawings and prints, and some fonds of architects (Chabard 2014, 55).

14. This is by no means an extensive list of the archival institutions in the field of architecture, but it provides an orientation of the various types of institutions that host collections of drawings, models, and entire archives, and the different institutional frameworks.

15. Martien de Vletter, interview with the author, June 15, 2015.

16. de Vletter, interview.

17. Zardini, interview.

18. Wigley and Koolhaas 2008, 167.

19. Lathrop 1977, 25.

20. Notable examples of recent anthropological studies of design, architecture, and spatial practices include Ingold 2007, 2011; Buchli 2013; Mack 2017. In spite of the growing interest of anthropologists in design issues in the past decade, architectural archiving has not been studied from an anthropological perspective.

21. The craftspeople of archiving followed in this book and their specific craftwork focuses on the objects in themselves, and on various impersonal practices, far from the domain of feelings (*Erlebnis*). Bridging the false dividing lines between practice and theory, technique and expression, maker and user, Sennett defines the work of craft as driven by constraints and resistance, as an art of managing ambiguities, manipulating tools, of routines and practical plays. He emphasizes the idea of experience as craft, as *Erfahrung* (Sennett 2008, 288).

22. Boyer 2008, 44.

23. Recent studies of "expertization" that relate to the themes of this book include Murphy 2015 and Yarrow 2019.

24. See Boyer 2008.

25. See Latour 1991.

26. See Barth 2002; Boyer 2005.

27. See Ryle 1984 [1949].

28. As shown by Hutchins (1995), the cognitive properties of the group differ significantly from the cognitive properties of an individual member. On cognition as embedded in social practices and distributed within group activities, see also Lave 1988.

29. Harris 2007, 6.

30. Foucault 1994, 131.

31. Foucault 1994, 155.

32. On the concepts of truth and knowledge production in architectural theory, see Sharr 2003.

33. In that regard architectural history is reminiscent of the sciences of the archives, as it depends on collections in the same ways as both natural and human sciences depend on collections. Archives provide crucial support for the process of creating scientific data, and scientific work consistently relies on the making and keeping of records. By exploring the practices, politics, and economics of the sciences of the archives, comparing patterns of how different sciences organized their record, Loraine Daston (2017) and her collaborators discuss how, through archiving, "the sciences choose to remember past findings and plan future research"; archives outlive individuals, organizations, and nations. Daston's volume presents a pioneering study of the role that science archives play in the development of natural and human sciences.

34. See Latour 2010; Ferraris 2007, 2013.

35. As the dossier lands in different hands, these hands in turn are endowed with different skills and manipulate various tools with different degree of resistance. The analysis of archiving expertise departs from here, inspired by Richard Sennett's (2008) analysis of skills as related to craftsmanship.

36. Lynch 1999, 83.

37. Tracing the institutionalization of the cultural field of architecture from 1975 to 1985 and analyzing the role of the first CCA exhibit, *L'architecture et son image*, in 1989, Pierre Chabard (2014) embarks in a *histoire croisée* of the CCA and the CCI. Overcoming purely internalist analyses of exhibitions and layering a social-historical perspective, Chabard claims that to "examine the architectural exhibition from an institutional angle invites us to look at it differently and forces us to consider it simultaneously from inside and from outside, at the same time in its autonomy, as a specific discursive form, as an authentic field of architectural action, but also within the multiple circumstances in which it sits and which overall determines it: namely, the sometimes competitive interconnected strategies of similar institutions (the Cci and the CCA), but also of different departments in the same institution (the Cci and the Mnam)" (49; my translation). He also argues for the importance of analyzing the tensions between the logics of capitalization, conservation, and valorization of a collection (whose form and content reflect the hazards of the market) and the logics of mediating via exhibitions an architectural culture on the move.

38. Giovanna Borasi, interview with the author, June 18, 2015.

39. Zardini, interview (emphasis added).

40. For example, *Archaeology of the Digital* was at the beginning a research project on the evolution of the relation between architecture and digital technology; then it became an exhibition, as well as involving an acquisition and research at the same time. See Zardini, interview.

41. See Garutti and Mihandoust 2015 and Garutti 2016, https://www.cca.qc.ca/en/events/52251/can-design-be-devious-the-story-of-the-robert-moses-bridges-over-the-long-island-parkways-and-other-explorations-of-unexpected-political-consequences-of-design.

42. Anne Beaulieu (2010) puts forward the concept of "co-presence" as a way to shape fieldwork. "Co-presence" is for her an interactive accomplishment by participants and ethnographers alike that does not share the unidirectional and ocular-centric connotations of witnessing, or interrogating. She shifts the focus on achieving co-presence by emphasizing that interaction is precarious. While physical co-location can be a resource for participants, it is not in itself a sufficient criterion for co-presence. Co-presence decentralizes the notion of space without excluding it; it enables a more symmetrical treatment of forms of interaction.

43. For an account of how ethnographers access the spaces and the streams of practices from which fact construction arises, see Knorr Cetina 1995.

44. On the ethnographic interview as a method, see Spradley 1979 and Van Maanen 2011.

45. The study includes fifty-two interviews with archivists, architects, conservators, cataloguers, digital specialists, librarians, and curators, conducted between 2015 and 2018, in English and French; the transcriptions amount to thousands of pages, without the ethnographic notes.

46. Evans and Jones (2011) review the literature on the walking interview in geography. According to them, walking interviews more efficiently capture the distinctive characteristics of place and contribute to a better understanding of place attachment. Regarding landscape anthropology, Gareth Doherty's (2016) insightful study traces the many different shapes and relational capacities of the color green. Green is a color that cannot be dissociated from the object, yet green is also social, political, cultural, and environmental at the same time. The relational capacity of green is narrated using the ethnographic techniques of *walking* as a way for situating the anthropologist *in the world* of the object, the landscape.

47. See Ingold and Vergunst 2008.

48. In my previous ethnographic studies (for instance, the study conducted at OMA, Yaneva 2009a, 2009b) the format of office-based, single-sited ethnography allowed following and depicting more specifically the changing agency of nonhumans—models, foam cutters, model-scopes, and drawings. The ethnography of archiving involves visiting different sites and practices and meeting a number of actors whose profiles and agency are to be introduced in the ethnographic account. Archiving requires a multi-sited and multi-siting, multi-actor ethnographic study; in each of the cases, and on each of the sites, new human and nonhuman aggregates are discovered.

49. I also visited the practice of Aimaro Isola in Turin, Italy, in the summer of 2018 to study his archive.

50. See Boyer and Howe 2015.

51. See Holbraad and Pedersen 2009.

52. See Deleuze 1983.

53. Deleuze 1983, 117.

54. Architectural theory generally embraces an understanding of buildings as having an objective reality "out there" while a number of subjective perspectives *to* buildings are being expressed, weighted, and reconciled. That is, it involves a "perspectival flexibility" that suggests that design has *a meaning* for many actors who express their diverging points of view. Stepping away from this dominant perspectivalism in architectural theory, we can foreground the practicalities, the materialities, the events, and the processes of transformation in buildings. Thus, variability is placed within things; the source of fluidity shifts from the many variable subjective viewpoints ("perspectival view") toward the multiple reality of the built object ("aperspectival objectivity"). On perspectival versus aperspectival objectivity, see Daston 1992. For a translation of this approach into architecture, see Yaneva 2017.

1. ARCHIVE FEVERS

1. Foucault 1972, 129.

2. Foucault 1994, 143.

3. See Fukuyama 1992.

4. Some of the very first moments of giving a value to archives in architecture occurred, for instance, at the *OMA/Progress* exhibition at the Barbican Art Gallery in London (October 6, 2011–February 19, 2012). The CCA exhibit *Out of the Box: Price, Rossi, Stirling +Matta-Clark* (October 23, 2003–September 6, 2004) also emphasizes the aesthetization of the archives, presenting them in a visually pleasing way.

5. For a thorough discussion of the relation between history and memory (and oblivion), see Paul Ricoeur 2004.

6. For Ricoeur, archiving and narrating otherwise are ways the historian can give expression to the voices of the abused and excluded. The historian does not merely oppose the manipulation and distortion of testimonies by telling the story differently, but also provides the space for the confrontation between opposing testimonies. The idea of providing a hospitable space is vital for fostering faithful testimony. This, however, is not a romanticized space in which opposing testimonies are forced into false harmony. And the historian is by no means a neutral observer in this process. He or she is an actor in the plot and also embedded in history (Kearney and Dooley 1999).

7. Ricoeur 1978, 68.

8. See Jordanova 2006.

9. See Jordanova 2012.

10. The archive is what "determines that all these things said do not accumulate endlessly in an amorphous mass, nor are they inscribed in an unbroken linearity, nor do they disappear at the mercy of chance external accidents; but they are grouped together in distinct figures, composed together in accordance with multiple relations, maintained or blurred in accordance with specific regularities" (Foucault 1972, 134).

11. Derrida 1995, 14.

12. Derrida, 1995, 10.

13. Derrida, 1995, 14.

14. See Agamben 1999.

15. Agamben 2006, 38.

16. Agamben 2006, 38.

17. Agamben 2006, 39.

18. See Enwezor 2008.

19. See Sekula 1986, 2003.

20. Sekula 2003, 444.

21. Sekula 2003, 451.

22. See Benjamin 1994.

23. Alphonse Bertillon was a French criminologist who developed an anthropometric system of identification based on the body in the late nineteenth century; Harold Colton was an archaeologist who developed a typological system for organizing and collecting ceramic wares in the Southwest of the United States in the early twentieth century.

24. On the definition of shadow archive, see Sekula 1986, 10.

25. See Foster 2004.

26. Thomas Richards (1993) established the origins of the "archival impulse" in Victorian England, during the prime of British imperialism.

27. See Foster 2004.

28. Foster 2004, 3.

29. Foster 2004, 22.

30. Of note here is Okwui Enwezor's provocative 2008 exhibition at the International Center of Photography, New York, *Archive Fever: Uses of the Document in Contemporary Art* (the title refers to Derrida's 1995 book, *Archive Fever*). More recently biennial curators have also given prominence to historical archives in their shows. For example, Massimiliano Gioni's Biennale incorporated an impressive amount of documentary materials—from photographs of the victims of atrocities in Cambodia to Paul Fusco's photos of Robert F. Kennedy's casket being transported to Arlington National Cemetery in Virginia; he also continued this emphasis in his 2013 Venice Biennale, which displayed such archives as a group of hundreds of small model houses built by an Austrian insurance clerk named Peter Fritz. Carolyn Christov-Bakargiev's much-praised 2012 exhibition *dOCUMENTA (13): The Uncommodifiable Quinquennial* in Kassel, Germany, also featured an extensive use of archives and artists who employ and research widely archives for their work.

31. For a reflection on the "anomic archive" in the arts and how randomness and arbitrary juxtaposition function as a form of socially enforced legitimation of anomie (not only as established aesthetic procedure), see Buchloh 1999.

32. See Downey 2015.

33. Downey 2015, 13. For a review of cutting-edge debates on "the archive" in other parts of the world, and particularly South Africa, see Hamilton 2002.

34. See Ghani 2015.

35. See Taylor 2006.

36. For a detailed account of this, see Downey 2015.

37. On issues of preservation of film archives, see Mattern 2017.

38. See Taylor 2003.

39. Taylor 2006, 68.

40. See Hacking 1990; Shapin 1994; Desrosières 1998; Patriarca 1998; Poovey 1998. On the power of "persuasive utterance" in the making of scientific truth-claims, see Norris 1995; Anderson 1991, 163–86.

41. See Sahlins 1992; Kirch 1992.

42. In 1961 archaeologists discovered a family archive of legal papyruses in a cave near the Dead Sea where their owner the Jewish woman Babatha, had hidden them in 135 CE. Esler (2017) engages in reading and analyzing the oldest four of these documents.

43. Esler 2017.

44. Wolcott 1999, 59. On making memos in ethnography, see Agar 1985.

45. Gracy 2004, 335.

46. Banks and Vokes 2010, 338.

47. See Banks and Vokes 2010.

48. See Decker 2013; Rowlinson, Hassard, and Decker 2014).

49. See Rowlinson, Hassard, and Decker (2014).

50. See Decker 2014.

51. Decker 2014, 520.

52. See Burton 2003. For a theoretical discussion of the specific historical conditions that structure the emergence of archives, see Burton 2005.

53. See Stoler 2002.

54. See Stoler 2009.

55. Stoler 2009, 20.

56. See Decker 2013; Stoler 2009, 9–10, 20.

57. See Mills 2013.

58. Gagen, Lorimer, and Vasudevan 2007.

59. See Moore 2010.

60. See Enigbokan 2019 and her website at archivingthecity.com. See also Enigbokan and Patchett 2012.

61. See Ashmore, Craggs, and Neate 2012.

62. See Larkham 2011.

63. See Gillette and Hurley 2018.

64. See Giuliano, Chakrabarti, and Rhoads 2016.

65. See Healthcott 2006.

66. See Zebracki 2018.

67. See Richards 1993.

68. The uniqueness of practice within the architectural archive becomes more evident when we consider a parallel history of scholarly discussion, that of the literary archive. A notable aspect of the architectural archive is that the architect is very often its author; that is why the comparison with literally studies imposes itself. Archivists of both literary and architectural archives have to contend with the specificities of a particular practice. How-

ever, architects produce a great multiplicity of documents, they work in *firms*, and their products do not seem to be the intimate accounts of personhood or concern for individuality that literary archives have. In architecture the concern is less about the author and more about the multiple realities of documents. If literary archives keep either an intended final work or something *behind* the final work that the author might want to keep private, in the architectural archive, there is not a "final" product, but a plurality of objects that show different states of a building-to-be. On issues related to the literary archive, see Skelton 1984; Tener 1984; Hobbs 2001; Tector 2006; Douglas and MacNeil 2009; McGill 2009.

69. For a detailed etymology of the term, see Echevarría 1990.

70. For an insightful study of the history of the Venice Architecture Biennale as a platform for discourse and display, as well as the postmodern movement more widely, see Szacka 2016.

71. See Lambert 1999.

72. While foundations have been set up to preserve the legacy of modernist architects such as Le Corbusier and Frank Lloyd Wright, prominent contemporary architects have also set up foundations in order to think and prepare for their own legacies in advance. Renzo Piano has his Fondazione Renzo Piano in Italy; Norman Foster, the Norman Foster Foundation in Madrid; Herzog & de Meuron, the Kabinett in Basel; and Zaha Hadid began her Zaha Hadid Foundation in 2013 prior to her death. Each of these foundations holds archives and libraries of the respective architects, with the aim of exhibiting and promoting the legacy of their work into posterity.

73. See Knight 1976.

74. Lathrop 1977, 25.

75. See Lathrop 1980.

76. Olsberg1996.

77. Olsberg 1996, 129.

78. See Olsberg 1996.

79. See Schrock 1996.

80. See Cox 1996.

81. See Cook 1996; Lathrop 1977.

82. Cook 1996, 139.

83. Bearman 1992, 34.

84. Belton 1996, 206.

85. Bartlett 1997, 456.

86. Lathrop 1996, 227.

87. See De Long 1996; Nelb 1996.

88. De Long 1996, 163.

89. Ragot 1996, 220.

90. Mitchell 1996, 203.

91. See Willis 1996.

92. See Thomas 1996.

93. See Carey 1996.

94. See Nowacki 1996.

95. Lövblad 2003, 138.

96. See Tatum 2002.

97. Tatum 2002, 27.

98. See Armstrong 2006.

99. See Pierce 2011.

100. See Davidson 2010.

101. Zardini 2010, 81.

102. Cohen 2010, 51.

103. Cohen 2010, 51

104. Berndt Fredriksson (2003), for example, looks at the emergence of the Swedish Foreign Service archive from the sixteenth century through the establishment of the Ministry of Foreign Affairs in 1840 and into the late twentieth century. He takes this study as an example of an empirical and "postmodernist" approach to archival science and as an alternative to the prevailing normative approach. Similarly, Thea Miller (2003) unfolds a long historical narrative of record-keeping practices in the administration in what is now Germany, from the medieval registers to the fourteenth-century registers, the emergence of a "registry" in the sixteenth century, and all the way through to the attempt to streamline the system of administrative archives in the early twentieth century and the use of information technology to organize electronic records in the late twentieth century.

105. Head 2010, 192.

106. Lemieux 2015, 28.

107. See Gracy 2004.

108. See Gracy 2003.

109. See Gracy 2007.

110. See Stevens, Flinn, and Shepherd 2010.

111. Stevens, Flinn, and Shepherd 2010, 62.

112. Huvila 2015, 122.

113. Huvila 2015, 135.

2. ARCHITECTURE AND THE "FEVER" OF ARCHIVING

1. For an examination of archival practice and its spatial repercussions, see Bailey and Miessen 2014. Questioning the processes that enable archives to become productive, the authors argue that a good archive offers an open framework that actively transforms itself, thus allowing for the constant production of new and surprising relationships and new perspectives on archival practice.

2. Peter Eisenman, interview with the author, October 18, 2016.

3. See Peyceré and Wierre 2008.

4. See Hennion and Latour 1993; Hennion and Latour 2003.

5. See Houdart and Minato 2009; Yaneva 2009a, 2009b; Jacobs and Merriman 2011; Loukissas 2012; Mommersteeg 2018. For more recent studies of the ecology of architectural practice, see Frichot 2018 and Yarrow 2019.

6. An exception is the study of Daniel Llach (2015), who traces the history of CAD and BIM, not as tools and design instruments but as important metaphors for rethinking the concepts of design, materiality and creativity.

7. Derrida 1995, 17.

8. He mentions only technologies from the 1990s: MCI or ATT telephone credit cards, portable tape recorders, computers, printers, faxes, televisions, teleconferencing, and above all email. This list can be updated today.

9. Beatriz Colomina argues famously that *L'Esprit Nouveau* produced Le Corbusier in the 1920s, that the brochures of Archigram produced Peter Cook in the 1970s, and that the pages of *Oppositions* and *October* produced the new avant-garde of contemporary architects (Colomina and Buckley 2010b).

10. Wigley and Koolhaas 2008, 173.

11. Wigley and Koolhaas 2008, 191.

12. Exhibitions, for instance, produce their own archives as they travel. Colomina's exhibition *Clip, Stamp, Fold* generated archives as it traveled from New York City (the Storefront of Art and Architecture), to Montreal (CCA), Barcelona, Oslo, and so on. At each of these sites, it generated new knowledge about magazines that existed in the local context

of these countries, and new archives were assembled and continued to travel (Colomina and Buckley 2010a).

13. See Lambert 1999, 313.

14. That is when we began witnessing a process of distanciation/alienation between the architects and their drawings; as integration of architecture in the field of cultural industry accelerated, the drawings became commercialized and a new scholarly field of "architectural studies" emerged (Chabard 2014, 2015). See also Szacka and Dadour 2015.

15. Eisenman, interview.

16. Another architect from this generation, Aldo Rossi, is known for producing drawings after the realization of projects, thus artificially generating more archives or collectibles.

17. We need to note that not all Eisenman's drawings in the CCA are signed (contrary to his recollections in this interview). Even though he did not sign everything, but maybe only some individual drawings that were on sale, as confirmed by the CCA, this was the start of the process of signing. It signaled a new awareness of the value of drawings as they gradually became "cultural merchandise" (Harris 1984, 78), which was a new phenomenon for both designers and art dealers. In a recent study Jordan Kaufman (2018) argued that between the 1970s and 1990s architectural drawings emerged as aesthetic objects and attained status as important cultural and historical artefacts.

18. I discussed this trend in interviews with Álvaro Siza and Peter Eisenman, to which I will refer to later in this book (see chapter 6).

19. For a detailed account of this historical moment, see Picon 2010.

20. See Lynn 1993.

21. For discussions on the history of architectural museums, see Szambien 1988; Harris 1989; Kaufman 1989; Lambert 1999; Cohen 2001.

22. Wigley 2005, 12.

23. Peter Eisenman loves collecting "vanguard stuff," as he calls the polemical didactic material, manifestos. He has futurist manifestos from the last thirty years and has collected *L'Esprit Nouveau*, little magazines, and so on. He donated approximately 3,000 items to the Yale library. He has about 5,000 books in his private library and is thinking about donating them as well (Eisenman, interview).

24. Eisenman, interview

25. Wigley 2005, 14.

26. Work on digital archives in architecture often revolves around issues of preservation and access, as well as the record life cycle, from initial production and use by the creator, to selection for and preservation within an archive, and finally to use by the researcher (Peyceré and Wierre 2008).

27. Foucault 1972, 127.

28. A few reflections only on the impact of Foucault and Derrida can be found in the architectural literature: Landau 1982; Rajchman 1988; Coyne 2011; Fontana-Giusti 2013.

29. We should note, however, that this reflexivity regarding the method of architectural history was present in architectural pedagogy in the past decade; a number of courses in postgraduate programs in architecture at Princeton University, Columbia University, among others, testify to this. Reinhold Martin's course "Research Practices: Archives, Objects, Histories" at Columbia University is representative.

30. Historians are the key users of the archives. However, illustrating how users of various archives interpret their making and unpacking the politics of archiving by creating a forum for makers and users to engage in discussions about the different readings of the CCA collection are beyond the scope of this book. In addition, very often makers are also users, while knowledgeable users of an archive can also become makers and contribute to

its further restructuring; for instance, the curatorial use of different archives results in numerous additions and reshaping of the CCA's collection, and it is on its own a fascinating story that also deserves to be told. Every use of the archives leaves imprints on their organization and epistemological structuring. Yet, unpacking all stories of use of the CCA collection (by historians, photographers, curators, practicing architects, renovators, artists, manufacturers) and all related processes would result in a different book.

31. Colomina 1994, 1–15.

32. For an analysis of how denying touch to "original" archival material is fundamental to the archive's mission, see Kleinman 2006.

33. In her writing on archives she is influenced by Alice Yaeger Kaplan (1990).

34. Colomina 1994, 9.

35. Colomina 1994, 9.

36. Eeva-Liisa Pelkonen's (2009) seminal study on Alvar Aalto recounts the meanderings performed by the architect across continents, geopolitical regimes, and cultural values, which greatly helped Aalto to perfect his art to the point that it became as powerful as the political power exercised by the state. She also reassembles an archive that will better help us apprehend his legacy. Antoine Picon (2009) reflects on the St. Simonians' architecture of utopia and the return of the archives, the "moment of paper." Mark Wigley's (2015) study of Buckminster Fuller also includes a reflection on the excessive "self-archiving habits" of the architect who managed to produce an extended autobiographical narrative. He denotes that Fuller was "symptomatically keeping everything in his chronological files" (Wigley 2015, 34). Buckminster Fuller regularly updated his "extended autobiographical narrative" to brief journalists before interviews in what Fuller called his "Memorandum of Activities: Richard Buckminster Fuller," which was appended to the "Dymaxion Index" that monitored his media coverage from 1947 onward (Wigley 2015, 23). He compiled a Dymaxion Chronofile that documented his entire life: it contained more than 140,000 papers and 1,700 hours of audio and video, all stretching to more than 1,400 linear feet of material. Thus, Fuller's life appears to be, according to Wigley, the "most documented life of all time." The files go back to when he was four years old, but he seriously started the archive only in 1917 when he was 22. From then until his death in 1983, he collected everything from each day, including ingoing and outgoing correspondence, newspaper clippings, drawings, blueprints, models, and even mundane ephemera such as dry-cleaning bills. In a recent study, my colleague from Manchester, Łukasz Stanek (2020), reflects on the formats and limitations of transnational archival research and on the structures of different textual and visual archives he consulted—institutional, official, governmental, and organizational, as well as private and partial, centralized or dispersed.

37. See Siddiqi 2017.

38. Siddiqi 2017, 1302.

39. See de Silva 1998.

40. See Orillard 2012.

41. See Dubowitz 2010, 2012.

42. Wigley 2018, 32.

43. See Burns 2013.

44. The use of photography to describe and document buildings should be complemented, Iain Borden (2007) suggests, by an alternative imaging to show how various political, social, and other meanings of architecture may be created by photographs as well as by the written word. Reflecting on the importance of photography archives that prolong the lives of built form, Pierluigi Serraino (2011) defines the Architecture and Photography Archive (APA) factor and its impact on the reliability and validity of the genealogies institutionalized in the defining narratives of the historians. He writes: "Architecture is dependent on photography to survive the passage of time. In turn, the latter

relies on the retrievability of the photographic archive for the recovery of its material and its insertion into architectural discourses" (Serraino 2011, 7).

45. See Baweja 2018.

46. See Heathcott 2007.

47. See Levine 2008.

48. Levine 2008, 17.

49. Kleinman 2006, 55.

50. The *libri delle case* are among the earliest illustrated inventories of architecture, preceded only by the drawings of fortifications in the cabinets of princes and of antiquities in the manuscripts of artists and architects. Before the middle of the sixteenth century, when the value of property was not in the income that it produced but the stability and status that it conferred, it was the land rather than the building that mattered most (Friedman 2012).

51. The structuring of archives around images introduced architects as new figures in the editorial team that produced the real estate documents. They were the great names of Roman design. They worked as measurers, estimators, administrators, and advisors in the building trades, and occasionally as participants in design competitions. They looked after the buildings of the institutions that employed them and were regularly the ones called on to prepare the house books (Friedman 2012).

52. Foucault, 1972, 129.

53. Friedman 2012, 129.

54. Friedman 2012, 130.

55. Historian of architecture Eeva-Liisa Pelkonen (2017) famously argued for a phenomenological engagement with the materials of architectural knowledge; using the analogy of a "soup," she stated in a provocative way that historians should allow themselves the time to "savor" the findings, to witness the granularity and the compositions, to "stay in the soup and enjoy the marvelous mixture of all its ingredients," just as a phenomenologist would do. The "soup" as a metaphor evokes the nonlinear nature of that immersive method of engagement with archival materials and suggests that as in any satisfactory culinary encounter, several flavors and themes seamlessly coexist; just as in cooking, the effect reveals the cause. This is, then, an appeal to avoid reducing archival material to mere historical evidence and looking for one cause, one meaning, and instead to embrace an experiential approach that accepts the multiplicity of meanings created through such an encounter.

3. A MORNING IN THE VAULTS

1. At the start of this chapter I reflect on previous fieldwork experiences that might suggest a "reflexivist" positioning of the anthropologist, evoking an "intersubjective" method of reflexivity. However, instead of turning myself as an the author into a transparent object for my own introspections, my aim is rather to engage in an "intra-objective" dialogue with the empirics of previous fieldwork, to be able to reach an "objectivity" by gradually absenting myself from the analysis that will follow.

2. I refer here to a two-year ethnographic study of the Office for Metropolitan Architecture of Rem Koolhaas in Rotterdam (OMA), which resulted in the books Yaneva 2009a and 2009b.

3. See Boyer and Howe 2015; Holbraad and Pedersen 2009.

4. Strathern 1999, 6. The "ethnographic moment" makes us dive into a pool of potential analogies to be drawn between past fieldwork experiences and future objects of comparative study.

5. This comparison is a-chronic, across time, providing an alternative to both a synchronic cross-cultural comparison (the OMA versus Eisenman's or Siza's firm cultures) or a diachronic comparison of different historical moments of one design practices (the

OMA in the 2000s versus the OMA in 2019); a "trans-temporal" comparison could overcome both the modernist clichés of cross-cultural comparison and the postmodernist preference for multi-sited fieldwork.

6. As Clifford Geertz (1988) terms this phenomenon when commenting on Malinowski's ethnographic diary.

7. Roland Barthes calls this problem the "diary disease" (1982, 491)—that is, the problem of insoluble doubt as to the value of what we write in a diary, the disdainful experience of a private "I" submitted to a public narrative use. This problem is also known as "the dilemma of Malinowski," "the descriptive participation," or "I, the witness."

8. On slowing down, see Stengers 2011 and Yaneva 2013.

9. Geertz 1973, 10.

10. Bergson 1991, 150.

11. Hastrup 1999, 45.

12. Elspeth Cowell, interview with the author, June 16, 2015.

13. Robert Desaulniers, interview with the author, June 17, 2015.

14. The expertise that is required to put an archive together also does not reside in any of the practitioners just as archiving does not reside in any place or situation. On multi-sited ethnography see Marcus 1995; on the methodology of shadowing, see Czarniawska 2004, 2007.

15. Mirko Zardini, interview with the author, June 15, 2015.

16. Although the different media of the different parts of the collection require specific treatment and numbering, the CCA's collection is considered as "one collection" and that is an important conceptual idea for everyone working here.

17. Giovanna Borasi, interview with the author, June 29, 2015.

18. Zardini, interview.

19. Pamela Casey, interview with the author, June 28, 2015.

20. Robert Desaulniers, interview with the author, June 17, 2015.

21. Casey, interview.

22. Casey, interview.

23. Borasi, interview.

24. Desaulniers, interview.

25. Deleuze and Krauss 1983, 53.

26. Borasi, interview.

27. Borasi, interview.

28. Borasi, interview.

29. Borasi, interview.

30. On the process of option making at the OMA, see Yaneva 2009a.

31. A building, as witnessed in office presentations, is an assembly of assemblages, pluralistically constituted, genuinely additive, marked by manyness. On the nature of a building as a "multiverse," see Yaneva 2017, 133–59.

32. Bergson, 1991, 162.

33. Borasi, interview.

34. Borasi, interview.

35. Lambert, interview.

36. Borasi, interview.

37. I will use the word "drop" here so as to depict a process of almost uncontrolled dripping of contextual elements that, just like small amounts of a liquid, were drawn into a roughly spherical mass by surface tension, and to distinguish it from "traces" as marks and clues that were intentionally left in these boxes as witnesses for context.

38. Borasi, interview.

39. Phyllis Lambert, interview with author, June 29, 2015.

40. The "leavings" of an architect can be various in nature. Historian David G. de Long (1996) worked with the archives of Bruce Goff and Louis I. Kahn, sorting materials from drawings through to musical records, photographs, and personal items such as clothes and pianos.

41. Lambert, interview.

42. For a discussion of architecture's autonomy as well as its various dependencies, see Till 2009. Till's ambition is to open up the discipline to dependency and to view this not as a threat but as an opportunity. He writes: "Architecture is thus shaped more by external conditions than by the internal processes of the architect. Architecture is defined by its very contingency, by its very uncertainty in the face of these outside forces" (Till 2009, 1).

43. Borasi, interview.

44. However, the definition of research differs from firm to firm. In the case of Abalos & Herreros's practice, research is very much related to teaching, and the archives contain slides and lecture materials.

45. See Till 2008. On some common myths in architecture, see Till 2009.

46. See Tarde, 2001.

47. I refer here to the "voices of silence" in Maurice Merleau-Ponty 1995, 39–83. For an insightful study of the philosophy of Merleau-Ponty for architects, see Hale 2016.

4. OPENING THE CRATES

1. In addition to Alexandre and Marie, there are two technicians working in the registrar's office, and the team's supervisor is Iglika Avramova. The registrar team meets in the registrar's office to plan work on a regular basis. It is also where the administrative work for loans is done, including negotiations with transport companies and customer services. Another person helps also during the summer because that is when many scholars visit. For instance, during my visit in June and July of 2015, there were about twenty-four researchers on the premises of the CCA.

2. Marie Gouret, interview with the author, June 17, 2015.

3. Deborah Poole (2005) calls this an "excess of description." Very often ethnographic literature recounts "the movement of images, and how images circulate in and out of archival collections of various kinds" (2005, 339). Poole gives an example of this from her own work, in which anthropological photographs in an archive become "part of a broader visual economy in which images of Andean peoples were produced and circulated internationally" (2005, 162).

4. The Museum System (TMS) is a collection management program that allows collection data to be easily and seamlessly integrated with other management systems. It also includes special software designed for managing collections at art museums and galleries, and for artist studios and estates to archive and track their art collections. In TMS collection information contains interlinked modules; when the information is entered once, it remains consistent and accessible. For more information, see http://www.gallerysystems.com/tms.

5. See Fraenkel 1992 and Gardey 2001.

6. Alexandre Phaneuf, interview with the author, June 17, 2015.

7. The collection is arranged according to these guiding codes, which correspond to the three departments. Archives like those of Cedric Price, James Stirling, and Aldo Rossi have a different numeration.

8. Phaneuf, interview.

9. While TMS is used to describe, catalogue, and manage objects, the CCA has adapted the system so that it can also describe archives. The plan is to migrate the archival data out of TMS in 2020 into an Archival Management System (AMS).

10. The object number is typically composed of the prefix "ARCH" and a number (e.g., 269524). It is independent of the hierarchy (fonds, series, subseries). It points to a sequential object number generated automatically by the system. The CCA started coding in this way so that if for any reason they have to change the order of files in the series, subseries or projects, the numbers on the objects do not have to be changed physically.

11. See CCA 2015.

12. Elspeth Cowell, interview with the author, June 16, 2015.

13. Mary Louise Gordon, interview with the author, June 17, 2015.

14. Gordon, interview.

15. Gordon, interview.

16. Phaneuf, interview.

17. On the practices of sorting and storing, see te Heesen 2002; Gardey 2008; Schaffer, Tresch, and Gagliardi, 2017.

18. Of the total collection of objects, 80 percent is stored in the CDC, not in the main CCA building. Yet, this does not tell the whole story: 100 percent of the photo collection, library collection, and prints and drawings collection is at CCA.

19. Very often the check is done during accessioning or inspection at the CDC by technicians and archivists.

20. Phaneuf, interview.

21. Phaneuf, interview.

22. Phaneuf, interview.

23. Phaneuf, interview.

24. Yaneva 2009b.

25. Design has a trajectorial nature (Yaneva 2009b), in spite of the common preconception in architecture studies of design as project-making and project realization, as a rational step-by-step linear process (see for example Jones 1970; Rowe 1987; Shoshkes 1989; Lawson 1994). The trajectorial understanding of design circumvents the prevailing linear rational schema of design process.

26. Gouret, interview.

27. Phaneuf, interview.

28. "The institutional archive is crucial as it is important to have a record of what happened," explains Louise Désy, a curator of photography at the CCA. In the addition to the reports and minutes produced on a daily basis, the CCA institutional archive also contains large numbers of photographs of different events at the CCA and parts of the institutional life. A person in charge of the collection services makes sure that every exhibit is photographed. A photographer also documents events and activities in the garden. The institutional archive of the CCA as an active institution is thus ever growing. Louise Désy, interview with the author, June 28, 2016.

29. This concept is introduced in Souriau 1956. Its use in architecture is further unpacked in Yaneva 2009b.

30. Phaneuf, interview.

31. The fact that architectural objects are placed in boxes of botanists bring us back to the comparison between butterflies and models, drawings and plants in a museum setting (see the introduction).

32. Phaneuf, interview.

5. POLITICS OF CARE

1. Latour 1999, 32.

2. Karen Potje, interview with the author, June 18, 2015.

3. Potje, interview.

4. Potje, interview.

5. An ethnographic visit to the basement of architect Aimaro Isola's practice, in the summer of 2018 in Turin, made me think about the conditions of storing archives; a damp basement is indeed very often where archives end up. Interviews with Aimaro Isola and his record manager, Marta Mancini, June 2018, Turin.

6. Karen Potje, interview with the author, June 28, 2016.

7. For an overview of the delicate material and ethical aspects of conservation of contemporary art pieces, see Chiantore, Rava, and Dell'Aquila 2012.

8. On the reversed relationship between copy and original, and the capacity of copy-making and reproduction to generate originals, see Hennion and Latour 1993.

9. Louise Désy, interview with the author, June 28, 2016.

10. Désy, interview.

11. See Crysler 2012.

12. Potje, interview, June 18, 2015.

13. Photographs are specific kinds of "active things." They require their own kinds of treatment, according to Louise Désy, curator of photography (hence responsible for the development and coordination of the activities related to the photography collection). She explains that photographs in archives or even in the library require a special temperature: "We have two vaults, one for the color material and one for the black and white. Already, at this level, there is a separation. It is important to recognize that the works on paper need a different temperature than the photography materials." In addition to the color separation, there is also a distinct separation between different processes: "You don't want to mix dye, chromogenic prints with other color materials," adds Louise. The boxes help maintain this separation. See Désy, interview.

14. For an overview of issues of pest management in museums, see Florian 1997.

15. Bugs (both paper-eating and wood-eating) are part of the lives of numerous collections. Yet, insects infect collections in different ways depending on the organic matter they contain. Natural history collections with large numbers of dried insects, usually stored in drawers, dry plant material in herbaria, stuffed animals, skins, and mounted specimens, fur and skeleton specimens are at a very high risk of infestation and damage. Second to these in terms of high-risk collections are ethnographic ones, which have similar materials: fur, feather, leather, plant materials, wood. They are followed by historic and modern art museums, and then libraries and archives. On the ways insects affect different types of collections, see Linnie 1987; Boersma et al. 2007; Querner 2015.

16. Karen Potje and David Stevenson, discussion with the author, June 18, 2015.

17. David Stevenson, interview with the author, June 28, 2015.

18. The exhibit *Rooms You May Have Missed: Bijoy Jain, Umberto Riva* included materials from the Indian practice Studio Mumbai/Bijoy Jain, some of which we have seen in the shipping area; the boxes received at the CCA contained insects when they arrived in the shipping space. This required immediate action to avoid putting the collection in danger.

19. Potje and Stevenson, discussion.

20. On the different techniques of detecting and preventing insects in collections, see Child 1999.

21. For a study of the role of instruments in architectural practice see Yaneva 2005. The Instruments project (http://soa.princeton.edu/content/instruments-project-princeton-conversations) pays attention to instrumental processes that are by design simultaneously material and metaphysical to explore the technical dimension of architecture.

22. Potje, interview, June 28, 2016.

23. Anne Gauthier, interview with the author, June 28, 2016.

24. Gauthier, interview.

25. Gauthier, interview.

26. See Simondon 1989.

27. Potje, interview, June 18, 2015.

28. See Simondon 1989.

29. Potje, interview, June 18, 2015.

30. David Stevenson, interview with the author, June 18, 2015.

31. Stevenson, interview, June 18.

32. Potje, interview, June 18, 2015.

33. It is important to clarify that only objects that are selected for a certain reason carry all those documents with them. Not all materials in the collection are accompanied by all these "passports" and "medical records" at all times.

34. Potje, interview, June 18, 2015.

35. Gauthier, interview.

36. Stevenson, interview, June 28.

37. It is reminiscent of the "failure of the technical gesture" described by Simondon (1989, 203), which decouples the technical act into two opposite realties: a figurative, subjective one (all the action schemes, habits, and gestures learned by humans) and the profound, objective reality (of qualities, dimensions, and properties of objects to which the technical gesture applies). The failure of the technical gesture separates what is blended in the repetitive act of making and archiving, mixed and coproduced in this process. In its normal functioning technology is an abstract system, often invisible; when it fails, it become visible, concrete, actual.

38. Potje, interview, June 28, 2016.

39. Stevenson, interview, June 28.

40. Gauthier, interview.

41. Potje, interview, June 28, 2016.

42. Karen Potje, interview with the author, June 28, 2016.

43. Gauthier, interview.

44. Potje, interview, June 28, 2016.

45. Potje, interview, June 18, 2015.

46. Potje, interview, June 18, 2015.

47. There is a strange fascination about paper in conservation. Different kinds of paper follow and support architectural drawings and collages throughout the conservation process. Paper multiplies here, taking on different forms, and appearing in different varieties. Karen uses different colors, different weights, different lengths of fibers. Japanese paper which is very thin, almost transparent, but strong and lightweight, is widely used for hinging or joining things, backing, and repairing. Kozo paper, in particular, is appropriate for almost any paper conservation technique because of its long strong fiber (10—15mm) and its malleability and wet strength. It is the best choice for protecting signatures, hinging, attaching covers to books, and repairing torn pages. Good-quality paper that is acid-free and has very long fibers that make them strong even though they are thin are highly appreciated in conservation.

48. Potje, interview, June 28, 2016.

49. Cellulose ethers are used as thickeners, anti-redeposition agents, and protective colloids for liquids in the food, paint, adhesive, and oil-drilling industries. In paper conservation, cellulose ethers have been used alone or with starch pastes for lining, hinging, and mending. Their moisture holding, surfactant, and anti-redeposition properties may be used to advantage as poultices for removing stains, old adhesives, and other accretions. Diluted solutions have been used for sizing or resizing paper.

50. Potje, interview, June 28, 2016.

51. Potje, interview, June 18, 2015.

52. Potje, interview, June 18, 2015.

53. On the politics of maintenance and repair, see Graham and Thrift 2007. On issues of care and urban repair, see Mattern 2018.

6. THE PLOT OF ARCHIVING

1. There was a market for books, prints and drawings, and photographs sold by dealers. Archives, however, were seldom sold by dealers or auctions.

2. Phyllis Lambert, interview with the author, June 29, 2016.

3. Donating and purchasing archives require different contractual relations. When the donor of the archive is alive the "copyright always stays with the donor and we ask them to transfer copyrights the day they die. And in the different countries you need to have different wordings in the will, etc." (Martien de Vletter, interview with the author July 11, 2016). Martien also explains at length that in the southern part of Europe, there are different export license rules and regulations. The practicalities of the shipping procedures are different, and the CCA very often needs an expert to work with.

4. Mirko Zardini, interview with the author, June 28, 2016.

5. Zardini, interview, June 28.

6. Zardini, interview, June 28.

7. Álvaro Siza, interview with the author, August 30, 2018.

8. Siza, interview.

9. Siza, interview.

10. For the online traces of this controversy, see Andrade 2014a, 2014b, 2014c.

11. Zardini, interview, June 28.

12. Mirko Zardini, interview with the author, June 15, 2015.

13. Recently Gulbenkian organized a large exhibition for modern and contemporary Portuguese architects; Serralves has also organized a number of exhibitions on architects and is currently preparing another one. The two also work together. Calouste Gulbenkian Foundation 2019; Siza, interview.

14. Elspeth Cowell, interview with the author, June 16, 2015.

15. Lambert, interview.

16. For more information on this CCA exhibit, *Corner, Block, Neighbourhood, Cities. Álvaro Siza in Berlin and The Hague*, September 24, 2015, to May 22, 2016, see the CCA website, https://www.cca.qc.ca/en/events/3509/corner-block-neighbourhood-cities-alvaro-siza-in-berlin-and-the-hague. For the archivist Pamela, who has worked for other institutions in the past, the link between archival material and exhibition material at the CCA is quite unique as "a lot of other archives don't have that angle" (Pamela Casey, interview with the author, June 28, 2016). Exhibits here act as vehicles to explore the archive and to actualize it; the intellectual lens of curating affords new readings and interpretations of the archive that could have structuring effects.

17. See the exhibit *NEIGHBOURHOOD: Where Álvaro Meets Aldo*, Portugal's Pavilion at the 2016 Venice Biennale, May 28–November 27, 2016.

18. In Holland, it was the Punt en Komma social housing project (1986–1988) that was part of the Schilderswijk neighborhood renewal project; and in Germany, the Wohnhaus Schlesisches Tor (Bonjour Tristesse) (1984) social housing project.

19. Giovanna Borasi, interview with author, June 18, 2015.

20. Casey, interview.

21. Siza, interview.

22. Borasi, interview.

23. In 2015, when the Siza archive was being packed in Portugal, other archives such as those of Abalos & Herreros archives and the Foreign Office Architects (FOA) archive of Farshid Moussavi and Alejandro Zaera-Polo were being processed in the off-site storage, the CDC.

24. Borasi, interview.
25. Siza, interview.
26. Peter Eisenman, interview with the author, October 18, 2016.
27. There are recent projects that the CCA does not have material for; for legal reasons this material needs to remain in the office of Siza in Portugal for some years. Peter Eisenman also explains that he keeps some of the material in his practice so that it can be used for exhibitions and also for legal reasons (Eisenman, interview).
28. Siza, interview.
29. For instance, books of Carlos Castanheira, who collaborates with Siza.
30. Siza, interview.
31. Recently Siza picked her up again to do the Giudecca project. So, she is on both sides now.
32. The Barcelona Meteorology Centre by Siza, built in 1992, or "the round building for Barcelona" as he calls it, was the one that prompted the use of computers in his office at the end of the 1980s. The restoration of the Chiado area in Lisbon (1989–1990) and the design of the Galician Center for Contemporary Art (1993) in Santiago de Compostela were also projects developed on the computer.
33. See *Álvaro Siza. Architecture 1980–1990*, 1990, Exposition coproduite par le Centre Georges Pompidou/Centre de création industrielle et le Secrétariat d'Etat à la culture du Portugal, Commande du Centre de création industrielle, 1992.
34. Siza, interview.
35. The CCA received mainly the "paper archive"; but they also received some hard drives from Siza with standardized computer and AutoCAD drawings, which need to be safeguarded.
36. Martien de Vletter interview with the author, June 15, 2015.
37. de Vletter, interview.
38. As the archivist and architect Magda jokes, "This is the only archive in the world where the two of them smoke!" (Magda Seifert, interview with the author, August 30, 2018). Chiara smokes both during the interview on the ground floor and while she shows me the locked drawers. I also find Siza smoking during the interview in his office.
39. de Vletter, interview.
40. If objects in museums are treated individually, collecting institutions deal with large amounts of objects. As Martien explains, "We are not checking every single object to see if it is folded, or if it has a staple in it, no. This is impossible. For example, the Cedric Price archive has about 20,000 drawings. But the Sterling archive has 80,000 drawings. It is impossible to check every single drawing for cracks" (de Vletter, interview).
41. Casey, interview
42. For instance, in the fonds of Abalos & Herreros, the architects continually refer back to their own work and borrowed ideas. They go back and go over older projects and pick and reuse themes and ideas. Sometimes it can be very hard for an archivist to understand the relations. The original order becomes difficult to grasp.
43. The sketchbooks contain most of what Siza does on a daily basis and constitute, in his own words, a good source for studying "the beginning of a project, the beginning of the thought process" (Siza, interview). They offer windows into the experiential side of his working processes. Full of pictures, sketches, notes, doodles, minutes of meetings and correspondence, they recreate this unique experience of Siza's day-to-day process of thinking architecture. Flipping through the sketchbooks, we imagine Siza taking a trip, sitting in a meeting, drawing faces and human bodies, animals; we picture unknown circumstances, daily impressions, intense working dynamics, all of these generating multiple versions of a building-to-be, all of them, all together giving hints to the daily moments of creativity. The travels, the encounters, the faces, the distant lands and landscapes, the ex-

citements and disappointments, all become visible in the densely filled sketchbooks. Here again we witness the mixture of architecture and context. Context is not outside, called upon to explain a drawing. It is a fusion of things and people, human experiences and crayon patterns. The sketchbook also acts as a hybridizer of architecture and society, actively mixing various layers of the working life of designers and salient aspects of their cultural worlds.

44. For a reflection on the type of "technology of history" inscribed in the filing cabinet—its specific design, materiality, and understanding of time—see Tagg 2012.

45. Other groupings are performed in other cases—for instance, separating the student's work from the practice work and from the work completed with different collaborators.

46. Chiara Porcu, interview with the author, August 30, 2018.

47. Porcu, interview.

48. Siefert, interview.

49. Siefert, interview

50. Casey, interview.

51. Casey, interview.

52. Casey, interview.

53. Porcu, interview

54. Deleuze and Krauss 1983, 53.

55. Deleuze 2000, 4.

56. See Deleuze 2000.

57. Siefert, interview.

58. Siefert, interview.

59. Porcu, interview.

60. Siza, interview.

61. Eisenman, interview.

62. Porcu, interview.

63. Casey, interview.

64. Adria Seccareccia has a background in history and holds an MA degree in library and information studies. Prior to the CCA, she worked at the archives of the Ohio Historical Society.

65. Robert Desaulniers, interview with the author, June 17, 2015.

66. Adria Seccareccia, interview with the author, June 29, 2016.

67. For more information on the projects Bonjour Tristesse (1982–1983) and Punt en Komma (1986–1989), see http://www.domusweb.it/en/news/2015/09/29/corner_block_neighbourhood_cities_alvaro_siza_in_berlin_and_the_hague_.html

68. Seccareccia, interview.

69. Seccareccia, interview.

70. Seccareccia, interview.

71. Desaulniers, interview.

72. If architects are still practicing, the CCA communicates more often with them. Very rarely do the archivists working for firms sit down with the CCA people to look at the archive together, says archivist Robert Desaulniers. If they do, these meetings usually include inspection of materials, and "sometimes you see their reaction: they are surprised. Things they have forgotten! Things they suddenly remember! Things they discard! They would focus on something that is very valuable for the processing of the archive" (Desaulniers, interview).

73. This dialogue is unique when the donor of an archive is alive. It is a more relaxed process. Martien explains, "It gives you time to reorganize, to go there and spend time in the office, to understand how it [the archive] was organized, and to maybe organize it in a way that would come to the CCA in an easier way. You have time to discuss with the donors

how they were doing things" (de Vletter, interview). When the archive arrives at the CCA and staff start cataloguing, they can still ask questions to the donors.

74. Seccareccia, interview.

75. Susan Leigh Star's (1989) analysis of working in archives and her observations on what it is to make a discovery within a collection is important in theorizing processes of classification and standardization. See also Star 2010.

76. Foucault 1972, 129.

7. THE LIFE OF AN OLD FLOPPY DISK

1. Some of the projects in this show, the third and last phase of the *Archaeology of the Digital* exhibition series called *Complexity and Convention*, include the Erasmus Bridge of UNStudio, Yokohama Terminal of Foreign Office Architects (FOA), the Carbon Tower of Testa & Weiser, the O/K Apartment by Kolatan/Mac Donald Studio, the Hypo Alpe-Adria Center by Morphosis, and the Eyebeam Atelier Museum competition entry by Preston Scott Cohen.

2. A walking interview in the gallery of *Archaeology of the Digital: Complexity and Convention* with David Stevenson, June 28, 2016.

3. The term "born-digital" refers to materials that originate in a digital form. This might include texts, images, drawings or recordings produced in digital form, rather than having been converted from print or analogue equivalents. The term is used in contrast to digital reformatting, or digitization, through which analogue materials become digital. The key issues related to born-digital material are digital preservation and intellectual property. See the dictionary entry for "born-digital" at the Society of American Archivists website: https://www2.archivists.org/glossary/terms/b/born-digital. Or for a lengthier engagement in issues related to born-digital archives, see Carroll et al. 2011.

4. Mirko Zardini, interview with the author, June 28, 2016.

5. Zardini, interview.

6. Recent work in the field has focused on issues of preservation and access to digital archives in the field of architecture (Peyceré and Wierre 2008). Analyzing the archives' record lifecycle, from initial production and use by the creator, to selection for and preservation within an archive, and finally to use by the researcher—the volume edited by Peyceré and Wierre (2008) explores the myriad issues related to the creation and the long-term preservation of digital architectural records. The volume reflects on how the dividing line between the architect and the archivist's work is becoming increasingly blurred and explores the changing relationship between the archivist and the researcher and how the "digital" upsets preexisting relations between the archive and architecture.

7. The *Archaeology of the Digital* was a three-phase exhibition series and research project at the CCA curated by Greg Lynn. The aim of the project was to explore the "digital" architectural cosmology that bloomed in the late 1980s and early 1990s. Each of the phases of the exhibition featured different projects and cut across different themes related to the "digital," digital technology and software, and the role of computation in architecture and design practices. The first exhibition, *Archaeology of the Digital* (2013), looked at projects associated with the emergence and establishment of the "digital" in architecture. The second exhibition, *Archaeology of the Digital: Media and Machines* (2014), turned to experiments with the digital, and how architects engaged more thoroughly with the digital. The third exhibition, *Archaeology of the Digital: Complexity and Convention* (2016) tackled five different themes: High-Fidelity 3D, Topology and Topography, Photorealism, Data, and Structure and Cladding (Lynn 2014).

8. Tim Walsh, interview with the author, June 27, 2016.

9. The CCA had tried to acquire, collect and exhibit all twenty-five projects. It has also released publications based on them and attempts to safeguard these born-digital proj-

ects. However, the CCA does not have enough resources to acquire the complete archives of each of the twenty-five architects chosen for the exhibition (e.g., the New York Stock Exchange project from Asymptote, the Hypo Alpe-Adria Center by Morphosis, the Erasmus Bridge by UNStudio). For Greg Lynn, each of these projects has value for the thinking and the development of architecture with the computer.

10. Martien de Vletter, interview with the author, June 15, 2015.

11. On issues of selection and preservation of digital material, see Burrows 2000.

12. For an overview of the limits and opportunities of digitizing heritage materials, see Ch'ng, Gaffney, and Chapman 2013.

13. Walsh, interview.

14. In a 2019 email, Tim Walsh mentioned that there are few archives that are purely physical or purely digital (Tim Walsh, personal communication with the author, February 4, 2019).

15. Walsh, interview.

16. Walsh, interview.

17. Walsh, interview.

18. Walsh, interview.

19. Walsh, interview.

20. Walsh, interview.

21. Walsh, interview.

22. Walsh, interview.

23. Walsh, interview.

24. The PERSIST project from UNESCO is part of the Action Plan for Strengthening the Memory of the World Program. For the project, UNESCO has partnered with the International Council on Archives (ICA) and the International Federation of Library Associations (IFLA). The project is in response to the emergence of the "information society" and seeks to establish the continuity of and access to information globally and to promote digital sustainability. The CCA is very interested in the UNESCO PERSIST project but is not a member and has no formal relationship with the project. For more information on the UNESCO PERSIST program, see https://unescopersist.org/about/.

25. ISAD(G) provides instructions of how to interpret the international standards for archival descriptions disrupted by the impact of digitized and born-digital records. See https://www.dpconline.org/news/dri-publishes-guidelines-for-isadg-and-encoded-archival-description.

26. For an extensive literature review on long-term preservation of 3D materials in architecture, see Thapa and Haddara 2013.

27. David explains: "A lot of the architects we are collecting now were people who were working twenty years ago, so I can say with almost certainty that they were not thinking about it then. Big modern firms are using software, which is integrated into the workflows and the systems of work that they have in place. They are thinking about that now, about long-term preservation and data integrity. They sometimes have people on staff who are working to do that in the bigger firms" (David Stevenson, interview with the author, June 18, 2015).

28. Walsh, interview.

29. Walsh, interview.

30. Walsh, interview.

31. Digitization projects involve both copyright and privacy issues, such as, for example, the question of whether or not to list addresses of residences (Shepherd 2002).

32. Walsh, interview.

33. The role of the office archivist in the future will be changing as well. Architectural firms will have more librarian-archivists, yet, none of them will have a specific mandate

to work with digital material. Archivists such as Chiara and Magda will train in setting out records management policies at firms introducing file-naming conventions and other organizational conventions. Yet, this will remain only one element of their overall work. The affiliated industries (such as the preservation of CAD and CAD modeling) will also inform their work to a great extent.

34. Digital objects do not respond well to benign neglect due to the constant evolution of technology and the degradation of storage media (Tibbo 2003).

35. Walsh, interview.

36. Stevenson, interview.

37. File normalization is the process of structuring a relational database in accordance with a series of "normal forms" to be able to reduce redundancy.

38. Stevenson, interview.

39. Walsh, interview.

40. Walsh, interview.

41. The meaning of "digital" is very broad here, and can refer to whatever is stored on computer networks/servers; videotapes and cassette tapes can be digital and analogue.

42. Stevenson, interview.

43. Stevenson, interview.

44. Karen Potje, interview with the author, June 18, 2015.

45. Stevenson, interview.

46. Stevenson, interview.

47. Potje, interview.

48. Stevenson, interview.

49. Walsh, interview.

CONCLUSION

1. See Aristotle 1995.

2. Giovanna Borasi, interview with the author, June 18, 2015.

3. Karen Potje, interview with the author, June 18, 2015.

4. Potje, interview.

5. David Stevenson, interview with the author, June 18, 2015.

6. Potje, interview.

7. Robert Desaulniers, interview with the author, June 17, 2015.

8. Attempting to move beyond the implied dichotomy of "knowing how" and "knowing that," anthropologist Trevor Marchand (2001) explores the common ground they share—both anchored in the body and within communicative processes. Yet, he goes in the direction of behavioral sciences to argue that the distinction between embodied knowledge and propositional or conceptual knowledge is not as deeply entrenched as once supposed. In his work on building-craft knowledge and apprenticeship, Marchand shows that knowledge is "enacted" via multiple modes of communication (including gestures and facial expressions) that respond dynamically to changing material and sensual and cognitive stimuli in the environment.

9. Jullien 1999, 32.

10. Architectural archival objects bear similarities to artistic objects insofar as the medium is often the same—commonly paper. As a result, the risks of exposure, dampness, and humidity are comparable. While medium, dimensions, fabric, and scale of objects all matter, the archival nature of architectural objects is of bigger concern than their architectural specificity. That is, archival materials come in huge quantities and in a specific condition while art objects exist in smaller crowds. The archival, we can argue, does not denote intrinsic quality; rather, it implies a specific modality of action: a huge quantity of objects that act in a similar way; they flock in sites, labs and workshops at the same time,

begging for attention, care, and treatment. Architectural collections, unlike art collections, require specific processes and contain objects like blueprints that can prove to be challenging (although an art collection can be equally challenging). There is also something very specific about the architectural material: its scale. While artistic and architectural prints may be made on paper, the techniques used for flattening paper vary. Whereas the paper of art objects can be flattened by humidifying or placed under blotters and weight, architectural objects will require a different technique due to the extensive use of tracing paper. Hard to preserve, tracing paper is moisture-sensitive, and if humidified and dried, it risks shrinking in one direction; that is, its scale can alter. Careful to prevent any scale modifications that could cause a change in the specificity of architectural works, friends of architectural objects focus on the particular procedural treatment of objects. For digital archivists, it is the architectural nature of CAD files that makes a difference in their work; yet, there, the comparison with technology imposes itself, moving the focus away from the arts.

11. Alexandre Phaneuf, interview with the author, June 17, 2015.

12. Phaneuf, interview.

13. Occasionally, they can grow attached to an architect's work that they have spent a lot of time archiving. As Adria explains, little by little, "you get an emotional attachment to it because you have been through all these images and drawings and photographs and buildings, and it will be impossible not to build an attachment." Adria Seccareccia, interview with the author, June 29, 2016.

14. Cognition is shaped by experience, at least to some considerable degree, as demonstrated by Cristina Grasseni's (2007) account of skilled vision among dairy farmers in northern Italy. She develops an ecological perspective by taking a detailed consideration of the ways in which everyday bodily practice, the use of relevant objects, and social training contribute to the configuration of specific ways of knowing; knowing is illuminated as a relational and material constitution of activities that are socially distributed and achieved through skilled practice.

15. Desaulniers, interview.

16. Boyer 2008, 39.

17. As advocated by Bruno Latour (1991).

18. For a discussion of reductionist and irreductionist approaches in Architecture see Yaneva 2012, 39–49.

19. The capitalization of knowledge, the accumulated knowledge via archiving, happens through what Bruno Latour (1987) calls "centers of calculation." These are venues in which knowledge production builds upon the accumulation of resources through circulatory movements to other places. These movements lead from the world to the inscriptions, and ultimately to new knowledge.

20. Both have been extensively studied by sociologists and historians of science: Latour and Woolgar 1979; Lynch 1993; Galison and Daston 2007.

21. See Latour 1996.

22. In fact, we can argue at a first glance that there is something of the spirit of the early modern *Wunderkammer* here, also known as "cabinets of curiosities" or "cabinets of wonder," which were encyclopedic collections of objects in Renaissance Europe whose categorical boundaries were not completely defined. The objects included belonged to natural history, geology, ethnography, archaeology, religion, art, and antiquity. *Wunderkammer* expresses the early modern culture of wonders; there, the objects are freed from the demands of utility; they bridge the natural and the artificial. The opposition between art and nature is also blurred (Daston and Park 1998).

23. The concept of *musée imaginaire* of Malraux (1949) rests on a philosophical view of art and art history as essentially arising out of dialogue between works. This dialogue

happens only if the artworks can be compared, which becomes possible thanks to the photographic representation, whether in the museum space or in the minds of individuals, in their imaginary. Malraux's privileging of curatorial over artistic production is a first instance of explicitly locating the creative act in the process of assembling, grouping, and displaying works of art.

24. Peter Christensen (2014) calls for the development of an institutional and archival culture that promotes both autographic and allographic understandings of architecture. Archives provide an opportunity to rethink the hegemonic system of canonization of architects. Instead of being ego-driven, the current practices of collecting institutions, argues Christensen, should rather prioritize the canonization of theoretical and technological movements within architectural history so that the process of collection of architecture can maintain its curatorial integrity.

25. See the analysis of minor literature of Kafka by Deleuze and Guattari (1986).

26. Borasi, interview.

27. Deleuze 1986, 43.

References

Agamben, Giorgio. 1999. *Remnants of Auschwitz. The Archive and Testimony.* Translated by Daniel Heller-Roazen. New York: Zone Books.

Agamben, Giorgio. 2006 [1989]. "The Archive and Testimony." In *The Archive. Documents of Contemporary Art*, edited by Charles Merewether, 38–40. London: Whitechapel Gallery.

Agar, Michael H. 1985. *Speaking of Ethnography.* London: Sage.

Anderson, Benedict. 1991. *Imagined Communities: Reflections on the Origin and Spread of Nationalism.* New York: Verso.

Andrade, Sérgio C. 2014a. "Siza dividido entre Portugal e o Canadá." *Ipsilon,* July 17.

Andrade, Sérgio C. 2014b. "Doações de Álvaro Siza excluem Matosinhos e a Universidade do Porto." *Ipsilon,* July 24.

Andrade, Sérgio C. 2014c. "Álvaro Siza: "Para os arquivos, quis instituições independentes, com autonomia." *Ipsilon,* August 5.

Aristotle. 1995. *The Complete Works of Aristotle.* Translated by Jonathan Barnes. Princeton, NJ: Princeton University Press.

Armstrong, Ann R. E. 2006. "Architectural Archives/Archiving Architecture: The Digital ERA." *Art Documentation: Journal of the Art Libraries Society of North America* 25 (2): 12–17.

Ashmore, Paul, Ruth Craggs, and Hannah Neate. 2012. "Working-With: Talking and Sorting in Personal Archives." *Journal of Historical Geography* 38 (1): 81–89.

Bailey, Stuart, and Markus Miessen, eds. 2014. *The Archives as a Productive Space of Conflict.* Berlin: Sternberg Press.

Banks, Marcus, and Richard Vokes. 2010. "Introduction: Anthropology, Photography and the Archive." *History and Anthropology* 21 (4): 337–49.

Barth, Fredrik. 2002. "An Anthropology of Knowledge." *Current Anthropology* 43 (1): 1–18.

Barthes, Roland. 1982. "Deliberations." In *A Barthes Reader*, edited by Susan Sontag, 479–544, New York: Hill and Wang.

Bartlett, Nancy. 1997. "The Records Continuum: Ian McLean and Australian Archives First Fifty Years." *The American Archivist* 60 (4): 456–58.

Baweja, Vandana. 2018. "Otto Koengisberger's Architectural Photographic Archive in India (1939–1951)." *Visual Resources* 34 (3-4): 315–346.

Bearman, David. 1992. "Documenting Documentation." *Archivaria* 34 (Summer): 33–49.

Beaulieu, Anne. 2010. "Research Note: From Co-Location to Co-Presence: Shifts in the Use of Ethnography for the Study of Knowledge." *Social Studies of Science* 40 (3): 453–70.

Belton, Tom. 1996. "By Whose Warrant? Analyzing Documentary Form and Procedure." *Archivaria* 41(Spring): 206–20

Benjamin, Walter. 1994 [1955]. *Illuminations.* Translated by Harry Zohn. New York: Schocken Books.

Bergson, Henri. 1991. *Matter and Memory.* Translated by Nancy Margaret Paul and W. Scott Palmer. New York: Zone Books.

Boersma, Foekje, Agnes W. Brokerhof, Saskia van den Berg, and Judith Tegetaers. 2007. *Unravelling Textiles: A Handbook for the Preservation of Textile Collections*. London: Archetype.

Borden, Iain. 2007. "Imaging Architecture: The Uses of Photography in the Practice of Architectural History." *Journal of Architecture* 12 (1): 57–77.

Boyer, Dominic. 2005. "Visiting Knowledge in Anthropology: An Introduction." *Ethnos* 70 (2): 141–48.

Boyer, Dominic. 2008. "Thinking through the Anthropology of Experts." *Anthropology in Action* 15 (2): 38–46.

Boyer, Dominic, and Cymene Howe. 2015. "Portable Analytics and Lateral Theory." In *Theory Can Be More than It Used to Be: Learning Anthropology's Method in a Time of Transition*, edited by Dominic Boyer, James D. Faubion, and George E. Marcus, 15–39. Ithaca, NY: Cornell University Press.

Buchli, Victor. 2013. *An Anthropology of Architecture*. London: Bloomsbury.

Buchloh, Benjamin H. D. 1999. "Gerhard Richter's 'Atlas': The Anomic Archive." *October* 88 (Spring): 117–145.

Burns, Karen. 2013. "Archive Stories/Symptomatic Histories: The Commemoration of Australian Frontier Space at Purrumbete, 1840–1902." *Architectural Theory Review* 18 (1): 83–104.

Burrows, Toby. 2000. "Preserving the Past, Conceptualizing the Future: Research Libraries and Digital Preservation." *Australian Academic & Research Libraries* 31 (4): 142–53.

Burton, Antoinette. 2003. *Dwelling in the Archive: Women Writing House, Home, and History in Late Colonial India*. Oxford: Oxford University Press.

Burton, Antoinette, ed. 2005. *Archive Stories: Fact, Fictions and the Writing of History*. Durham, NC: Duke University Press.

Calouste Gulbenkian Foundation. N.d. "Online Access to the Álvaro Siza Archive." https://gulbenkian.pt/en/news-en/online-access-to-the-alvaro-siza-archive/ (accessed May 15, 2019).

Canadian Centre for Architecture. N.d. "Institutional Overview." https://web.archive.org/web/20120201201054/http://www.cca.qc.ca/en/collection/294-institutional-overview (accessed May 17, 2017).

Carey, Alice. 1996. "The Importance of Construction Documents to Restoration Architects." *The American Archivist* 59 (2): 176–84.

Carroll, Laura, Erika Farr, Peter Hornsby, and Ben Ranker. 2011. "A Comprehensive Approach to Born-Digital Archives." *Archivaria* 72 (Fall): 61–92.

Ch'ng, Eugene, Vincent Gaffney, and Henry Chapman, eds. 2013. *Visual Heritage in the Digital Age*. London: Springer.

Chabard, Pierre. 2011. "Du dessin à l'image: crises à la surface de l'architecture." In *Architecture 80, une chronique métropolitaine: les voies de la postmodernité (1980–1990)*, edited by Soline Nivet, and Lionel Engrand, 106–19, Paris: Pavillon de l'Arsenal.

Chabard, Pierre. 2014. "Entre collection et médiation: stratégies institutionnelles autour de l'architecture au début des années 1980." *Les Cahiers du Musée National d'Art Moderne* 129 (Autumn): 52–63.

Chabard, Pierre. 2015. "Ce que l'exposition fait à l'architecture: le cas du CCI dans les années 1980." In *L'objet de l'exposition: l'architecture exposée*, edited by Stéphane Doré, and Frédéric Herbin, 22–29. Bourges: Ensa Bourge.

Chiantore, Oscar, Antonio Rava, and Valeria Dell'Aquila. 2012. *Conserving Contemporary Art: Issues, Methods, Materials, and Research*. Los Angeles: Getty Conservation Institute.

Child, R. E. 1999. "Insect Pests in Archives: Detection, Monitoring and Control." *Journal of the Society of Archivists* 20 (2): 141–48.

Christensen, Peter. 2014. "Conceptual Problems in the Collection of Architects' Archives." In *Architekturmuseum der Technischen Universität München: Die Sammlung*, edited by Andres Lepik, 217–237. Ostfildern: Hatje Cantz Verlag.

Cohen, Jean-Louis. 2001. "Exposer l'architecture." In *Une Cité à Chaillot: Avant-première*, edited by Jean-Louis Cohen, and Claude Eveno, 31–44. Paris: Editions de l'Imprimeur.

Cohen, Jean-Louis. 2010. "Mirror of Dreams." *Log* 20 (Fall): 49–53.

Colomina, Beatriz. 1994. *Privacy and Publicity: Modern Architecture as Mass Media* Cambridge, MA: MIT Press.

Colomina, Beatriz, and Craig Buckley. 2010a. "The Exhibition as Archive." In *Clip/Stamp/Fold: The Radical Architecture of Little Magazines 196X–197X*, edited by Beatriz Colomina, and Craig Buckley, 16–18. Madrid: Actar.

Colomina, Beatriz, and Craig Buckley, eds. 2010b. *Clip/Stamp/Fold: The Radical Architecture of Little Magazines 196X–197X*. Madrid: Actar.

Côme, Tony. 2013. "L'architecture à tout prix." *Criticart* 12 (Autumn): 18–32.

Cook, Terry. 1996. "Building and Archives: Appraisal Theory for Architectural Records." *The American Archivist* 59 (2): 136–43.

Cox, Richard J. 1996. "The Archival Documentation Strategy and Its Implications for the Appraisal of Architectural Records." *The American Archivist* 59 (2): 144–54.

Coyne, Richard. 2011. *Derrida for Architects*. London: Routledge.

Crysler, C. Greig. 2012. "Time's Arrows: Spaces of the Past." In *Handbook of Architectural Theory*, edited by Greig Crysler, Stephen Cairns, and Hilde Heynen, 289–308. Thousand Oaks, CA: Sage.

Cuff, Dana. 1992. *Architecture: The Story of Practice*. Cambridge, MA: MIT Press.

Czarniawska, Barbara. 2004. "On Time, Space, and Action Nets." *Organization* 11 (6): 773–91.

Czarniawska, Barbara. 2007. *Shadowing, and Other Techniques for Doing Fieldwork in Modern Societies*. Copenhagen: Copenhagen Business School Press.

Daston, Lorraine. 1992. "Objectivity and the Escape from Perspective." *Social Studies of Science* 22 (4): 597–618.

Daston, Lorraine, ed. 2017. *Science in the Archives: Pasts, Presents, Futures*. Chicago: University of Chicago Press.

Daston, Lorraine, and Katharine Park. 1998. *Wonders and the Order of Nature, 1150–1750*. New York: Zone Books.

Davidson, Cynthia. 2010. Untitled Editorial. *Log* 20 (Fall): n. p.

De Long, David G. 1996. "The Historian's View." *The American Archivist* 59 (2): 156–64.

de Silva, Minette. 1998. *The Life and Work of an Asian Woman Architect*. Kandy, Sri Lanka: The de Silva Trust.

Decker, Stephanie. 2013. "The Silence of the Archives: Business History, Postcolonialism and Archival Ethnography." *Management & Organizational History* 8 (2): 155–73.

Decker, Stephanie. 2014. "Solid Intentions: An Archival Ethnography of Corporate Architecture and Organizational Remembering." *Organization* 21 (4): 514–42.

Deleuze, Gilles. 1983. *Cinéma. I. L'Image-mouvement*. Paris: Les Éditions de Minuit.

Deleuze, Gilles. 1986. *Foucault*. Paris: Les Éditions de Minuit.

Deleuze, Gilles. 2000. *Proust and Signs: The Complete Text*. Translated by Richard Howard. Minnesota: University of Minnesota Press.

Deleuze, Gilles, and Félix Guattari. 1986. *Kafka: Toward a Minor Literature*. Translated by Dana Polan. Minneapolis: University of Minnesota Press.

Deleuze, Gilles, and Rosalind Krauss. 1983. "Plato and the Simulacrum." *October* 27 (Winter): 45–56.

Derrida, Jacques. 1995. "Archive Fever: A Freudian Impression." Translated by Eric Prenowitz. *Diacritics* 25 (2): 9–63.

Desrosières, Alain. 1998. *The Politics of Large Numbers: A History of Statistical Reasoning.* Cambridge, MA: Harvard University Press.

Doherty, Gareth. 2016. *Paradoxes of Green: Landscapes of a City-State.* Oakland: University of California Press.

Douglas, Jennifer, and Heather MacNeil. 2009. "Arranging the Self: Literary and Archival Perspectives on Writers' Archives." *Archivaria* 67 (Spring): 25–39.

Downey, Anthony. 2015. "Contingency, Dissonance, and Performativity: Critical Archives and Knowledge Production in Contemporary Art." In *Dissonant Archives*, edited by Anthony Downey, 13–42. London: I. B. Tauris.

Dubowitz, Lilly. 2010. "In Search of a Forgotten Architect." *AA Files* 61: 3–17.

Dubowitz, Lilly. 2012. *In Search of a Forgotten Architect: Stefan Sebök 1901–1941.* London: Architectural Association.

Echevarría, Roberto González. 1990. *Myth and Archive: A Theory of Latin American Narrative.* Cambridge: Cambridge University Press.

Edwards, Elizabeth. 1992. *Anthropology and Photography, 1860–1920.* London: Yale University Press in association with the Royal Anthropological Institute.

Enigbokan, Adeola. 2019. "Archiving the City: Bio." Blog. April 27. https://archivingthecity .com/about/.

Enigbokan, Adeola, and Merle Patchett. 2012. "Speaking with Specters: Experimental Geographies in Practice." *Cultural Geographies* 19 (4): 535–46.

Enwezor, Okwui. 2008. "Archive Fever: Photography between History & the Monument." In *Archive Fever: Uses of the Document in Contemporary Art*, edited by Okwui Enwezor and Willis E. Hartshorn, 11–51. New York: International Center of Photography.

Esler, Philip F. 2017. *Babatha's Orchard: The Yadin Papyri and an Ancient Jewish Family Tale Retold.* Oxford: Oxford University Press.

Evans, James, and Phil Jones. 2011. "The Walking Interview: Methodology, Mobility and Place." *Applied Geography* 31 (2): 849–58.

Ferraris, Maurizio. 2007. "Documentality, or Why Nothing Social Exists beyond the Text." In *Cultures. Conflict—Analysis—Dialogue, Proceedings of the 29th International Ludwig Wittgenstein-Symposium in Kirchberg, Austria*, edited by C. Kanzian and E. Runggaldier, 385–40. Vienna: Publications of the Austrian Ludwig Wittgenstein Society, New Series 3.

Ferraris, Maurizio. 2013. *Documentality: Why It Is Necessary to Leave Traces.* New York: Fordham University Press.

Florian, Mary-Lou E. 1997. *Heritage Eaters: Insects & Fungi in Heritage Collections.* London: James & James.

Fontana-Giusti, Gordana. 2013. *Foucault for Architects.* London: Routledge.

Forgey, Benjamin. 1989. "In Montreal, the Temple of Architecture." *Washington Post*, May 6.

Foster, Hal. 2004. "An Archival Impulse." *October* 110 (Autumn): 3–22.

Foucault, Michel. 1972. *The Archaeology of Knowledge.* New York: Pantheon.

Foucault, Michel. 1994. *The Order of Things. An Archeology of the Human Sciences.* New York: Vintage.

Fraenkel, Béatrice. 1992. *La signature. Gensèe d'un signe.* Paris: Éditions Gallimard.

Fredriksson, Berndt. 2003. "Postmodernist Archival Science—Rethinking the Methodology of a Science." *Archival Science* 3 (2): 177–97.

Frichot, Hélène. 2018. *Creative Ecologies. Theorizing the Practice of Architecture.* London: Bloomsbury.

Friedman, David. 2012. "Visual Documents, Property Archives, and the Map of the City of Rome: 1563–1712." *Journal of the Society of Architectural Historians* 71 (3): 278–305.

Fukuyama, Francis. 1992. *The End of History and the Last Man*. New York: Free Press.

Gagen, Elizabeth, Hayden Lorimer, and Alex Vasudevan, eds. 2007. "Practicing the Archive: Reflections on Methods and Practice." *Historical Geography Research Series* 40.

Galison, Peter, and Lorraine Daston. 2007. *Objectivity*. Cambridge, MA: MIT Press.

Gardey, Delphine. 2001. *La dactylographe et l'expéditionnaire: Histoire des employés de bureau, 1890–1930*. Paris: Belin.

Gardey, Delphine. 2008. *Ecrire, calculer, classer. Comment une révolution de papier a transformé les sociétés contemporaines (1800–1940)*. Paris: La Découverte.

Garutti, Francesco. 2016. *Can Design Be Devious? The Story of the Robert Moses Bridges over the Long Island Parkways, and Other Explorations of Unexpected Political Consequences of Design*. Montreal: Centre for Canadian Architecture.

Geertz, Clifford. 1973. *The Interpretation of Cultures: Selected Essays*. New York: Basic Books.

Geertz, Clifford. 1988. *Works and Lives: The Anthropologist as Author*. Stanford, CA: Stanford University Press.

Ghani, Mariam. 2015. "Field Notes for 'What We Left Unfinished': The Artist and the Archive." In *Dissonant Archives: Contemporary Visual Culture and Contested Narratives in the Middle East*, edited by Anthony Downey, 43–64. London: I. B. Tauris.

Gillette, Maris Boyd, and Andrew Hurley. 2018. "Vision, Voice and the Community Landscape: The Missouri Place Stories Pilot Project." *Landscape and Urban Planning* 173 (May): 1–8.

Giuliano, Genevieve, Sandip Chakrabarti and Mohja Rhoads. 2016. "Using Regional Archived Multimodal Transportation System Data for Policy Analysis of the LA Metro Expo Line." *Journal of Planning Education and Research* 36 (2): 195–209.

Gracy, Karen F. 2003. "Documenting the Process of Film Preservation." *Moving Image* 3 (1): 1–41.

Gracy, Karen F. 2004. "Documenting Communities of Practice: Making the Case for Archival Ethnography." *Archival Science* 4 (3-4): 335–65.

Gracy, Karen F. 2007. *Film Preservation: Competing Definitions of Value, Use, and Practice*. Chicago: Society of American Archivists.

Graham, Stephen, and Nigel J. Thrift. 2007. "Out of Order: Understanding Repair and Maintenance." *Theory, Culture & Society* 24 (3): 1–25.

Grasseni, Cristina. 2007. "Communities of Practice and Forms of Life: Toward a Rehabilitation of Vision? In *Ways of Knowing: New Approaches in the Anthropology of Knowledge and Learning*, edited by Mark Harris, 203–22. New York: Berghahn Books.

Hacking, Ian. 1990. *The Taming of Chance*. New York: Cambridge University Press.

Hale, Jonathan. 2016. *Merleau-Ponty for Architects*. London: Routledge.

Hamilton, Carolyn, ed. 2002. *Refiguring the Archive*. Dordrecht: Kluwer Academic.

Harris, John. 1984. "Le dessin d'architecture: une nouvelle marchandise culturelle." In *Images et imaginaires d'architecture: dessin, peinture, photographie, arts graphiques, théâtre, cinéma en Europe aux xix e et xx e siècles*, edited by Jean Dethier, 74–78. Paris: Centre Georges Pompidou-CCI.

Harris, John. 1989. "Storehouses of Knowledge: The Origins of the Contemporary Architectural Museum." In *Canadian Centre for Architecture: Buildings and Gardens*, edited by Larry Richards, 15–32. Montreal: Canadian Centre for Architecture.

Harris, Mark, ed. 2007. *Ways of Knowing: New Approaches in the Anthropology of Experience and Learning*. Oxford: Berghahn.

Hastrup, Kirsten. 1999. "The Ethnographic Present: A Reinvention." *Cultural Anthropology* 5 (1): 45–61.

Head, Randolph. 2010. "Preface: Historical Research on Archives and Knowledge Cultures: An Interdisciplinary Wave." *Archival Science* 10 (3): 191–94.

Heathcott, Joseph. 2006. "Curating the City: Challenges for Historic Preservation in the Twenty-First Century." *Journal of Planning History* 5 (1): 75–83.

Heathcott, Joseph. 2007. "Reading the Accidental Archive: Architecture, Ephemera, and Landscape as Evidence of an Urban Public Culture." *Winterthur Portfolio* 41 (4): 239–68.

Hennion, Antoine, and Bruno Latour. 1993. "Objet de science, objet d'art: note sur les limites de l'anti-fétichisme." *Sociologie de l'Art* 6: 5–24.

Hennion, Antoine, and Bruno Latour. 2003. "How to Make Mistakes on So Many Things at Once—and Become Famous for It." In *Mapping Benjamin: The Work of Art in the Digital Age*, edited by Hans Ulrich Gumbrecht, and Michael Marrinan, 91–97. Stanford, CA: Stanford University Press.

Hobbs, Catherine. 2001. "The Character of Personal Archives: Reflections on the Value of Records of Individuals." *Archivaria* 52 (Fall): 126–35.

Holbraad, Martin, and Morten Axel Pedersen. 2009. "Planet M: The Intense Abstraction of Marilyn Strathern." *Anthropological Theory* 9 (4): 371–94.

Houdart, Sophie, and Chihiro Minato. 2009. *Kuma Kengo. An Unconventional Monograph*. Paris: Editions Donner Lieu.

Hutchins, Edwin. 1995. *Cognition in the Wild*. Cambridge, MA: MIT Press.

Huvila, Itso. 2015. "Another Wood between the Worlds? Regimes of Worth and the Making of Meanings in the Work of Archivists." *Information Society* 31 (2): 121–38.

Ingold, Tim. 2007. *Lines: A Brief History*. London: Routledge.

Ingold, Tim. 2011. *Redrawing Anthropology: Materials, Movements, Lines*. Farnham: Ashgate.

Ingold, Tim, and Jo Lee Vergunst. 2008. *Ways of Walking: Ethnography and Practice on Foot*. London: Ashgate.

Jacobs, Jane M., and Peter Merriman, eds. 2011. "Practising Architectures." Special issue, *Social & Cultural Geography* 12 (3).

Jones, Christopher L. 1970. *Design Methods: Seeds of Human Futures*. London: Wiley-Interscience.

Jordanova, Ludmila. 2006. *History in Practice*. London: Bloomsbury.

Jordanova, Ludmila. 2012. *The Look of the Past: Visual and Material Evidence in Historical Practice*. Cambridge, UK: Cambridge University Press.

Jullien, François. 1999. *The Propensity of Things: Toward a History of Efficacy in China*. Translated by Janet Lloyd. New York: Zone Books.

Kaplan, Alice Yaeger. 1990. "Working in the Archives." *Yale French Studies* (77): 103–16.

Kauffman, Jordan. 2018. *Drawing on Architecture: The Object of Lines, 1970–1990*. Cambridge, MA: MIT Press.

Kaufman, Edward N. 1989. "The Architectural Museum from World's Fair to Restoration Village." *Assemblage* 9 (June): 20–39.

Kearney, Richard, and Mark Dooley. 1999. *Questioning Ethics: Contemporary Debates in Philosophy*. London: Routledge.

Kirch, Patrick Vinton 1992. *Anahulu: The Anthropology of History in the Kingdom of Hawaii*, vol. 2, *The Archaeology of History*. Chicago: University of Chicago Press.

Kleinman, Kent. 2006. "Archiving/Architecture." In *Archives, Documentation, and Institutions of Social Memory: Essays from the Sawyer Seminar*, edited by Francis X. Blouin Jr. and William G. Rosenberg, 54–60. Ann Arbor: University of Michigan Press.

Knight, James. 1976. "Architectural Records and Archives in Canada: Toward a National Programme." *Archivaria* 3 (Winter): 62–72.

Knorr Cetina, Karin. 1995. "Laboratory Studies—The Cultural Approach to the Study of Science." In *Handbook of Science and Technology Studies*, edited by Sheila Jasanoff, Gerald E. Markle, James C. Petersen, and Trevor Pinch, 140–66. London: Sage.

Lambert, Phyllis. 1999. "The Architectural Museum: A Founder's Perspective." *Journal of the Society of Architectural Historians* 58 (3): 308–15.

Landau, Royston. 1982. "Notes on the Concept of an Architectural Position." *AA Files* 1 (Winter): 111–14.

Larkham, Peter, J. 2011. "Hostages to History? The Surprising Survival of Critical Comments about British Planning and Planners, c. 1942–1955." *Planning Perspectives* 26 (3): 487–91.

Lathrop, Alan K. 1977. "The Archivist and Architectural Records." *Georgia Archive* 5 (2): 25–32.

Lathrop, Alan K. 1980. "The Provenance and Preservation of Architectural Records." *The American Archivist* 43 (3): 325–38.

Lathrop, Alan K. 1996. "Appraisal of Architectural Records in Practice: The Northwest Architectural Archives." *The American Archivist* 59 (2): 222–27.

Latour, Bruno. 1987. *Science in Action*. Cambridge, MA: Harvard University Press.

Latour, Bruno. 1991. *We Have Never Been Modern*. Cambridge, MA: Harvard University Press.

Latour, Bruno. 1999. *Politiques de la Nature*. Paris: Editions La Découverte.

Latour, Bruno. 1996. "Ces réseaux que la raison ignore: laboratoires, bibliothèques, collections." In *Le pouvoir des bibliothèques. La memoire des livres dans la culture occidentale*, edited by Marc Baratin, and Christian Jacob, 23–46. Paris: Albin Michel.

Latour, Bruno. 2010. *The Making of Law: An Ethnography of the Conseil d'État*. Cambridge: Polity.

Latour, Bruno, and Peter Weibel, eds. 2002. *Iconoclash: Beyond the Image Wars in Science, Religion, and Art*. Cambridge, MA: MIT Press.

Latour, Bruno, and Steve Woolgar. 1979. *Laboratory Life: The Social Construction of Scientific Facts*. Beverly Hills, CA: Sage.

Lave, Jean. 1988. *Cognition in Practice: Mind, Mathematics, and Culture in Everyday Life*. Cambridge: Cambridge University Press.

Lawson, Bryan. 1994. *Design in Mind*. Oxford: Butterworth Architecture.

Lemieux, Victoria L. 2015. "Visual Analytics, Cognition and Archival Arrangement and Description: Studying Archivists' Cognitive Tasks to Leverage Visual Thinking for a Sustainable Archival Future." *Archival Science* 15 (1): 25–49.

Levine, Neil. 2008. "Building the Unbuilt: Authenticity and the Archive." *Journal of the Society of Architectural Historians* 67 (1): 14–17.

Linnie, Martyn Joseph. 1987. "Pest Control. A Survey of Natural History Museums in Great Britain and Ireland." *International Journal of Museum Management and Curatorship* 6 (3): 277–90.

Llach, Daniel. 2015. *Builders of the Visions: Software and the Imagination of Design*. London: Routledge.

Loukissas, Yanni. 2012. *Co-Designers. Cultures of Computer Simulation in Architecture*. London: Routledge.

Lövblad, Håkan. 2003. "Monk, Knight or Artist? The Archivist as a Straddler of a Paradigm." *Archival Science* 3 (2): 131–55.

Lynch, Michael. 1993. *Scientific Practice and Ordinary Action: Ethnomethodology and Social Studies of Science*. Cambridge: Cambridge University Press.

Lynch, Michael. 1999. "Archives in Formation: Privileged Spaces, Popular Archives and Paper Trails." *History of the Human Sciences* 12 (2): 65–87.

Lynn, Greg. 1993. "Introduction: Folding in Architecture." *Architectural Design Profile 102*, 63 (3–4): 8–15.

Lynn, Greg. 2014. *Archaeology of the Digital*. Montreal: Canadian Centre for Architecture.

Mack, Jennifer. 2017. *The Construction of Equality: Syriac Immigration and the Swedish City*. Minneapolis: University of Minnesota Press.

Malraux, André. 1949. *The Psychology of Art*, vol. 1: *Museum without Walls*. Translated by Stuart Gilbert. New York: Pantheon.

Marchand, Trevor. 2001. *Minaret Building and Apprenticeship in Yemen*. New York: Routledge.

Marcus, George E. 1995. "Ethnography in/of the World System: The Emergence of Multi-Sited Ethnography." *Annual Review of Anthropology* 24 (October): 95–117.

Mattern, Shannon. 2017. "Extract and Preserve: Underground Repositories for a Posthuman Future." *New Geographies* 9 (December): 54–65.

Mattern, Shannon. 2018. "Maintenance and Care." *Places Journal* (November). https://placesjournal.org/article/maintenance-and-care/.

McGill, Robert. 2009. "Biographical Desire and the Archives of Living Authors." *Auto/Biography Studies* 24 (1): 129–45.

Merleau-Ponty, Maurice. 1995. *Signs: Studies in Phenomenology and Existential Philosophy*. Translated by Richard G. Mc Gleary. Evanston, IL: Northwestern University Press.

Mihandoust, Shahab, dir. 2015. *Misleading Innocence (Tracing What a Bridge Can Do)*. Montreal: Canadian Montreal Centre for Architecture. https://www.cca.qc.ca/en/events/52259/misleading-innocence-tracing-what-a-bridge-can-do.

Miller, Thea. 2003. "The German Registry: The Evolution of a Recordkeeping Model." *Archival Science* 3 (1): 43–63.

Mills, Sarah. 2013. "Cultural-Historical Geographies of the Archive: Fragments, Objects and Ghosts." *Geography Compass* 7 (10): 701–13.

Mitchell, William J. 1996. "Architectural Archives in the Digital Era." *The American Archivist* 59 (2): 200–4.

Mommersteeg, Brett. 2018. "The Garden of Bifurcating Paths: Towards a Multi-Sited Ecological Approach to Design." *Ardeth* 2 (Spring): 219–38.

Moore, Francesca P. L. 2010. "Tales from the Archive: Methodological and Ethical Issues in Historical Geography Research." *Area* 42 (3): 262–70.

Murphy, Keith M. 2015. *Swedish Design: An Ethnography*. Ithaca, NY: Cornell University Press.

Nelb, Ryan Tawny. 1996. "Architectural Records Appraisal: Discussion of Problems and Strategies for the Documenting Michigan Architecture Project." *The American Archivist* 59 (2): 228–39.

Norris, Christopher. 1995. "Truth, Science, and the Growth of Knowledge." *New Left Review* 210: 105–23.

Nowacki, James N. 1996. "In Search of the Past: A Lawyer's Perspective." *The American Archivist* 59 (2): 186–91.

Olsberg, Nicholas. 1996. "Documenting Twentieth-Century Architecture: Crisis and Opportunity." *The American Archivist* 59 (2): 128–35.

Orillard, Clément. 2012. "Gordon Cullen beyond *The Architectural Review*: Some New Perspectives from His Personal Archives." *Journal of Architecture* 17 (5): 719–31.

Patriarca, Silvana. 1998. *Numbers and Nationhood: Writing Statistics in Nineteenth-Century Italy*. Cambridge: Cambridge University Press.

Pelkonen, Eeva-Liisa. 2009. *Alvar Aalto: Architecture, Modernity, and Geopolitics*. New Haven, CT: Yale University Press.

Pelkonen, Eeva-Liisa. 2017. "Making Effect." Lecture at the meeting of ResArc, ArkDes, the Swedish Centre for Architecture and Design, Stockholm, September 14–17.

Peyceré, David, and Florence Wierre, eds. 2008. *Architecture and Digital Archives, Architecture in the Digital Age: A Question of Memory*. Gollion, Switz.: Infolio.

Picon, Antoine. 2009. *Saint-Simon and the Architecture of Utopia*. Farnham: Ashgate.

Picon, Antoine. 2010. *Digital Culture in Architecture: An Introduction for the Design Profession*. Basel: Birkhäuser.

Pierce, Kathryn. 2011. "Collaborative Efforts to Preserve Born-Digital Architectural Records: A Case Study Documenting Present-Day Practice." *Art Documentation: Journal of the Art Libraries Society of North America* 30 (2): 43–48.

Poole, Deborah. 2005. "An Excess of Description: Ethnography, Race, and Visual Technologies." *Annual Review of Anthropology* 34 (October): 159–79.

Poovey, Mary. 1998. *A History of the Modern Fact: Problems of Knowledge in the Sciences of Wealth and Society*. Chicago: Chicago University Press.

Querner, Pascal. 2015. "Insect Pests and Integrated Pest Management in Museums, Libraries and Historic Buildings." *Insects* 6 (2): 595–607.

Ragot, Gilles. 1996. "The Hennebique Archives: Toward a New Corpus for Contemporary Architectural History." *The American Archivist* 59 (2): 214–22.

Rajchman, John. 1988. "Foucault's Art of Seeing." *October* 44 (Spring): 88–117.

Richards, Thomas. 1993. *The Imperial Archive: Knowledge and the Fantasy of Empire*. London: Verso.

Ricoeur, Paul. 1978. "Archives, Documents, Traces." *Inscriptions,* 66–69. http://artsites.ucsc.edu/sdaniel/230/Ricoeur_archive.pdf.

Ricoeur, Paul. 2004. *Memory, History and Forgetting*. Translated by Kathleen Blamey and David Pellauer. Chicago: University of Chicago Press.

Rowe, Peter G. 1987. *Design Thinking*. Cambridge, MA: MIT Press.

Rowlinson, Michael, John Hassard, and Stephanie Decker. 2014. "Strategies for Organizational History: A Dialogue between Historical Theory and Organization Theory." *Academy of Management Review* 39 (3): 250–74.

Ryle, Gilbert. 1984 [1949]. *The Concept of Mind*. Chicago: Chicago University Press.

Schaffer, Simon, John Tresch, and Pasquale Gagliardi, eds. 2017. *Aesthetics of Universal Knowledge*. London: Palgrave Macmillan.

Sahlins, Marshall. 1992. *Anahulu: The Anthropology of History in the Kingdom of Hawaii*, vol. 1, *Historical Ethnography*. Assisted by Dorothy B. Barrère. Chicago: University of Chicago Press.

Schrock, Nancy Carlson. 1996. "Preservation Factors in the Appraisal of Architectural Records." *The American Archivist* 59 (2): 206–13.

Sekula, Allan. 1986. "The Body and the Archive." *October* 39 (Winter): 3–64.

Sekula, Allan. 2003. "Reading an Archive: Photography between Labor and Capitalism." In *The Photography Reader*, edited by Liz Wells, 443–52. New York: Routledge.

Sennett, Richard. 2008. *The Craftsman*. New Haven, CT: Yale University Press.

Serraino, Pierluigi. 2011. "[A]rchitecture + [P]hotography + [A]rchive: The APA Factor in the Construction of Historiography." *Journal of Art Historiography* 5 (December): 1–14.

Shapin, Steven. 1994. *A Social History of Truth: Civility and Science in Seventeenth-Century England*. Chicago: Chicago University Press.

Sharr, Adam. 2003. "CAN ARCHITECTURE LIE? On Truth, Knowledge and Contemporary Architectural Theory." *Architectural Theory Review* 8 (2): 164–72.

Shepherd, Kelcy. 2002. "Selecting and Shaping Digital Projects: A Blueprint for Architectural Archives." *Art Documentation: Journal of the Art Libraries Society of North America* 21 (2): 18–20.

Shoshkes, Ellen. 1989. *The Design Process*. New York: Whitney Library of Design.

Siddiqi, Anooradha Iyer. 2017. "Crafting the Archive: Minnette De Silva, Architecture, and History." *Journal of Architecture* 22 (8): 1299–1336.

Simondon, Gilbert. 1989. *Du mode d'existence des objets techniques*, rev. ed. Paris: Aubier.

Skelton, Robin. 1984. "The Acquisition of Literary Archives." *Archivaria* 18 (Summer): 214–19.

Souriau, Etienne. 1956. "Du mode d'existence de l'œuvre à faire." *Bulletin de la société française de philosophie* 25 (February): 4–44.

Spradley, James. 1979. *The Ethnographic Interview*. Belmont, CA: Wadsworth.

Stanek, Łukasz. 2020. *Architecture in Global Socialism: Eastern Europe, West Africa, and the Middle East in the Cold War*. Princeton, NJ: Princeton University Press.

Star, Susan Leigh. 1989. "Institutional Ecology, 'Translations' and Boundary Objects: Amateurs and Professionals in Berkeley's Museum of Vertebrate Zoology." *Social Studies of Science* 19 (3): 387–420.

Star, Susan Leigh. 2010. "This Is Not a Boundary Object: Reflections on the Origin of a Concept." *Science, Technology, & Human Values* 35 (5): 601–17.

Stengers, Isabelle. 2011. "Another Science Is Possible! A Plea for Slow Science." Inaugural Lecture Chair, Willy Calewaert, 2011–2012 (VUB), presented at the Faculté de Philosophie et Lettres, Université Libre de Bruxelles, Brussels, December 13.

Stevens, Mary, Andrew Flinn, and Elizabeth Shepherd. 2010. "New Frameworks for Community Engagement in the Archive Sector: From Handing Over to Handing On." *International Journal of Heritage Studies* 16 (1–2): 59–76.

Stoler, Ann. 2002. "Colonial Archives and the Arts of Governance." *Archival Science* 2 (1–2): 87–109.

Stoler, Ann. 2009. *Along the Archival Grain: Epistemic Anxieties and Colonial Common Sense*. Princeton, NJ: Princeton University Press.

Strathern, Marilyn. 1999. *Property, Substance, and Effect: Anthropological Essays on Persons and Things*. London: The Athlone Press.

Szacka, Léa-Catherine. 2016. *Exhibiting the Postmodern: The 1980 Venice Architecture Biennale*. Venice: Marsilio.

Szacka, Léa-Catherine, and Stéphanie Dadour. 2015. "Lexposition comme vecteur de changement de paradigme: le cas de la Biennale d'architecture de Venise et de l'exposition House Rules." In *L'objet de l'exposition: l'architecture exposée*, edited by Stéphane Doré, and Frédéric Herbin, 38–46. Bourges: Ensa Bourge.

Szambien, Werner. 1988. *Le musée d'architecture*. Picard: France.

Tagg, John. 2012 "The Archiving Machine; or, The Camera and the Filing Cabinet." *Grey Room* 47 (Spring): 24–37.

Tamen, Miguel. 2001. *Friends of Interpretable Objects*. Cambridge, MA: Harvard University Press.

Tarde, Gabriel. 2001 [1903]. *Les lois de l'imitation*. Paris: Les empêcheurs de penser en rond.

Tatum, Laura. 2002. "Documenting Design: A Survey of State-of-the-Art Practice for Archiving Architectural Records." *Art Documentation: Journal of the Art Libraries Society of North America* 21 (2): 25–31.

Taylor, Diana. 2003. *The Archive and the Repertoire: Performing Cultural Memory in the Americas*. Durham, NC: Duke University Press.

Taylor, Diana. 2006. "Performance and/as History." *The Drama Review* 50 (1): 67–86.

Tector, Amy. 2006. "The Almost Accidental Archive and Its Impact on Literary Subjects and Canonicity." *Journal of Canadian Studies* 40 (20): 96–108.

te Heesen, Anke. 2002. *The World in a Box: The Story of an Eighteenth-Century Picture Encyclopedia*. Chicago: Chicago University Press.

Tener, Jean. 1984. "Problems of Literary Archives: A Commentary." *Archivaria* 18 (Summer): 228–31.

Thapa, Devinder, and Moutaz Haddara. 2013. "Long-Term Preservation of 3D Architectural Building Data: A Literature Review." In *NOKOBIT*, edited by Terje Fallmyr, 117–131. Trondheim: Stiftelsen og Akademika forlag.

Thomas, Christopher. 1996. "A Historian's Experience of Architectural Collections." *The American Archivist* 59 (2): 166–75.

Tibbo, Helen R. 2003. "On the Nature and Importance of Archiving in the Digital Age." *Advances in Computers* 57 (December): 1–67

Till, Jeremy. 2008. "Three Myths and One Model." *Building Material* 17 (Dublin): 4–10.

Till, Jeremy. 2009. *Architecture Depends*. Cambridge, MA: MIT Press.

Van Maanen, John. 2011. *Tales of the Field: Writing Ethnography*. Chicago: Chicago University Press.

Wigley, Mark. 2005. "Unleashing the Archive." *Future Anterior: Journal of Historic Preservation, History, Theory, and Criticism* 2 (2): 10–15.

Wigley, Mark. 2015. *Buckminster Fuller Inc. Architecture in the Age of Radio*. Zurich: Lars Muller Publishers.

Wigley, Mark. 2018. *Cutting Matta-Clark, The Anarchitecture Investigation*. Zurich: Lars Müller.

Wigley, Mark, and Rem Koolhaas. 2008. *Casa da Musica/Porto*. Porto: Fundação Casa da Música.

Willis, Alfred. 1996. "The Place of Archives in the Universe of Architectural Documentation." *The American Archivist* 59 (2): 192–98.

Wolcott, Harry. 1999. *Ethnography: A Way of Seeing*. Walnut Creek, CA: Alta Mira Press.

Yaneva, Albena. 2005. "Scaling Up and Down: Extraction Trials in Architectural Design." *Social Studies of Science* 35 (6): 867–94.

Yaneva, Albena. 2009a. *The Making of a Building: A Pragmatist Approach to Architecture* Oxford: Peter Lang.

Yaneva, Albena. 2009b. *Made by the Office for Metropolitan Architecture. An Ethnography of Design*. Rotterdam: 010 Publishers.

Yaneva, Albena. 2012. *Mapping Controversies in Architecture*. Farnham: Ashgate.

Yaneva, Albena. 2013. "Actor-Network-Theory Approach to Archaeology of Contemporary Architecture." In *Oxford Handbook of the Archaeology of the Contemporary World*, edited by Paul Graves-Brown, Rodney Harrison, and Angela Piccini, 121–35. Oxford: Oxford University Press.

Yaneva, Albena. 2017. *Five Ways to Make Architecture Political. An Introduction to the Politics of Design Practice*. London: Bloomsbury.

Yarrow, Thomas. 2019. *Architects: Portraits of a Practice*. Ithaca, NY: Cornell University Press.

Zardini, Mirko. 2010. "Exhibiting and Collecting Ideas: A Montreal Perspective." *Log* 20 (Fall): 77–84.

Zebracki, Martin. 2018. "Urban Preservation and the Querying Spaces of (Un)Remembering: Memorial Landscapes of the Miami Beach Art Deco Historic District." *Urban Spaces* 55 (10): 2261–85.

Index

digital files; digital technology; digitization of archives
concretization, 117
conservation of archival objects, 104–6, 128–30; bugs and, 110–13, 211n13; condition reporting and, 113–17, 214n40; digital files, 165–66, 168–69, 172, 175–76; knowledge in, 126–27, 129–30; and mistakes and accidents, 121–22; paper and, 212nn47,49; photographs and, 211n13; tests and instruments for, 120–21; time and, 106–10; treatments and stabilization in, 117–20, 128, 130; treatments compared to surgeries in, 122–26
consignation, power of, 27
contamination, 94–95
Cook, Terry, 36
copies, 70–78, 109–10, 143–46, 150, 167–69
co-presence, 17, 199n42
copyright issues, 168–69
Cormier, Ernest, 76–77
Cowell, Espeth, 63, 122, 134
Cox, Richard, 36
Craggs, Ruth, 34
Cullen, Gordon, 50

Dagbert, Caroline, 85
dampness, 109
Daston, Loraine, 199n33
Davidson, Cynthia, 39
Davies, Kimberly, 15–16, 104
Decker, Stephanie, 33
De Long, David G., 37, 209n40
Derrida, Jacques, 25, 26–27, 45
Desaulniers, Robert, 63, 69, 70, 97, 152–53, 155, 186, 188, 197n3, 215n72
design practices and processes: architects' awareness of archiving, 107–9; archiving in, 43–48, 74; connection between archiving and, 146–51; dynamic intensity of, 72–73; as related to architects, 181–82; trajectorial nature of, 210n25. See also drawings
De Silva, Minnette, 50
Désy, Louise, 109, 210n28, 211n13
de Vletter, Martien, 7, 119, 138–40, 161, 213n3, 214n40, 215–16n73
"diary disease," 208n7
digital archives: issues concerning, 205n26; as "object-centric," 176–79; versus paper archives, 169–71; physical materials in, 172–75, 217n14; processing of, 171–72. See also computerization
digital files: alteration of, 176; organization of, 164; preservation of, 165–66, 168–69, 172,

175–76; transmission of, 163–64, 171–72. See also computerization
digital technology, 38–39, 159–62, 166–69, 170–71. See also computerization
digitization of archives: versus born-digital archives, 160–61; fear of, 162–66; and time and cycles of obsolescence, 166–69. See also computerization
Doherty, Gareth, 200n46
dossiers, 12
Downey, Anthony, 30
drawings: conservation of, 107–8; as related to architects, 181–82, 205n14; signed, 46, 205n17. See also design practices and processes
Dubowitz, Lilly, 50–51
duplications, 70–78, 109–10, 143–46, 150, 167–69

Edwards, Elizabeth, 32
"Egyptologists," archivists compared to, 148, 149, 173, 189
Eisenman, Peter, 43, 46, 47, 136, 150, 205n17, 205n23
Eisenman, Peter, archive, 7, 174
empirical turn, in archival scholarship, 25, 35–41
en attente, 96–98
Enigbokan, Adeola, 34
Esler, Philip, 32
ethanol, 125, 126
ethnographic moment, 61, 207n4
ethnographic montage, 21
ethnographic photography archives, 32–33, 86
ethnographic sketching, 20–21
Evans, James, 200n46
exhibition, connection between collection and, 39–40
expertization, 9, 10
eye strain, 121–22

failure of the technical gesture, 212n37
fax machine, 45–46
"fonds," 197n3. See also archive(s)
Foreign Office Architects (FOA), 88, 164
Foster, Hal, 29
Foucault, Michel, 11, 24, 26
Fredriksson, Berndt, 204n104
Freud, Sigmund, 45
Friedman, David, 53
Fuller, Buckminster, 206n36
Fundação Calouste Gulbenkian, 133, 213n13

.

CPSIA information can be obtained
at www.ICGtesting.com
Printed in the USA
LVHW090729041020
667770LV00017B/96